Learn, Teach...

Succeed...

With **REA's GACE Middle Grades Mathematics 013** test prep, you'll be in a class all your own.

WE'D LIKE TO HEAR FROM YOU!

Visit **www.rea.com** to send us your comments
or email us at **info@rea.com**

GACE® MIDDLE GRADES MATHEMATICS (013)

GEORGIA ASSESSMENTS FOR THE CERTIFICATION OF EDUCATORS®

 TestWare® Edition

Dana Sparkman, Ph.D.
Former Assistant Professor
Georgia Southern University
Statesboro, Georgia

Research & Education Association

Visit our Educator Support Center: www.rea.com/teacher
Updates to the test and this book: www.rea.com/gace.htm

Research & Education Association
61 Ethel Road West
Piscataway, New Jersey 08854
E-mail: info@rea.com

Georgia GACE® Middle Grades Mathematics Test (013) With TestWare® on CD-ROM

Library of Congress Control Number 20100928193

ISBN-13: 978-0-7386-0829-7
ISBN-10: 0-7386-0829-7

For all references in this book, Georgia Assessments for the Certification of Educators® and GACE® are trademarks, in the U.S. and/or other countries, of the Georgia Professional Standards Commission and Pearson Education, Inc., or its affiliates.

Windows® is a registered trademark of Microsoft Corporation.

The Mathematics Test Objectives presented in this book were created and implemented by the Georgia Professional Standards Commission and Pearson Education, Inc. For further information visit the GACE website at www.gace.nesinc.com.

REA® and TestWare® are registered trademarks of Research & Education Association, Inc.

E10-0101

About the Author

Dr. Dana Sparkman has devoted her career to the education of teachers. Dr. Sparkman earned her Ph.D. with a major in Elementary Education, from the University of Alabama. As an Assistant Professor in the Department of Teaching and Learning at Georgia Southern University, Dr. Sparkman taught a full range of mathematics courses for future teachers. She has been a member of the Georgia Council of Teachers of Mathematics, and the Georgia Educational Research Association. Dr. Sparkman is a member of the National Council of Teachers of Mathematics and the National School Science and Mathematics Association. She often presents papers at international and national conferences. A recent family move has brought her to the University of West Alabama, where she is an Assistant Professor of Elementary Education.

Acknowledgments

We would like to thank REA's Larry B. Kling, Vice President, Editorial, for supervising development; Pam Weston, Vice President, Publishing, for setting the quality standards for production integrity and managing the publication to completion; John Paul Cording, Vice President, Technology, for coordinating the design, development, and testing of REA's TestWare®; Alice Leonard, Senior Editor, for project management and preflight editorial review; Kathleen Casey, Senior Editor, for post-production quality assurance; Heena Patel, software project manager, for her software testing efforts; and Christine Saul, Senior Graphic Artist, for cover design.

We gratefully acknowledge Mel Friedman, Senior Math Editor, for ensuring the integrity of the mathematics in this publication.

We also gratefully acknowledge Ashwath Narayana C and Jay G of Transcend Creative Services (TCS Publishing) for managing the page composition and typesetting; Susanne Holland for technical editing; Marianne L'Abbate for copyediting; and Stephanie Reymann for creating the index.

About Research & Education Association

Founded in 1959, Research & Education Association is dedicated to publishing the finest and most effective educational materials—including software, study guides, and test preps—for students in middle school, high school, college, graduate school, and beyond.

REA's Test Preparation series includes books and software for all academic levels in almost all disciplines. Research & Education Association publishes test preps for students who have not yet completed high school, as well as for high school students preparing to enter college. Students from countries around the world seeking to attend college in the United States will find the assistance they need in REA's publications. For college students seeking advanced degrees, REA publishes test preps for many major graduate school admission examinations in a wide variety of disciplines, including engineering, law, and medicine. Students at every level, in every field, with every ambition can find what they are looking for among REA's publications.

REA's practice tests are always based upon the most recently administered exams and include every type of question that you can expect on the actual exams.

REA's publications and educational materials are highly regarded and continually receive an unprecedented amount of praise from professionals, instructors, librarians, parents, and students. Our authors are as diverse as the fields represented in the books we publish. They are well-known in their respective disciplines and serve on the faculties of prestigious high schools, colleges, and universities throughout the United States and Canada.

Today, REA's wide-ranging catalog is a leading resource for teachers, students, and professionals.

We invite you to visit us at *www.rea.com* to find out how "REA is making the world smarter."

Contents

Introduction

About This Book and TestWare®

REA's *GACE (013) Middle Grades Mathematics Test* is a comprehensive guide designed to assist you in preparing to take this GACE test. To help you to succeed in this important step toward your teaching career in Georgia schools, this test guide features:

- An accurate and complete overview of the GACE (013) Middle Grades Mathematics Test

- The information you need to know about the exam

- A targeted review of each subarea

- Tips and strategies for successfully completing standardized tests

- Diagnostic tools to identify areas of strength and weakness

- Two full-length, true-to-format practice tests, in this book and on CD, based on the most recently administered GACE (013) Middle Grades Mathematics test

- Detailed explanations for each answer on the practice tests. These allow you to identify correct answers and understand not only why they are correct but also why the other answer choices are incorrect.

When creating this test prep, the author and editors considered the most recent test administrations and professional standards. They also researched information from the Georgia Professional Standard Commission, professional journals, textbooks, and educators. The result is the best GACE test preparation materials based on the latest information available.

About Test Selection

The GACE (013) Middle Grades Mathematics Test is conducted during morning test sessions. Test sessions are four hours in length.

About the GACE 013 Middle Grades Mathematics Test

The purpose of the GACE (013) Middle Grades Mathematics Test is to assess the knowledge and skills of prospective Georgia mathematics teachers in the middle school.

What Does the Test Cover?

The following table lists the objectives used as the basis for the GACE (013) Middle Grades Mathematics Test and the approximate number of questions in each subarea. A thorough review of all the specific skills is the focus of this book.

Test Overview Chart:

Subareas	Approximate Number of Selected Response Questions	Range of Objectives	Constructed-Response Assignments
Numbers and Operations	14	0001 – 0003	
Measurement and Geometry	14	0004 – 0006	1
Patterns, Algebra, and Functions	14	0007 – 0009	1
Data Analysis and Probability	9	0010 – 0011	
Mathematical Processes and Perspectives	9	0012 – 0013	
Total	60		2
Percentage of Test Score	80%		20%

How Is the GACE 013 Middle Grades Mathematics Test Scored?

Your total test score will be a scaled score. A scaled score combines your correct answers to the scorable questions on the selected-response section of the test with the scores you received on the constructed-response questions. The scale runs from 100 to 300, with 220 being the passing score.

When Will I Receive My Score Report, and What Will It Look Like?

Reporting of Scores. Your scores are reported directly to the Georgia Standards Commission and are automatically added to your certification application file.

Unofficial test scores are posted on the Internet at 5:00 p.m. Eastern Time on the score report dates listed on http://www.gace.nesine.com/Ga4_testdates.asp.

Can I Retake the Test?

Retaking a Test. If you wish to retake a test, you may do so at a subsequent test administration. Please consult the GACE website at **www.gace.nesinc.com** for information about test registration. The GACE website also includes information regarding test retakes and score reports.

Who Administers the Test?

The Georgia Professional Standards Commission (GaPSC) has contracted with the Evaluation Systems group of Pearson to assist in the development and administration of the Georgia Assessments for the Certification of Educators® (GACE®).

When and Where is the Test Given? How Long Will it Take?

The GACE is administered seven times a year at five locations across the state, as detailed on the GACE website. The 013 Middle Grades Mathematics test is available during the morning sessions on all test days EXCEPT May and June.

To receive information on upcoming test dates and locations, you may contact the test administrator at:

Georgia Assessments for the Certification of Educators

Pearson
P.O. Box 226
Amherst, MA 01004-9013
Telephone: 413-256-2892 or (866) 565-4894
Fax: 413-256-7077
Website: www.gace.nesinc.com

The tests are scheduled to be completed within a maximum of four hours.

How to Use This Book and TestWare®

When Should I Start Studying?

It is never too early to start studying for the GACE 013 Middle Grades Mathematics Test. The earlier you begin, the more time you will have to sharpen your skills. Do not procrastinate! Cramming is not an effective way to study because it does not allow you the time you need to think about the content, review the content required in the objectives, and take the practice tests.

What Do the Review Sections Cover?

The targeted review in this book is designed to help you sharpen the skills you need to approach the GACE 013 Middle Grades Mathematics Test, as well as provide strategies for attacking the questions.

Each teaching area included in the GACE 013 Middle Grades Mathematics Test is examined in a separate chapter. The skills required for all areas are extensively discussed to optimize your understanding of what the examination covers.

Your schooling has taught you most of the information you need to answer the questions on the test. The education classes you took should have provided you with the know-how to make important decisions about situations you will face as a teacher. The review sections in this book are designed to help you fit the information you have acquired into the objectives specified on the GACE. Going over your class notes and textbooks together with the reviews provided here will give you an excellent springboard for passing the examination.

Studying for the GACE 013 Middle Grades Mathematics Test

Choose the time and place for studying that works best for you. Some people set aside a certain number of hours every morning to study, while others prefer to study at night before going to sleep. Other people study off and on during the day—for instance, while waiting for a bus or during a lunch break. Only you can determine when and where your study time will be most effective. Be consistent and use your time efficiently. Work out a study routine and stick to it.

When you take the practice tests, simulate the conditions of the actual test as closely as possible. Turn off your television and radio, and sit down at a table in a quiet room, free from distraction. On completing a practice test, score it and thoroughly review the explanations to the questions you answered incorrectly; however, do not review too much at any one time. Concentrate on one problem area at a time by reviewing the question and explanation, and by studying the review in this guide until you are confident that you have mastered the material.

Keep track of your scores so you can gauge your progress and discover general weaknesses in particular sections. Give extra attention to the reviews that cover your areas of difficulty, so you can build your skills in those areas. Many have found the use of study or note cards very helpful for this review.

How Can I Use My Study Time Efficiently?

The following study schedule allows for thorough preparation for the GACE 013 Middle Grades Mathematics Test. The course of study presented here is seven weeks, but you can condense or expand the timeline to suit your personal schedule. It is vital that you adhere to a structured plan and set aside ample time each day to study. The more time you devote to studying, the more prepared and confident you will be on the day of the test.

Study Schedule

Week 1	After having read this first chapter to understand the format and content of this exam, take the first practice test on the CD. The scores will indicate your strengths and weaknesses. Make sure you simulate real exam conditions when you take the tests. Afterward, score them and review the explanations, especially for questions you answered incorrectly. Use index cards to track the information about which you need to learn more.
Week 2	Review the explanations for the questions you missed, and review the appropriate chapter sections. Useful study techniques include highlighting key terms and information, taking notes as you review each section, and putting new terms and information on your index cards to help retain the information.
Week 3 and Week 4	Reread all your index cards, refresh your understanding of the objectives included in the exam; study the chapters in this book, especially those that cover the areas in which you feel weak; review your college textbooks, and read over notes you took in your college classes. This is also the time to consider any other supplementary materials that your counselor or the Georgia Professional Standards Commission suggests. Review the department's Website at http://www.gace.nesinc.com. Make additional notes as needed.
Week 5	Begin to condense your notes and findings. A structured list of important facts and concepts, based on your index cards and the GACE 013 Middle Grades Mathematics objectives, will help you thoroughly review for the test. Review the answers and explanations for any questions you missed.
Week 6	Have someone quiz you using the index cards you have amassed. Take the second practice test on the CD, adhering to the time limits and simulated test day conditions.
Week 7	Using all your study materials, review areas of weakness revealed by your score on the second set of practice tests. Then retake sections of the practice tests that are printed in this book, as needed.

Test-Taking Tips

Although you may not be familiar with tests like the GACE, this book will acquaint you with this type of exam and help alleviate your test-taking anxieties. By following the seven suggestions listed here, you can become more relaxed about taking the GACE, as well as other tests.

Tip 1. Become comfortable with the format of the GACE. When you are practicing, stay calm and pace yourself. After simulating the test only once, you will boost your chances of doing well, and you will be able to sit down for the actual GACE with much more confidence.

Tip 2. Read all the possible answers. Just because you think you have found the correct response, do not automatically assume that it is the best answer. Read through each choice to be sure that you are not making a mistake by jumping to conclusions.

Tip 3. Use the process of elimination. Go through each answer to a question and eliminate as many of the answer choices as possible. If you can eliminate two answer choices, you have given yourself a better chance of getting the item correct, because only two choices are left from which to make your guess. Do not leave an answer blank. It is better to guess than not to answer a question on the GACE test because there is no additional penalty for wrong answers.

Tip 4. Place a question mark in your answer booklet next to the answers you guessed, and then recheck them later if you have time.

Tip 5. Work quickly and steadily. You will have four hours to complete the test, so the amount of time you spend will depend upon whether you take both subtests in one test session. Taking the practice tests in this book or on the CD will help you learn to budget your precious time.

Tip 6. Learn the directions and format of the test. This will not only save time but also will help you avoid anxiety (and the mistakes caused by being anxious).

Tip 7. When taking the multiple-choice portion of the test, be sure that the answer oval you fill in corresponds to the number of the question in the test booklet. The multiple-choice test is graded by machine, and marking one wrong answer can throw off your answer key and your score. Be extremely careful.

The Day of the Test

Before the Test

On the morning of the test, be sure to dress comfortably so you are not distracted by being too hot or too cold while taking the test. Plan to arrive at the test center early. This will allow you to collect your thoughts and relax before the test and will also spare you the anguish that comes with being late. You should check your GACE Registration Bulletin to find out what time to arrive at the center.

What to Bring

Before you leave for the test center, make sure that you have your admission ticket. Your admission ticket lists your test selection, test site, test date, and reporting time. See the Test Selection http://www.gace.nesinc.com/GA4_whattobring.asp.

You must also bring two pieces of personal identification. One must be a current, government-issued identification, in the name in which you registered, bearing your photograph and signature, and one additional piece of identification (with or without a photograph). If the name on your identification differs from the name in which you are registered, you must bring official verification of the change (e.g., marriage certificate, court order).

You must bring several sharpened No. 2 pencils with erasers, because none will be provided at the test center. If you like, you can wear a watch to the test center. However, you cannot wear one that makes noise, because it might disturb the other test takers. Dictionaries, textbooks, notebooks, calculators, cell phones, beepers, PDAs, scratch paper, listening and recording devices, briefcases, or packages are not permitted. Drinking, smoking, and eating during the test are prohibited. You may not bring any visitors, including relatives, children, and friends.

You may bring a water bottle into the testing room, as long as it is clear without a label but with a tight lid. During testing, you will have to store your bottle under your seat.

Use of Calculators

One of several models of Texas Instruments products will be provided to you at the test site. Instructions for using these calculators will _not_ be provided at the test site. You may _not_ use your own calculator _or_ calculator manual. Because of this, it is imperative that you visit the GACE site to verify the latest models to be used — and then become familiar with them. http://www.gace.nesinc.com/GA4_testselection.asp

Security Measures

As part of the identity verification process, your thumbprint will be taken at the test site. Thumbprints will be used only for the purpose of identity verification. If you do not provide a thumbprint, you will not be permitted to take the test and you will not receive a refund or a credit for the fee paid.

Enhanced security measures, including additional security screenings, may be required by test site facilities. If an additional screening is conducted, only screened persons will be admitted to the test site. If you do not proceed through the security screening, you will not be allowed to test and you will not receive a refund or credit of any kind.

Late Arrival Policy

If you are late for a test session, you may not be admitted. If you are permitted to enter, you will not be given any additional time for the test session. You will be required to sign a statement acknowledging this.

If you arrive late and are not admitted, you will be considered absent and will not receive a refund or credit of any kind. You will need to register and pay again to test at a future administration.

Absentee Policy

If you are absent, you will not receive a refund or credit of any kind. You will need to register and pay again to test at a future administration.

A day or so before your scheduled test, be sure and check the GACE website for any changes to the Test Site Rules. http://www.gace.nesinc.com/GA4_siterules.asp

During the Test

The GACE 013 Middle Grades Mathematics Test is given in one sitting, with no breaks. However, during testing, you may take restroom breaks. Any time that you take for restroom breaks is considered part of the available testing time. Procedures will be followed to maintain test security. Once you enter the test center, follow all the rules and instructions given by the test supervisor. If you do not, you risk being dismissed from the test and having your score canceled.

When all the materials have been distributed, the test instructor will give you directions for completing the informational portion of your answer sheet. Fill out the sheet carefully, because the information you provide will be printed on your score report.

Once the test begins, mark only one answer per question, completely erase unwanted answers and marks, and fill in answers darkly and neatly.

After the Test

When you finish your test, hand in your materials and you will be dismissed. Then, go home and relax—you deserve it!

CHAPTER

1

Numbers and Operations

The Real Numbers and Integers

Real numbers can be represented on a real number line, which has an infinite number of points and extends endlessly in both directions. Each point on the line is associated with a real number.

On a number line, we select a point and label it with the number 0. Any point on the line can then be labeled with a real number, depending on its position. Numbers to the right of 0 on the number line are positive. On the number line shown in Figure 1.1, the point 4 units to the right of 0 is +4 (the + sign is usually assumed, so +4 is written simply as 4). Conversely, numbers to the left of 0 on the number line are negative. Therefore, the point 3 units to the left of 0 is −3.

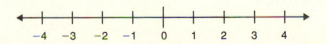

Figure 1.1

The number line in Figure 1.1 represents the subset of real numbers called **integers**.

Integers consist of negatives, positives, and zero. The set of integers can be represented as {. . . −4, −3,

−2, −1, 0, 1, 2, 3, 4, . . .}. There are several subsets of integers as well, as illustrated in the following table.

Subsets of Integers	Definition of the Subset
Whole numbers	The set of integers starting with 0 and increasing: {0, 1, 2, 3, . . .}
Positive integers or natural numbers	The set of integers starting with 1 and increasing: {1, 2, 3, . . .}
Negative integers	The set of integers starting with −1 and decreasing: {−1, −2, −3, . . .}
Prime numbers	The set of positive integers greater than 1 that are divisible only by 1 and themselves: {2, 3, 5, 7, 11, . . .}
Even integers	The set of integers divisible by 2: {. . . , −4, −2, 0, 2, 4, . . .}
Odd integers	The set of integers not divisible by 2: {. . . , −3, −1, 1, 3, 5, . . .}

Figure 1.2 shows the relationship among the different types of numbers.

1

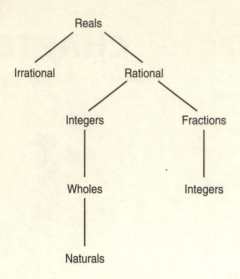

Figure 1.2

There are three standard properties of equality involving real numbers.

1. Reflexive Property

   For each real number a, $a = a$.

2. Symmetric Property

   For real numbers a and b, if $a = b$, then $b = a$.

3. Transitive Property

   For real numbers a, b, and c, if $a = b$ and $b = c$, then $a = c$.

Rational and Irrational Numbers

The set of real numbers is made up of **rational numbers** and **irrational numbers**. A rational number is a number that can be written in fractional form ($\frac{a}{b}$), where a is any integer, and b is any integer except zero. This group includes fractions and decimals that end. An irrational number is a number that cannot be written in simple fractional form. Irrational numbers include many radical numbers and decimal numbers that do not repeat in a pattern and do not end.

Here are some examples of rational numbers: 3, 6, -8, -15, $\frac{2}{3}$, $-\frac{1}{2}$, $\frac{9}{4}$, and 4.589.

Here are some examples of irrational numbers (the symbol $\approx$ means "is approximately equal to"): pi (π) ≈ 3.14159, $\sqrt{2} \approx 1.41421$, and $\sqrt{5} \approx 2.23607$.

EXAMPLE 1

List the numbers $\frac{1}{2}$, 0.2, $\sqrt{2}$, 2, from least to greatest.

SOLUTION

$\frac{1}{2} = 0.5$ and $\sqrt{2} \approx 1.414$.

Therefore, the numbers from least to greatest are 0.2, $\frac{1}{2}$, $\sqrt{2}$, 2.

Absolute Value

The **absolute value** of a given number is the distance between that number and zero on the number line. It is represented by the symbol $||$. Examples are:

$|7| = 7$ and $|-5| = 5$.

There are several rules related to absolute values.

1. $|-A| = A$

2. $|A| \geq 0$, equality holding only if $A = 0$

3. $\left|\dfrac{A}{B}\right| = \dfrac{|A|}{|B|}$, $B \neq 0$

4. $|AB| = |A| \times |B|$

5. $|A^2| = A^2$

EXAMPLE 2

Calculate the value of $|-8| + |-13|$.

SOLUTION

$|-8| + |-13| = 8 + 13 = 21$.

EXAMPLE 3

Calculate the value of $|4 - 9| - |-7 - 2|$ $+ |-5 + 6|$.

SOLUTION

$$|4-9| - |-7-2| + |-5+6| = |-5| - |-9| + |1|$$
$$= 5-9 +1=-3.$$

Place Value for Whole Numbers

Our number system is devised such that the place that a digit holds in a number reveals the value of the digit. For example, in the number 386, the 3 is in the hundreds place, so the value of that digit is 300.

Large numbers are placed into groups of three called periods, which are separated by commas. When reading each period, use the same pattern of hundreds, tens, and ones.

Billions Period			Millions Period			Thousands Period			Ones Period		
Hundreds	Tens	Ones	Hundreds	Tens	Ones	Hundreds	Tens	Ones	Hundreds	Tens	Ones
	2	1,	3	4	9,	0	2	7,	4	1	8

In the number on the chart, the digit 3 is in the hundred millions place; therefore, the value of the digit 3 is 300 million, or 300,000,000. The entire number is read as "Twenty one billion, three hundred forty nine million, twenty seven thousand, four hundred eighteen."

Prime and Composite Numbers

A prime number is a whole number that has exactly two factors, 1 and itself. The numbers 7, 11, 17, and 23 are examples of prime numbers. The number 2 is the only even prime.

Composite numbers are whole numbers that have more than two different factors.

The number 6 is a composite number because its factors are 1, 2, 3, and 6. The number 20 is also a composite number because its factors are 1, 2, 4, 5, 10, and 20.

The number 1 is neither prime nor composite.

The Fundamental Theorem of Arithmetic

The fundamental theorem of arithmetic states that any number can be subdivided uniquely (except for order) into a product of prime numbers. The following examples illustrate a method by which this prime factorization can be done.

EXAMPLE 4

Write the prime factorization of 24.

SOLUTION

We begin with two numbers whose product is 24, such as 4 and 6. So, $24 = 4 \times 6$. Then, because $4 = 2 \times 2$ and $6 = 2 \times 3$, we can write $24 = 2 \times 2 \times 2 \times 3$. The answer is more commonly written as $2^3 \times 3$.

EXAMPLE 5

Write the prime factorization of 60.

SOLUTION

Select two numbers whose product is 60. Let's choose 6 and 10. Then $60 = 6 \times 10$. Because $6 = 2 \times 3$ and $10 = 2 \times 5$, we can express 60 as $2 \times 3 \times 2 \times 5$, which is equivalent to $2^2 \times 3 \times 5$.

We usually write the prime factorization in ascending order of the bases with the associated exponents. Also, there is usually more than one way to write a number as a product of two factors. The final prime factorization is always unique. In Example 5, we could have written $60 = 15 \times 4 = 3 \times 5 \times 2 \times 2$. The final answer is still $2^2 \times 3 \times 5$.

EXAMPLE 6

Write the prime factorization of 45.

SOLUTION

$45 = 5 \times 9 = 5 \times 3 \times 3 = 3^2 \times 5.$

EXAMPLE 7

Write the prime factorization of 100.

SOLUTION

$100 = 10 \times 10 = 2 \times 5 \times 2 \times 5 = 2^2 \times 5^2$.

Greatest Common Factor

Using the fundamental theorem of arithmetic to determine the prime factorization of numbers is helpful when finding the greatest common factor (GCF) of numbers. The GCF is the largest number that is a factor of two or more whole numbers.

EXAMPLE 8

Find the greatest common factor for 16 and 40.

SOLUTION

First, write each number in prime factorization form: $16 = 2 \times 8 = 2 \times 2 \times 2 \times 2 = 2^4$ and $40 = 4 \times 10 = 2 \times 2 \times 2 \times 5 = 2^3 \times 5$. Our next step is to determine the largest factor in both numbers. This is done by identifying common bases and using the lowest exponent present for each base. The only common base for 16 and 40 is 2, for which the lowest exponent is 3. So the GCF is $2^3 = 8$.

EXAMPLE 9

Find the greatest common factor for 90 and 72.

SOLUTION

$90 = 2 \times 3 \times 3 \times 5 = 2 \times 3^2 \times 5$ and $72 = 2 \times 2 \times 2 \times 3 \times 3 = 2^3 \times 3^2$. The common bases are 2 and 3. For the base 2, the lowest exponent is 1. For the base 3, both numbers contain 3^2, so the lowest exponent is 2. Therefore, the GCF is $2 \times 3^2 = 18$.

NOTE:

If there is no common base for the given numbers, the GCF becomes 1. As an example, $9 = 3^2$ and $35 = 5 \times 7$. So the GCF of 9 and 35 must be 1.

Least Common Multiple

Sometimes it is necessary to find the least common multiple (LCM) of numbers.

The LCM is the smallest number that is a multiple of a given set of numbers. There are three steps involved in finding the LCM of two numbers.

EXAMPLE 10

Find the least common multiple for 18 and 20.

SOLUTION

First, find the prime factorization of each number: $18 = 2 \times 3^2$ and $20 = 2^2 \times 5$.

Second, identify each different base in these numbers, including bases that appear in both numbers. The bases are 2, 3, and 5.

Third, use each base with the highest exponent found in either number. For both bases 2 and 3, the highest exponent present is 2. For the base 5, the highest exponent is 1. Therefore, the LCM is $2^2 \times 3^2 \times 5 = 180$.

EXAMPLE 11

Find the least common multiple of 12 and 105.

SOLUTION

$12 = 2^2 \times 3$ and $105 = 3 \times 5 \times 7$. The four different bases are 2, 3, 5, and 7. For each of 3, 5, and 7, the highest exponent is 1. For the base 2, the highest (and only) exponent is 2. Therefore, the LCM is $2^2 \times 3 \times 5 \times 7 = 420$.

EXAMPLE 12

Find the LCM of 11, 28, and 80.

SOLUTION

The number 11 is already in prime factorization form; $28 = 2^2 \times 7$ and $80 = 2^4 \times 5$. The four different bases are 2, 5, 7, and 11. Each of the bases 5, 7, and 11 occurs only once. The highest exponent for the base 2 is 4. Therefore, the LCM = $2^4 \times 5 \times 7 \times 11 = 6160$.

NOTE:

If there is no common base for the given numbers, the LCM is simply the product of the numbers. As an example, the LCM for the numbers 20 and 21 is $(20)(21) = 420$.

Divisibility Rules

In many types of problems, such as finding the prime factorization of a number, it is helpful to know whether some numbers are divisible by other numbers. The following are basic divisibility rules:

1. A number is divisible by 2 if the last digit is even.
2. A number is divisible by 3 if the sum of the digits in the number is divisible by 3.
3. A number is divisible by 4 if the number made by the last two digits is divisible by 4.
4. A number is divisible by 5 if the number ends in 0 or 5.
5. A number is divisible by 6 if the number is divisible by 2 and 3.
6. A number is divisible by 9 if the sum of the digits in the number is divisible by 9.
7. A number is divisible by 10 if the last digit is 0.

EXAMPLE 13

Given the five-digit number 43,10_, how many different units digits are possible in order for this number to be divisible by 3?

SOLUTION

The sum of the digits shown is 8. We can add any digit, as long as the final sum is divisible by 3. There are three acceptable digits, namely, 1, 4, and 7. Each of the numbers 43,101, and 43,104, and 43,107 are divisible by 3.

EXAMPLE 14

If the six-digit number 112,_86 is divisible by both 6 and 9, what digit(s) is(are) possible for the hundreds place?

SOLUTION

Divisibility by 6 implies divisibility by 2 and by 3. Because the divisibility rule for 9 already includes the divisibility rule for 3, we need an even number for which the sum of its digits is 9. The given number is already even, and the sum of the digits shown is 18. If we replace the placeholder for the hundreds digit by either a 0 or 9, the sum of the digits will be either 18 or 27. Note that the numbers 112,086 and 112,986 are divisible by both 6 and 9.

EXAMPLE 15

Given the five-digit number 32,5_0, how many different tens digits are possible for this number to be divisible by 8?

SOLUTION

Because the rightmost three digits must represent a number that is divisible by 8, there are only two choices for the tens digit, namely, 2 or 6. Note that 32,520 and 32,560 are each divisible by 8.

Exponents

Mathematics problems often contain exponents. Exponential notation is an abbreviated way to show repeated multiplication. When repeated multiplication is indicated, the number is said to be raised to a power. In the expression $a^n = b$, a represents the base, n is the exponent or power that tells the number of times the base is to be multiplied by itself, and b is the product of the multiplication. In the expression 2^3, 2 is the base and 3 is the exponent. This means that 2 is multiplied by itself 3 times ($2 \times 2 \times 2$), and the product is 8.

An exponent may be either positive or negative. A negative exponent is defined as follows: If $n > 0$, then $a^{-n} = \dfrac{1}{a^n}$, provided that $a \neq 0$. Thus, $3^{-2} = \dfrac{1}{3^2} = \dfrac{1}{9}$.

An exponent of 0 gives a result of 1, as long as the base is not equal to 0:

$$a^0 = 1, a \neq 0.$$

An exponent may also be a fraction. If m and n are positive integers, $a^{\frac{m}{n}} = \sqrt[n]{a^m}$. Here, the numerator remains as the exponent of a, and the denominator tells what root to take.

EXAMPLE 16

What is the value of $8^{\frac{2}{3}}$?

SOLUTION

$$8^{\frac{2}{3}} = \sqrt[3]{8^2} = \sqrt[3]{64} = 4$$

EXAMPLE 17

What is the value of $\left(\dfrac{1}{16}\right)^{\frac{3}{2}}$?

SOLUTION

$$\left(\frac{1}{16}\right)^{\frac{3}{2}} = \left(\sqrt{\frac{1}{16}}\right)^3 = \left(\frac{1}{4}\right)^3 = \frac{1}{64}.$$

If the exponent is negative, we can still evaluate the expression.

EXAMPLE 18

What is the value of 7^{-3}?

SOLUTION

$$7^{-3} = \frac{1}{7^3} = \frac{1}{343}$$

EXAMPLE 19

What is the value of $(8)^{\frac{-1}{3}}$?

SOLUTION

$$(8)^{\frac{-1}{3}} = \frac{1}{(8)^{\frac{1}{3}}} = \frac{1}{\sqrt[3]{8}} = \frac{1}{2}.$$

If the base is negative, be extra careful in evaluating the expression, especially with regard to the sign of the answer.

EXAMPLE 20

What is the value of $(-2)^{-4}$?

SOLUTION

$$(-2)^{-4} = \frac{1}{(-2)^4} = \frac{1}{16}.$$

EXAMPLE 21

What is the value of $\left(-\dfrac{1}{9}\right)^{-3}$?

SOLUTION

$$\left(-\frac{1}{9}\right)^{-3} = \frac{1}{\left(-\frac{1}{9}\right)^3} = \frac{1}{-\frac{1}{729}} = -729.$$

There are several rules related to simplifying numbers with exponents.

1. $a^m \times a^n = a^{m+n}$

2. $(a^m)^n = a^{mn}$

3. $\dfrac{a^m}{a^n} = a^{m-n}$

4. $(ab)^m = a^m b^m$

5. $(a/b)^n = a^n / b^n$, if $b \neq 0$.

EXAMPLE 22

What is the value of $2^2 \times 2^3$?

SOLUTION

$2^2 \times 2^3 = 2^{2+3} = 2^5 = 32$.

EXAMPLE 23

What is the simplified expression for $(y^3)^4$?

SOLUTION

$(y^3)^4 = y^{3 \times 4} = y^{12}$

EXAMPLE 24

What is the value of $\dfrac{2^7}{2^3}$?

SOLUTION

$\dfrac{2^7}{2^3} = 2^{7-3} = 2^4 = 16$.

EXAMPLE 25

What is the simplified expression for $(2x)^3$?

SOLUTION:

$(2x)^3 = 2^3 x^3 = 8x^3$.

EXAMPLE 26

What is the value of $\left(\dfrac{2}{3}\right)^3$?

SOLUTION

$\left(\dfrac{2}{3}\right)^3 = \dfrac{2^3}{3^3} = \dfrac{8}{27}$.

Real Number Properties and Operations

Addition and multiplication are particularly important operations, and many properties about these operations have been determined and named. Because addition and multiplication are so closely related, the properties for each operation are similar. Following are the most important properties of real numbers. In each property, a, b, and c represent real numbers.

1. Closure Property of Addition

   $a + b$ is a real number.

2. Closure Property of Multiplication

   ab is a real number.

3. Commutative Property of Addition

   $a + b = b + a$.

4. Commutative Property of Multiplication

   $ab = ba$.

5. Associative Property of Addition

   $(a + b) + c = a + (b + c)$.

6. Associative Property of Multiplication

   $(ab)c = a(bc)$.

7. Identity Property of Addition

   $a + 0 = 0 + a = a$.

8. Identity Property of Multiplication

   $a \times 1 = 1 \times a = a$.

9. Inverse Property of Addition

   There exists a real number $-a$ such that $a + (-a) = -a + a = 0$.

10. Inverse Property of Multiplication

    There exists a real number a^{-1} such that $a \times a^{-1} = a^{-1} \times a = 1$.

11. Distributive Property of Multiplication over Addition

    $a(b + c) = ab + ac$.

The operations of subtraction and division are also important, but less so than addition and multiplication. Following are the definitions for these operations, for any real numbers a, b, and c.

$$a - b = c \text{ if and only if } b + c = a.$$

$$\frac{a}{b} = c \text{ if and only if } bc = a.$$

The definition of division eliminates division by 0. Therefore, $\frac{5}{0}$ is undefined, $\frac{0}{0}$ is undefined, but $\frac{0}{5} = 0$.

In many instances, it is possible to perform subtraction by converting a subtraction statement to an addition statement. Thus, $a - b = a + (-b)$. Likewise, a division statement may be converted to a multiplication statement.

$$\frac{a}{b} = a \times b^{-1}, \text{ provided } b \neq 0.$$

EXAMPLE 27

The statement $(4)(7 + 5) = (4)(7) + (4)(5)$ illustrates which property of real numbers?

SOLUTION

This is the Distributive Property of Multiplication over Addition.

EXAMPLE 28

The statement $\frac{1}{2} + (-\frac{1}{2}) = 0$ illustrates which property?

SOLUTION

This is the Inverse Property of Addition. Remember that fractions may be used as examples of real numbers.

EXAMPLE 29

The statement $(0.4 \times 8) \times \frac{1}{3} = 0.4 \times (8 \times \frac{1}{3})$ illustrates which property?

SOLUTION

This is the Associative Property of Multiplication. As in Example 28, we may use any type of real number.

Operations Involving Real Numbers

The rules for performing operations on integers, fractions, and decimals in which at least one is negative are the same as performing operations on positive numbers, except you must pay close attention to the sign (positive or negative value of each number) and the sign of the answer. The rule for multiplication and division is that two positives or two negatives result in a positive answer, whereas a combination of a positive number and a negative number results in a negative number. Here are some examples: $\frac{-15}{-5} = 3$, $7 \times (-2) = -14$, and $\frac{-51}{3} = -17$.

Adding and subtracting with positive and negative numbers is somewhat different. Positive numbers in an equation can be viewed as "gaining" whereas negative numbers can be viewed as "losing." Here are some illustrations:

$17 + 4 = 21$ (started with 17, gained 4)

$17 - 4 = 13$ (started with 17, lost 4)

$17 + (-4) = 13$ (started with 17, added a loss of 4)

$17 - (-4) = 21$ (started with 17, took away a loss of 4)

Be careful: Adding or "gaining" -4 is like losing 4. Subtracting or "losing" -4 is like gaining 4.

EXAMPLE 30

What is the value of $24 + (-8) - 6$?

SOLUTION

First, combine the negative terms $(-8 - 6)$, which results in -14. Then subtract to get $24 - 14 = 10$.

EXAMPLE 31

What is the value of $29 - (-5)$?

SOLUTION

Subtracting a negative number is equivalent to taking away a loss, which means a gain. You can think of the problem as $29 + (+5)$. Therefore, the answer is 34.

EXAMPLE 32

What is the value of $(-3)(-3)(-\frac{3}{4})$?

SOLUTION

The product of two negatives is a positive. By multiplying this product by a third negative, the answer must be negative. The problem simplifies to $(9)(-\frac{3}{4}) = -\frac{27}{4}$.

Order of Operations

Mathematical expressions and equations often include more than one operation. When simplifying those expressions and equations, there is a specific order in which each operation is done. This is called the **order of operations**, and the steps are as follows:

1. Perform the operations inside parentheses and other grouping symbols. Remember, a fraction bar is a grouping symbol.

2. Clear the exponents or roots.

3. Multiply and divide, from left to right.

4. Add and subtract, from left to right.

The mnemonic statement "**P**lease **e**xcuse **m**y **d**ear **A**unt **S**ally" stands for **p**arentheses, **e**xponents, **m**ultiply, **d**ivide, **a**dd, **s**ubtract. This can help with remembering the order of operations.

EXAMPLE 33

What is the value of $(3 + 2) \times 4 - 3$?

SOLUTION

First, perform the operation inside the parentheses to get $5 \times 4 - 3$. Then multiply from left to right to

get $20 - 3$. Finally, subtract from left to right to get the answer of 17.

EXAMPLE 34

What is the value of $(7 - 5)^2 + 20 \div 5 + 1$?

SOLUTION

Perform the operation inside the grouping symbols (parentheses and the division bar) to get $2^2 + 4 + 1$. Next, evaluate the term with the exponents and add to get $4 + 4 + 1 = 9$.

EXAMPLE 35

What is the value of $7 + 4 \times 3 - 1 \div 3$?

SOLUTION

First, do the multiplication to get $7 + 12 - 1 \div 3$. Second, do the division so that the example reads as $7 + 12 - \frac{1}{3}$. Finally, add and subtract from left to right to get the answer of $18\frac{2}{3}$.

EXAMPLE 36

What is the value of $4(3 + 1) \div (2^3 \times 3)$?

SOLUTION

Simplify each set of parentheses to get $4(4) \div (8 \times 3) = 4(4) \div (24)$. The answer is found by dividing 16 by 24 to get $\frac{16}{24} = \frac{2}{3}$.

Decimals

When we divide the denominator of a fraction into the numerator, the result is a decimal. Decimals are a way of representing fractions by using a denominator that is a power of ten (such as tenths, hundredths, and thousandths). Decimal numbers are written with a decimal point. Whereas whole numbers are placed to the left of the decimal point, decimal numbers are placed to the right of the decimal point. Starting from the decimal point and going to the right, the first six placeholders are tenths, hundredths, thousandths, ten thousandths, hundred thousandths, and millionths. As an example, for the number 0.325894, the value of the digit 2 is hundredths, the value of the digit 8 is ten thousandths, and the value of the digit 4 is millionths.

Decimals have equivalent fractional forms. Here are some examples: $0.3 = \dfrac{3}{10}$, $0.35 = \dfrac{35}{100}$, $0.027 = \dfrac{27}{1000}$, and $0.00009 = \dfrac{9}{100,000}$.

Both whole numbers and decimals may be written with exponents. With whole numbers, the exponents are positive; with decimals, the exponents are negative. Tens may be written as 10^1. Tenths may be written as 10^{-1}. Hundreds may be written as 10^2. Hundredths may be written as 10^{-2}. Thousands may be written as 10^3. Thousandths may be written as 10^{-3}.

Operations with Decimals

To add or subtract decimal numbers, arrange them vertically, with the decimal points aligned. Then add or subtract them as with whole numbers. In the case of a whole number, the decimal point is "understood;" therefore, you may place a decimal point at the end of the whole number so that it is easy to align with the other decimal numbers.

To multiply decimal numbers, arrange the numbers vertically, with alignment on the right side. Multiply the numbers as if they were whole numbers. Count the numbers behind the decimal point in each number being multiplied. That indicates how many numbers should be behind the decimal point in the product.

EXAMPLE 37

What is the product of 2.051 and 3.2?

SOLUTION

2.051 (3 decimal places)

×   3.2 (1 decimal place)

  4102

61530

65632

The final answer is 6.5632 (4 decimal places).

One way to check whether your decimal point is in the correct place is to determine whether your answer is reasonable. In the above example, consider the whole numbers in the factors (2 and 3). Multiplying 2 × 3 would result in the product of 6, which is an approximation of the product of the given problem. Knowing this approximation helps you to be certain that your decimal point is in the correct place.

To divide decimal numbers, set up the problem as you would a traditional whole-number division problem. In the divisor, move the decimal point all the way to the right, making it appear as a whole number. Count the number of places the decimal point was moved. Move the decimal point to the right the same number of places in the dividend. Move the decimal point directly upward, and write it in the quotient spot. Finally, divide the numbers as if they were whole numbers to arrive at the answer.

EXAMPLE 38

Divide 24.3 by 3.24.

SOLUTION

Because the divisor (3.24) has two decimal places, move the decimal point two places to the right to get 324. This means that we must move the decimal point of the dividend (24.3) two places to the right to get 2430. (Note that a zero had to be included.) The rest of the division is shown below.

$$
\begin{array}{r}
7.5 \\
3.24\,\overline{)\,24.30\,0} \\
22\ 68 \\
\hline
16\ 20 \\
16\ 20 \\
\hline
0
\end{array}
$$

The final answer is 7.5.

Comparing Decimals

When comparing two numbers with decimals to determine which is larger, compare the numbers, starting with the tenths place. Whichever number has the larger digit in this place indicates the largest number. If the digits are the same, look to the hundredths place, and so on.

EXAMPLE 39

Compare the numbers 0.825 and 0.619. Also compare the numbers 0.705 and 0.761.

SOLUTION

Because 8 is larger than 6, we conclude that 0.825 is greater than 0.619. Comparing 0.705 and 0.761, we see that both numbers have 7 in the tenths place, so we compare the digits in the hundredths place. Because 6 is larger than 0, we conclude that 0.761 is greater than 0.705.

EXAMPLE 40

List these decimals from least to greatest: 0.357, 0.3, 0.369, 0.356, 0.0367

SOLUTION

It may be helpful to list decimals vertically so that it is easier to compare digits. Also, you may add enough zeroes at the end of decimal numbers so that visually they appear the same length.

0.3570

0.3000

0.3690

0.3560

0.0367

The smallest number is 0.0367, then 0.3, then 0.356, then 0.357, then 0.369.

Rounding Decimals

Some problems require rounding of decimal numbers. The rules for rounding decimal numbers are the same as those for rounding whole numbers. Find the "place" to which you are being asked to round. Look at the digit to the right of that place. If the digit is 5 or greater, round the digit up to the next number. If the digit is less than 5, round the digit down one number.

EXAMPLE 41

Round off 3.284 to the nearest hundredth.

SOLUTION

The digit 8 is in the hundredths place. Look at the digit to the right. It is less than 5, so rounding 3.284 to the nearest hundredth results in 3.28.

EXAMPLE 42

Round off 14.5728 to the nearest tenth.

SOLUTION

The digit 5 is in the tenths place. Look at the digit to the right. It is greater than 5, so round the tenths digit up. Therefore, rounding this number to the nearest tenth results in 14.6.

EXAMPLE 43

Round off 2.3796 to the nearest hundredth.

SOLUTION

Find the digit in the hundredths place, which is 7. Look to the place to the right; the digit in that place is 9, which tells us to round up the tenths place. Therefore, 2.3796 rounded off to the nearest hundredth is 2.38.

Sometimes more than one adjustment needs to be made in the rounding off process. Here are two such examples.

EXAMPLE 44

Round off 0.971 to the nearest tenth.

SOLUTION

The digit in the hundredths place (7) is at least 5, so we must increase the digit in the tenths place. Because the tenths place digit is 9, it becomes 0, which forces the units digit to change to 1. Thus, the answer becomes 1.0.

EXAMPLE 45

Round off 7.0029 to the nearest hundredth.

SOLUTION

The digit in the thousandths place (2) is less than 5, so we do not change the digit in the hundredths place. The final answer is 7.00, which *cannot* simply be written as 7.

Decimals as Rational or Irrational Numbers

Remember that **rational numbers** can be written in the form $\frac{a}{b}$ (as long as $b \neq 0$). Therefore, we can express any rational number as a decimal by dividing the numerator by the denominator. The result is either a **terminating decimal** (which means that $\frac{a}{b}$ has a remainder of 0 at some point) or a **repeating decimal** (which means that, when a is divided by b, the decimal has a repeating pattern). Examples of terminating (rational) decimals are: 0.25, which has a fractional equivalent of $\frac{1}{4}$, and 0.675, which has a fractional equivalent of $\frac{27}{40}$.

Examples of repeating decimals are $0.\overline{2}$, which has a fractional equivalent of $\frac{2}{9}$, and $0.\overline{142857}$, which has a fractional equivalent of $\frac{1}{7}$.

Irrational numbers are numbers in which the decimal form is nonterminating and nonrepeating. Examples are $\sqrt{2}$ and $\sqrt[3]{4}$. For these numbers, your calculator will display several decimal places, but there is no pattern and they do not terminate. We can check that $\sqrt{2} \approx 1.4142$ and that $\sqrt[3]{4} \approx 1.5874$.

Scientific Notation

We often use decimal numbers that are very small or very large. In such cases, use scientific notation. Write it as a product of two factors, namely, a decimal number between 1 and 10 multiplied by a power (exponent) of ten. If the number already lies between 1 and 10, the power of 10 to use is zero. For example, $7.4 = 7.4 \times 10^0$.

EXAMPLE 46

Write 41,700,000 in scientific notation.

SOLUTION

Write the first factor as a decimal between 1 and 10, which becomes 4.17. Then write the second factor as a power of ten, which is 10^7. The answer is 4.17×10^7.

To be sure that the exponent is correct, count the number of digits between the decimal point in 4.17 to the end of 41,700,000. If the decimal point comes after the 4, there are 7 places to the end of 41,700,000. Therefore, the exponent must be 7.

EXAMPLE 47

Write the number 187,500,000,000 using scientific notation.

SOLUTION

Write the first factor as a decimal between 1 and 10, which is 1.875. Next, count the number of places the decimal point must be moved from 1.875 to

187,500,000,000. Because the number of places is 11, the answer becomes 1.875×10^{11}.

EXAMPLE 48

Write the number 0.00035 in scientific notation.

SOLUTION

Write the first factor as a decimal between 1 and 10, which is 3.5. Write the second factor as a power of ten. Because it is a decimal less than 1, the exponent is negative. There are four places between 0.00035 and 3.5, so the second factor must be 10^{-4}. Thus, the answer is 3.5×10^{-4}.

Percent

Percent is a way to represent numbers where the whole is considered 100%. The word *percent* means "per 100." Fractions with a denominator of 100 can be written as a percent. Decimals can also be written easily as a percentage simply by moving the decimal point.

There are three types of percent problems: finding a percentage of a given number, finding what percentage one number is of another number, and finding the total when the percentage is known.

Finding a Percentage of a Number

For problems like this, first write the percent as a decimal. Then multiply the decimal and the given number. Place the decimal point in the correct place.

EXAMPLE 49

What is 40% of 30?

SOLUTION

Write the 40% as the decimal 0.40. Then multiply this number by 30. The answer is $(0.40)(30) = 12$.

EXAMPLE 50

What is 0.64% of 600?

SOLUTION

Write 0.64% as the decimal 0.0064 and multiply by 50. The answer is $(0.0064)(600) = 3.84$.

Finding the Percentage That One Number Is of Another Number

For problems like this, set up an equation that will state that n percent times the total number is the missing number. It helps to write the percent number as a fraction or decimal.

EXAMPLE 51

What percent of 150 is 25?

SOLUTION

Write the equation: $\frac{n}{100} \times 150 = 25$. Next, solve this equation, which can be rewritten as $1.5n = 25$. Then $n = 16.67$. Thus, 25 is 16.67% of 150.

EXAMPLE 52

What percent of 18 is 25.2?

SOLUTION

Write the equation $\frac{n}{100} \times 18 = 25.2$. Simplify this equation to $0.18n = 25.2$. Thus, $n = 140$, which means that 25.2 is 140% of 18.

Finding the Total When the Percent Is Known

For problems like this, set up a proportion. Percentage is $\frac{n}{100}$; therefore, set it equal to the given number over the unknown number, and then solve the proportion.

EXAMPLE 53

> 24 is 30% of what number?

SOLUTION

Write the proportion as $\dfrac{24}{n} = \dfrac{30}{100}$. Solve this proportion by cross-multiplying to get $30n = 24 \times 100 = 2,400$. Thus, $n = 80$.

EXAMPLE 54

> 32 is 220% of what number?

SOLUTION

Write the proportion as $\dfrac{32}{n} = \dfrac{220}{100}$. We can reduce the fraction on the right side to $\dfrac{11}{5}$ so that the proportion simplifies to $\dfrac{32}{n} = \dfrac{11}{5}$. Cross-multiply to get $11n = 160$. To the nearest hundredth, the answer is 14.55.

Equivalent Forms of Numbers

Some problems may require given numbers to be converted into an equivalent form to make the problem easier to solve.

1. To convert a fraction to a decimal, divide the numerator by the denominator. As an example, $\dfrac{1}{5}$ can be written as follows:

    $$5\overline{)\begin{array}{l} 0.2 \\ 1.0 \\ \underline{1.0} \\ 0 \end{array}}$$

    Thus, $\dfrac{1}{5} = 0.2$.

2. To convert a decimal to a percent, move the decimal point two places to the right. In effect, this is the same as multiplying the decimal by 100. As an example, $0.25 = 25\%$.

3. To convert a percent to a decimal, move the decimal point two places to the left. This is the same as dividing the percent by 100. As an example, $35\% = 0.35$. In this example, the decimal point is understood to be to the right of the digit 5 in 35%.

4. To convert a decimal to a fraction, use the given decimal, and make it a fraction over the power of ten that is indicated by the decimal. As an example, in the number 0.25, the decimal ends in the hundredths place. Therefore, 25 would be the numerator of the fraction, and 100 would be the denominator. So $0.25 = \dfrac{25}{100}$, which can be reduced to $\dfrac{1}{4}$.

EXAMPLE 55

> Express $3\dfrac{4}{10}$ as a decimal and as a percent.

SOLUTION

Because the fraction has a denominator of 10, the decimal form becomes 3.4. The equivalent form as a percent is found by moving the decimal point two places to the right and adding any necessary zeros. Thus, $3.4 = 340\%$.

EXAMPLE 56

> Express 0.009 as a percent and as a fraction.

SOLUTION

By moving the decimal point two places to the right, 0.009 is converted to its equivalent form as a percent: 0.9%. As a fraction, 0.009 can be written as $\dfrac{9}{1000}$.

EXAMPLE 57

> Express 42% as a decimal and as a fraction.

SOLUTION

Move the decimal point two places to the left so that 42% can be written as 0.42. The symbol % means "hundredths;" 42% is equivalent to $\frac{42}{100}$. We then reduce this fraction to its final answer of $\frac{21}{50}$.

Radicals

The square root of a number is a number that, when multiplied by itself, results in the original number. That is, if $a^2 = b$, then a is a square root of b. As an example, because $3^2 = 9$, this means that 3 is a square root of 9. A second square root of 9 is -3 because $(-3)^2 = 9$. Each positive number has two real roots; the positive root is considered the principal root. There are no real square roots for negative numbers.

A radical sign shows that the root of a number or expression will be taken. The radicand is the number of which the root will be taken. The index tells how many times the root needs to be multiplied by itself to equal the radicand. If no index is indicated, calculate the square root.

As an example, for the radical $\sqrt[4]{81}$, 4 is the index and 81 is the radicand. Also, $\sqrt[4]{81} = 3$ because $3 \times 3 \times 3 \times 3 = 81$. Note that 3 is the principal fourth root of 81. If we wanted the answer of -3, we would use the expression $-\sqrt[4]{81}$.

As a second example, for the radical $\sqrt[5]{32}$, 5 is the index and 32 is the radicand. Also, $\sqrt[5]{32} = 2$ because $2 \times 2 \times 2 \times 2 \times 2 = 32$. Note that $(-2) \times (-2) \times (-2) \times (-2) \times (-2) = -32$, which means that $\sqrt[5]{-32} = -2$.

Operations with Radicals

To multiply two or more radicals, use the following rule: $\sqrt[n]{a} \times \sqrt[n]{b} = \sqrt[n]{ab}$. If there are numbers outside the radical sign, multiply them together as usual. Then multiply the radicands and simplify.

EXAMPLE 58

Simplify $\sqrt{2} \times \sqrt{24}$.

SOLUTION

$$\sqrt{2} \times \sqrt{24} = \sqrt{48} = \sqrt{16} \times \sqrt{3} = 4\sqrt{3}$$

EXAMPLE 59

Simplify $3\sqrt[3]{2} \times 5\sqrt[3]{24}$.

SOLUTION

$$3\sqrt[3]{4} \times 5\sqrt[3]{24} = 15\sqrt[3]{96} = 15\sqrt[3]{8} \times \sqrt[3]{12}$$
$$= 15 \times 2 \times \sqrt[3]{12} = 30\sqrt[3]{12}.$$

To divide radicals, multiply both the numerator and the denominator by a quantity that will rationalize the denominator. With square roots, the simplest procedure is to multiply both numerator and denominator by the given radical. With cube roots, we must find a multiple of the radicand for which the cube root is a rational number.

EXAMPLE 60

Simplify $\dfrac{3\sqrt{5}}{5\sqrt{6}}$.

SOLUTION

$$\frac{3\sqrt{5}}{5\sqrt{6}} = \frac{3\sqrt{5} \times \sqrt{6}}{5\sqrt{6} \times \sqrt{6}} = \frac{3\sqrt{30}}{5 \times 6} = \frac{3\sqrt{30}}{30} = \frac{\sqrt{30}}{10}.$$

EXAMPLE 61

Simplify $\dfrac{28\sqrt[3]{54}}{7\sqrt[3]{2}}$.

SOLUTION

$$\frac{28\sqrt[3]{54}}{7\sqrt[3]{2}} = \frac{28\sqrt[3]{54} \times \sqrt[3]{4}}{7\sqrt[3]{2} \times \sqrt[3]{4}} = \frac{28\sqrt[3]{216}}{7\sqrt[3]{8}} = \frac{28 \times 6}{7 \times 2} = 12.$$

Note that, for Example 61, another approach would be to divide separately the rational numbers and the radical numbers. Then $\frac{28}{7} = 4$ and $\frac{\sqrt[3]{54}}{\sqrt[3]{2}} = \sqrt[3]{27} = 3$. Our final answer is still 12. Also, note that we did not simply multiply the numerator and denominator by $\sqrt[3]{2}$. Had we used this multiplier, the denominator would have been $\sqrt[3]{4}$, an irrational number.

To add or subtract radicals, the radicals <u>must</u> have the same index and the same radicand. Add or subtract the coefficients, but leave the radicands alone.

The similarities of the radicands may be determined once the radicals are simplified.

EXAMPLE 62

Simplify $3\sqrt{5} - 5\sqrt{5} + 2\sqrt{8} + 3\sqrt{18}$.

$4\sqrt{2} + 9\sqrt{2}$

$-2\sqrt{5} + 13\sqrt{2}$

SOLUTION

The first two radicals can be combined as $-2\sqrt{5}$, whereas the third and fourth radicals must be simplified. So $3\sqrt{5} - 5\sqrt{5} + 2\sqrt{8} + 3\sqrt{18} = -2\sqrt{5} + 2 \times \sqrt{4} \times \sqrt{2} + 3 \times \sqrt{9} \times \sqrt{2} = -2\sqrt{5} + 4\sqrt{2} + 9\sqrt{2} = -2\sqrt{5} + 13\sqrt{2}$.

EXAMPLE 63

Simplify $6\sqrt{12} - \sqrt{3} + \sqrt[3]{125} + \sqrt[3]{16}$.

$12\sqrt{3}.$

$11\sqrt{3}$ $+$ $5 + 2\sqrt[3]{2}$

SOLUTION

$6\sqrt{12} - \sqrt{3} + \sqrt[3]{125} + \sqrt[3]{16}$

$= 6 \times \sqrt{4} \times \sqrt{3} - \sqrt{3} + 5 + \sqrt[3]{8} \times \sqrt[3]{2}$

$= 12\sqrt{3} - \sqrt{3} + 5 + 2\sqrt[3]{2} = 11\sqrt{3} + 5 + 2\sqrt[3]{2}.$

Chapter 1 Quiz

1. If there exist positive integers a and b such that $8a + 12b = c$, then c must be divisible by:

   (A) 3   (C) 18

   (B) 4   (D) 24

2. What is the value of 6% × 6%?

   (A) 0.0036%   (C) 3.6%

   (B) 0.36%   (D) 36%

3. A number line with a linear inequality is shown below.

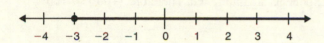

   Which of these statements describes this inequality?

   (A) All numbers less than or equal to −3.

   (B) All numbers greater than or equal to −3.

   (C) All numbers less than −3.

   (D) All numbers greater than −3.

4. Which of the following is an irrational number?

   (A) $\sqrt{3}$ (C) $\dfrac{13}{16}$

   (B) $\sqrt{4}$ (D) −1.27

5. A man buys a book for $20. When he wants to sell it, he wants to offer a discount of 40% on his selling price for the book. Because he wants to make a final profit of 50% on his purchase price, at what price should he originally mark it?

   (A) $25   (C) $40

   (B) $30   (D) $50

6. In July 2004, there were approximately 293,000,000 people living in the United States. How is this number written in scientific notation?

   (A) 29.3×10^7 (C) 2.93×10^8

   (B) 293.0×10^6 (D) 29.3×10^9

7. Which one of the following is equivalent to 100^{18}?

   (A) $(100^6)^3$ (C) $(10^6)^3$

   (B) $100^6 \times 100^3$ (D) $10^6 \times 10^3$

8. A number is considered perfect if it is the sum of its positive integer factors, except itself. For example, 6 is a perfect number because $6 = 1 + 2 + 3$. Which one of the following is a perfect number?

   (A) 36   (C) 20

   (B) 28   (D) 12

9. What percent of 150 is 12?

   (A) 20   (C) 10

   (B) 16   (D) 8

10. What is the simplified form for $\dfrac{\sqrt{75x^7}}{\sqrt{3x}}$?

   (A) $25x^5$ (C) $5x^3$

   (B) $5x^5$ (D) $25x^4$

Chapter 1 Quiz Solutions

1. (B)

Because 8 and 12 are each divisible by 4, c must also be divisible by 4.

2. (B)

First, change each 6% to 0.06. Then, multiply $(0.06)(0.06) = 0.0036 = 0.36\%$.

3. (B)

Because the black dot is on -3, the solution must include this number. The arrow points to the right; thus, all numbers greater than or equal to -3 must be included.

4. (A)

An irrational number is one that cannot be written as the quotient of two integers. Choice (B) is wrong because $\sqrt{4} = 2$ (or $\frac{2}{1}$). Choice (C) is wrong because it is already written as a quotient of two integers. Choice (D) is wrong because $-1.27 = \frac{-127}{100}$, which is a quotient of two integers. But $\sqrt{3}$ cannot be written as a quotient of two integers.

5. (D)

A 50% profit on the cost would be ($20)(0.5), which equals $10. Ten dollars, when added to the original cost of the book equals $30. Thus, $30 represents the selling price. Because $30 represents a 40% discount from the marked price, $30 is actually 60% of the marked price. The marked price is therefore found by dividing $30 by 0.60, which is $50.

6. (C)

First, move the decimal point so that the number reads as 2.93. Then count the number of decimal places that the decimal point moves from 2.93 to 293,000,000. The decimal point moves eight places to the right. Thus, in scientific notation, this number is 2.93×10^8.

7. (A)

When an expression involving a base and an exponent is raised to an exponent, the base remains the same, and the exponents are multiplied. Therefore, $(100^6)^3 = 100^{18}$.

8. (B)

The factors of 28, other than itself, are 1, 2, 4, 7, and 14. Note that $1 + 2 + 4 + 7 + 14 = 28$. Answer choice (A) is wrong because $36 \neq 1 + 2 + 3 + 4 + 6 + 9 + 12 + 18$. Answer choice (C) is wrong because $20 \neq 1 + 2 + 4 + 5 + 10$. Answer choice (D) is wrong because $12 \neq 1 + 2 + 3 + 4 + 6$.

9. (D)

First, set up the equation $\frac{n}{100} \times 150 = 12$. This equation simplifies to $1.5n = 12$. Thus, $n = 8$.

10. (C)

When simplifying expressions such as this one, try to find common factors in the various terms. You see that both 75 and 3 contain 3. Take advantage of this by rewriting the expression this way:

$$\frac{\sqrt{25} \times \sqrt{3} \times \sqrt{x^6} \times \sqrt{x}}{\sqrt{3} \times \sqrt{x}}$$

Then cancel like terms so that the answer reads as $\sqrt{25x^6}$, which simplifies to $5x^3$.

Measurement and Geometry

The Customary System of Measurement

Some problems may require you to make conversions for units of measurement (distance, volume, and mass) in both the customary system and the metric system. Following are the most common conversions within each system, including some basic conversions between metric units and customary units.

Distance	1 foot = 12 inches
	1 yard = 3 feet
	1 mile = 5,280 feet
	1 inch = 2.54 centimeters
Capacity (volume)	1 gallon = 4 quarts
	1 quart = 2 pints
	1 pint = 16 fluid ounces
	1 pint = 2 cups
	1 liter = 1.06 quarts
Mass	1 pound = 16 ounces
	1 ton = 2,000 pounds
	1 kilogram = 2.2 pounds

To convert within the standard system, we must multiply or divide. When we convert from a smaller unit to a larger unit (such as inches to feet), we divide. For example, when converting 36 inches to feet, divide 36 by 12 (because there are 12 inches in one foot) for the answer of 3 feet. When converting from a larger unit to a smaller unit (such as gallons to quarts), multiply. For example, when converting 5 gallons to quarts, multiply 5 gallons by 4 quarts (because there are 4 quarts in a gallon), arriving at an answer of 20 quarts.

EXAMPLE 1

12 ft. = _____ yd.

SOLUTION

We are converting from a smaller unit to a larger unit, so we use division. Because 3 feet is equivalent to 1 yard, 12 feet $= \dfrac{12}{3} = 4$ yards.

EXAMPLE 2

64 oz. = _____ lbs.

SOLUTION

We are converting from a smaller unit to a larger unit, so we use division. Because 16 ounces is equivalent to 1 pound, 64 ounces $= \frac{64}{16} = 4$ pounds.

EXAMPLE 3

7 gal. = _____ qt.

SOLUTION

We are converting from a larger unit to a smaller unit, so we use multiplication. Because 4 quarts is equivalent to 1 gallon, the answer is $7 \times 4 = 28$ quarts.

EXAMPLE 4

Convert 13 feet 7 inches to inches.

SOLUTION

First, convert feet to inches. Because we are converting from a larger unit (feet) to a smaller unit (inches), we use multiplication. Then add the remaining 7 inches. So 13 feet $\times$ 12 inches/foot = 156 inches and 156 inches + 7 inches = 163 inches.

EXAMPLE 5

You have decided to install decorative tiles to line one border of your flower garden. The border measures 15 feet in length. Each tile measures 6 inches in length, and you want to leave 3 inches of space between each tile. How many tiles will you need to construct the border?

SOLUTION

First, convert the 15-foot border to inches: 15 feet $\times$ 12 inches/foot = 180 inches. For each tile, you will need to consider 6 inches plus the 3 inches of space (9 inches total). Then determine how many 9-inch segments are in 180 (180/9 = 20). Thus, you will need 20 tiles to construct the border.

EXAMPLE 6

12 quarts = _____ liters.

SOLUTION

We are converting from a smaller unit to a larger unit, so we use division. Because 1 liter is equivalent to 1.06 quarts, 12 quarts is equivalent to $\frac{12}{1.06} \approx 11.32$ liters.

EXAMPLE 7

9.5 kilograms = _____ pounds.

SOLUTION

One kilogram is larger than one pound. Therefore, 9.5 kilograms is equivalent to $(9.5)(2.2) = 20.9$ pounds.

The Metric System of Measurement

The metric system is built on the base of 10, which makes it simpler to understand than the standard system. Knowing the following prefixes will help:

kilo-	=	$\times 1{,}000$
hecto-	=	$\times 100$
deka-	=	$\times 10$
deci-	=	$\times 0.10 \left(\frac{1}{10}\right)$
centi-	=	$\times 0.01 \left(\frac{1}{100}\right)$
milli-	=	$\times 0.001 \left(\frac{1}{1000}\right)$

Metric Units

In the metric system, the basic unit of length is the meter, which is a little longer than a yard in the standard system. Using the prefixes above, a kilometer is 1,000 meters, and a millimeter is $\frac{1}{1{,}000}$ of a meter.

The basic unit of capacity in the metric system is the liter, which is a little more than a quart in the standard system. A hectoliter is 100 liters, and a centiliter is $\frac{1}{100}$ of a liter.

The basic unit of weight in the metric system is the gram, which is about the weight of a single paper clip. A kilogram is 1,000 grams, and a milligram is $\frac{1}{1,000}$ of a gram.

Converting Within the Metric System

The metric system is built on the base of 10, and to convert within this system, all that is required is to move the decimal point. It may be helpful to use the graphic organizer of a metric chart to help.

EXAMPLE 8

Convert 4 kilometers to meters.

SOLUTION

Just as with our customary system of measurement, we note that we are changing from a larger unit to a smaller unit. Thus, we use multiplication. The answer is $4 \times 1,000 = 4,000$ meters.

EXAMPLE 9

Convert 320 milligrams to dekagrams.

SOLUTION

One milligram is 0.001 of a gram, and a dekagram is equivalent to 10 grams. This implies that one milligram is 0.0001 of a dekagram. Thus, we can use division. The answer is $\frac{320}{10,000} = 0.0320$ dekagrams. (We can also write the answer as 0.032.)

EXAMPLE 10

Convert 123 milliliters to liters.

SOLUTION

We are converting from a smaller unit to a larger unit, which implies the use of division. Thus, the answer is $\frac{123}{1000} = 0.123$.

EXAMPLE 11

Convert 45.6 meters to centimeters.

SOLUTION

We are converting from a larger unit to a smaller unit, which means multiplication. In this case, the answer is $45.6 \times 100 = 4,560$.

Estimation Strategies Related to Measurement

You may be asked to estimate the measurement of figures or items and determine whether an estimate is reasonable. In these cases, the following estimation strategies may be helpful:

1. Use benchmarks or referents. Suppose that you are nearly 6 feet tall (benchmark). About three people of the same height, standing on each other's shoulders would reach the ceiling. Therefore, the ceiling in this room must be about 18 feet tall. As another example, you know that an angle with a square corner measures 90°. If an angle is about half that size, it must measure about 45°.

2. Estimate in chunks. Seven cubes fit alongside the edge of a box. There is room for about 8 rows of cubes. Therefore, about 56 cubes will fit inside the box.

3. Estimate by subdividing. That length of rope is too long to estimate accurately. Suppose that you fold it in half, then fold it in half again. At this point, suppose that each small segment is about 3 feet. Therefore, the rope is about 12 feet long.

Perimeter

Many geometry problems require the determination of the length of sides. The distance around a polygon (a closed figure with line segments as sides) is called the **perimeter**. To find the perimeter of a polygon, simply add the lengths of the sides.

EXAMPLE 12

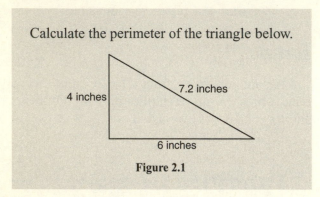

Calculate the perimeter of the triangle below.

4 inches 7.2 inches 6 inches

Figure 2.1

SOLUTION

To find the perimeter of a triangle, simply add the length of all three sides. Thus, the perimeter is 4 + 6 + 7.2 = 17.2 inches.

EXAMPLE 13

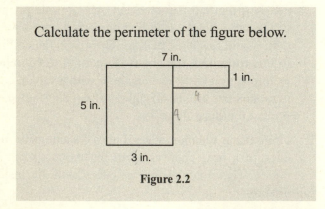

Calculate the perimeter of the figure below.

7 in. 1 in. 5 in. 3 in.

Figure 2.2

SOLUTION

First, look at the large rectangle. We know that the base is 3 inches, so the opposite side will also be 3 inches. Because the entire top segment is 7 inches, and the part of that which makes up the large rectangle is 3 inches, we know the remaining part of that segment is 4 inches. Therefore, the bottom segment of the small rectangle is also 4 inches. Follow the same proce-

dure with the side of the large rectangle that measures 5 inches. We know that the opposite side is 5 inches as well, 1 inch of which is made up of the side of the small rectangle. Therefore, the remaining portion of that segment is 4 inches. Here are the individual measurements for the length and width of each rectangle.

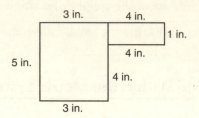

3 in. 4 in. 1 in. 5 in. 4 in. 4 in. 3 in.

Figure 2.3

Add the lengths of all these sides. Thus, the perimeter is 3 in. + 4 in. + 1 in. + 4 in. + 4 in. + 3 in. + 5 in. = 24 inches.

Area of Plane Figures

Sometimes we are asked to calculate the number of square units inside a figure, or its **area**. We use different formulas to determine the area of different polygons; however, area is always reported in square units, regardless of the shape of the polygon. Later in this chapter, you will find information on finding the area of a variety of plane figures.

Solid Figures

When working with solid (three-dimensional) figures, you may be asked to find the surface area and volume. **Surface area** is the number of square units that make up all the faces of the figure. **Volume** is the amount of space that a three-dimensional figure takes up. A variety of formulas help with finding the surface area and the volume of these figures. Remember that area is reported in square units, whereas volume is reported in cubic units.

Cube

A cube is a solid figure that has six square faces and twelve edges. Each of the edges is the same length. To find the surface area of a cube, use the formula $A = 6a^2$, where a is the length of any edge. To find the volume of a cube, use the formula $V = a^3$, where a is the length of any edge. Figure 2.4 shows a cube with an edge of length a.

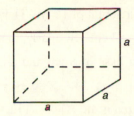

Figure 2.4

EXAMPLE 14

One face on a cube has a surface area of 25 square inches. Find the volume of the cube.

SOLUTION

First, determine the length of one edge of the cube. Because we know the area of one of the faces is 25, we know that the length of one of the edges is 5 (because the formula for the area of a square is $A = s^2$, where s is the length of one of the edges). Then, substitute the value of the edge into the formula for finding the volume of a cube. Using $V = a^3$, where a is the length of any edge, we find that $V = 5^3 = 125$ in³.

Rectangular Prism

A rectangular prism is a solid figure that has six rectangular faces and twelve edges. Opposite edges are congruent. Figure 2.5 shows a rectangular prism with length, width, and height represented by $l, w,$ and h, respectively.

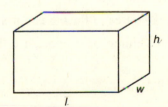

Figure 2.5

To find the surface area of a rectangular prism, use the following formula:

$$SA = 2lw + 2wh + 2lh$$

To find the volume of a rectangular prism, multiply the length, the width, and the height ($V = lwh$).

EXAMPLE 15

Suppose that a box has a length of 10 cm, a width of 8 cm, and a height of 5 cm. How many 1-cm cubes can fit in the box?

SOLUTION

Using the formula $V = lwh$ and substituting the known values, $V = (10)(8)(5) = 400$ cubic centimeters. Thus, 400 1-cm cubes can fit in the box.

EXAMPLE 16

Suppose that a box has a length of 15 inches and a width of 10 inches. If the surface area is 750 square inches, what is the height?

SOLUTION

Using the formula $SA = 2lw + 2wh + 2lh$ and substituting known values, $750 = (2)(15)(10) + (2)(10)(h) + (2)(15)(h)$. This equation simplifies to $750 = 300 + 20h + 30h$. Then $450 = 50h$, so $h = 9$ inches.

Pyramid

A **pyramid** is a figure that has a polygonal base (usually a square or a rectangle) and four triangular faces. To find the surface area of a pyramid, add the area of all five of its faces (the four triangles plus the base).

To find the volume of a pyramid, use the formula $V = \frac{1}{3}Bh$, where B is the area of the base and h is the height.

Figure 2.6 shows a pyramid with a trapezoidal base.

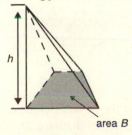

area B

Figure 2.6

EXAMPLE 17

Given a pyramid whose base is a square, suppose that the edge of one of the bases is 12 inches and the height is 9 inches. What is the volume of this pyramid?

SOLUTION

Here is a diagram of this pyramid:

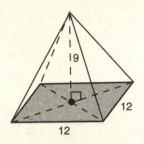

Figure 2.7

To find the volume of a pyramid, use the formula $V = \frac{1}{3}Bh$. The area of the base is $12^2 = 144$ square inches. Because the height is 9 inches, the volume is $\frac{1}{3} \times 144 \times 9 = 432$ cubic inches.

EXAMPLE 18

Given a pyramid whose base is a rectangle, suppose that the length is 8 cm, the width is 6 cm, and the lateral height is 14 cm. What is the surface area?

SOLUTION

Here is a diagram of this pyramid:

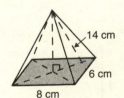

Figure 2.8

First note that the lateral height is the distance from the vertex to any edge of the base. By definition, the seg-

ment that represents this lateral height is perpendicular to the edge to which it is drawn. The area of the base is $8 \times 6 = 48$ cm². Two of the faces are triangles with a base of 6 cm and a height of 14 cm. Their combined area is $2 \times \frac{1}{2} \times 6 \times 14 = 84$ cm². Similarly, there are two triangular faces with a base of 8 cm and a height of 14 cm. Their combined area is $2 \times \frac{1}{2} \times 8 \times 14 = 112$ cm². Thus, the total surface area is $48 + 84 + 112 = 244$ cm².

Cone

A cone is a solid figure that has a circular base and an apex point. In a regular cone, a line drawn perpendicular to the base from the apex passes through the center of the base. It is defined as a solid of the form described by the revolution of a right-angled triangle about one of the sides adjacent to the right angle.

Figure 2.9 illustrates a cone in which r is the radius of the base, h is the (vertical) height from the apex to the base, and s is the slant height.

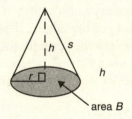

Figure 2.9

To find the surface area of a cone, use the following formula:

Surface area $= \pi r^2 + \pi r s$

This may also be written as:

Surface area $=$ area of the base $+ \pi r s$

To find the volume of a cone, use the following formula:

$$V = \frac{1}{3}\pi r^2 h$$

EXAMPLE 19

Calculate the volume of a cone that has a height of 6 cm and whose radius is 4 cm.

SOLUTION

By substitution,

$$V = \frac{1}{3}\pi(4^2)(6) = 32\pi cm^3 \approx 100.53 cm^3.$$

EXAMPLE 20

The surface area of a cone is 80π square inches. If the slant height is 11 in., what is the radius?

SOLUTION

By substitution, $80\pi = \pi r^2 + 11\pi r$, which can be simplified to $80 = r^2 + 11r$. Rearranging and factoring leads to $(r + 16)(r - 5) = 0$. The only positive answer is $r = 5$. (Disregard the value of -16.)

Cylinder

A cylinder is a solid figure that has two congruent and parallel circular bases. It is defined as the surface formed by the set of lines perpendicular to a plane, which pass through a given circle in that plane. Figure 2.10 shows a cylinder with a radius of r and a height of h. This is called a right circular cylinder.

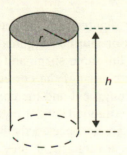

Figure 2.10

To find the surface area (SA) of this cylinder, use the formula $SA = 2\pi r^2 + 2\pi rh$.

To find the volume of a cylinder that has radius r and height h, use the following formula: $V = \pi r^2 h$.

EXAMPLE 21

Calculate the volume of the cylinder shown below in Figure 2.11.

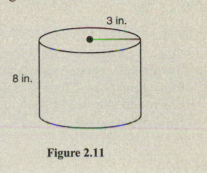

3 in.

8 in.

Figure 2.11

SOLUTION

$\pi\ 3^2\ 8$

By substitution, $V = \pi(3^2)(8) = 72\pi \approx 226.19$ cubic inches.

EXAMPLE 22

Using the diagram in Example 21, what is the surface area?

SOLUTION

By substitution, $SA = 2\pi(3^2) + 2\pi(3)(8) = 66\pi \approx 207.35$ square inches.

Sphere

A sphere is a solid figure made up of all points that are a given distance from a given point in three-dimensional space. Figure 2.12 shows a sphere with a radius of r and a diameter of d.

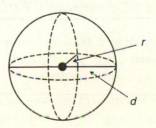

Figure 2.12

To find the surface area of a sphere with radius r, use the following formula:

$$SA = 4\pi r^2$$

EXAMPLE 23

You are creating a model for science class. In this model, you have a sphere with a radius measurement of 5 inches. How much material would you need to buy to cover the surface of this sphere?

SOLUTION

By substitution, $SA = 4\pi(5^2) = 100\pi \approx 314.16$ square inches.

To find the volume of a sphere with radius r, use the following formula:

$$V = \frac{4}{3}\pi r^3$$

EXAMPLE 24

To the nearest integer, the volume of a sphere is 400 cubic inches. To the nearest hundredth, what is the length of the diameter?

SOLUTION

By substitution, $400 = \frac{4}{3}\pi r^3$. Then $r^3 = \frac{300}{\pi}$, so $r = \sqrt[3]{\frac{300}{\pi}} \approx 4.57$ inches. Thus, the diameter is approximately $(2)(4.57) \approx 9.14$ inches.

Nets of Three-Dimensional Figures

A **net** is simply a two-dimensional pattern of a three-dimensional shape. This flat pattern can be folded into a space figure that it represents.

Using nets allows us to examine the faces and edges of a three-dimensional figure. Nets may also make it easier to determine the surface area of a three-dimensional figure by looking at it in two dimensions rather than three.

EXAMPLE 25

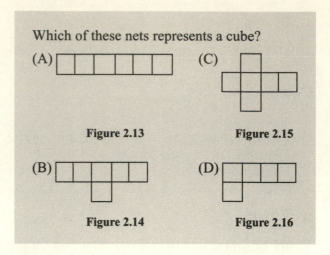

Which of these nets represents a cube?

(A)   (C)

Figure 2.13   **Figure 2.15**

(B)   (D)

Figure 2.14   **Figure 2.16**

SOLUTION

(C)

Net A does not make a cube. If the net were folded, the first and the fifth squares would collide.

Net B does not make a cube. If the net were folded, the first and last squares would collide.

Net C will make a cube.

Net D will not make a cube because it has only five squares.

Similarity and Congruence

In geometry, figures may sometimes be referred to as **congruent** or **similar**. Figures are congruent if they are exactly the same shape and exactly the same size. Figures are similar if the corresponding (matching) angles are congruent and the corresponding sides are proportional. Although similar figures must have the same shape, they are not necessarily the same size. Note that if two figures are congruent, they are automatically similar. Figures 2.17 and 2.18 show pairs of congruent squares and triangles, respectively.

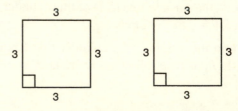

Figure 2.17

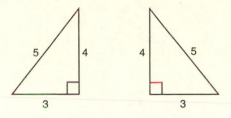

Figure 2.18

Figures 2.19 and 2.20 show similar rectangles and triangles, respectively.

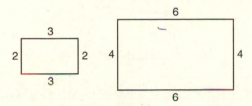

Figure 2.19

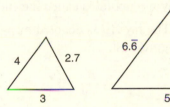

Figure 2.20

Note that the corresponding sides are in proportion. In Figure 2.19, $\frac{2}{4} = \frac{3}{6}$. In Figure 2.20, $\frac{4}{6.6} = \frac{3}{5} = \frac{2.7}{4.5}$.

Scale Factors and Proportions

It is possible to compare similar figures using the **scale factor**. The scale factor is the ratio of the lengths of two corresponding segments in two similar geometric figures. The scale factor is often used in drawing diagrams or maps; the ratio of the length of a line on a scaled diagram or map to the corresponding length of the real object is the scale factor. Look at Figure 2.21 below.

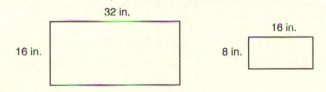

Figure 2.21

To find the scale factor, compare the corresponding sides. In the large rectangle, the top segment is 32 inches; in the small rectangle, the corresponding segment is 16 inches. Therefore, the scale factor is $\frac{32}{16} = 2$.

Understanding scale factors can be helpful when determining the area of similar figures. The ratio of the areas of two similar figures is the square of the scale factor. In Figure 2.21, the area of the small rectangle is $(16)(8) = 128$ square inches. We know that the scale factor is 2; therefore, the area of the large rectangle is the square of that ($2^2 = 4$). So the area of the large rectangle is 4 times that of the small one ($128 \times 4 = 512$ square inches). Note that we can easily check this answer because $(32)(16) = 512$.

Scale factors can also help with finding the volume of similar figures. The ratio of the volumes of two similar space figures is the cube of the scale factor. Consider the cubes shown in Figure 2.22.

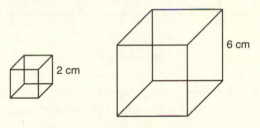

Figure 2.22

The cubes are similar, and the scale factor is 3 because the ratio of the large cube to the small cube is 6:2, or 3:1. The volume of the small cube is 8 cubic inches. The volume of the large cube, then, is the cube of the scale factor (3^3), in this case 27 times the volume of the small cube. Therefore, the volume of the large cube is 216 cubic centimeters. This can be verified because $6^3 = 216$.

Definitions and Properties of Basic Geometric Figures

Geometry has a foundation of several common terms. We accept these terms implicitly so that we may use them to define other terms. Let's look at these basic terms.

Point: A point is simply a place in space. It does not have any dimensions; you cannot measure a point, but you can name where it is, and you can draw its representation. •P designates point P.

Plane: A plane is defined as a series of points lying on a flat surface that extends indefinitely in all directions. In geometric notation, a plane is typically represented as a closed, four-sided figure known as a parallelogram, and it is named by placing a capital letter in one of the corners. Plane geometry is concerned with two-dimensional figures—those that lie in a plane. Figure 2.23 shows plane *P*.

Figure 2.23

Line: A line is a series of adjacent points that extends indefinitely. A line can be either curved or straight; unless otherwise stated, however, the term *line* refers to a straight line. We denote a line by naming two points on it. Consider Figure 2.24.

Figure 2.24

This drawing can be named as line *XZ* or as line *ZX*. Symbolically, we write $\overleftrightarrow{XZ}$ or $\overleftrightarrow{ZX}$. Some lines have particular properties that make them different from other lines. **Parallel lines** lie in the same plane and never cross because they are the same distance apart. Parallel lines are designated by the symbol ∥. Thus, $\overleftrightarrow{AB} \parallel \overleftrightarrow{CD}$ means that lines AB and CD are parallel to each other. Parallel lines AB and CD are shown below in Figure 2.25.

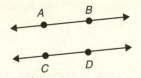

Figure 2.25

Perpendicular lines are lines that form right angles where they intersect. Perpendicular lines are designated by the symbol ⊥. Therefore, $\overleftrightarrow{AB} \perp \overleftrightarrow{CD}$ means that line AB is perpendicular to line CD. Figure 2.26 shows perpendicular lines AB and CD. Note the right-angle symbol that appears where the two lines intersect.

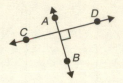

Figure 2.26

Line Segment: If *A* and *B* are two points on a line, then the **line segment** *AB* is the set of points on that line between and including *A* and *B*, which are called the endpoints. This is shown in Figure 2.27.

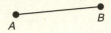

Figure 2.27

The line segment is referred to as $\overline{AB}$ or as $\overline{BA}$.

Ray: Let *A* be the dividing point on a line. Then a **ray** is the set of all the points on a half-line and the dividing point itself. The dividing point is called the endpoint or vertex of the ray. The ray *AB* is denoted by $\overrightarrow{AB}$, and is shown below in Figure 2.28.

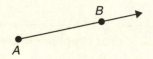

Figure 2.28

Note that $\overrightarrow{AB}$ is *not* equivalent to $\overrightarrow{BA}$. Also, the arrow over the letters *always* points to the right, no matter which way the ray faces.

Angles: An **angle** is a union of two rays having the same endpoint. An angle, such as the one illustrated in Figure 2.29, can be referred to by:

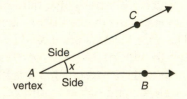

Figure 2.29

(a) a capital letter that names its vertex, ∠*A*.

(b) a lowercase letter or number placed inside the angle, ∠*x*.

(c) three capital letters, where the middle letter is the vertex and the other two letters are not on the same ray, i.e., ∠CAB or ∠BAC, both of which represent the angle illustrated in Figure 2.29.

Categories of Angles

An **acute angle** is an angle whose measure is greater than 0° but less than 90°.

A **right angle** measures exactly 90°.

An **obtuse angle** is an angle whose measure is greater than 90° but less than 180°.

A **straight angle** is an angle whose measure is exactly 180°. A straight angle is actually a straight line.

A **reflex angle** is an angle whose measure is greater than 180° but less than 360°.

Some angles are defined by their relationship to other angles. Two angles are considered **congruent** if they have the same angle measure.

If the sum of the measures of two angles is exactly 90°, they are called **complementary angles.**

If the sum of the measures of two angles is exactly 180°, they are called **supplementary angles.**

Vertical angles are two angles with a common vertex and with sides that are two pairs of opposite rays.

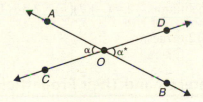

Figure 2.30

In Figure 2.30, $\overrightarrow{AB}$ and $\overrightarrow{CD}$ intersect at point O. Opposite pairs of angles, in this case, α and $\alpha *$ are called **vertical angles**, and they always have equal measures.

Polygons

Points, lines, and angles are all used to make **plane figures**, which are two-dimensional. Plane figures that

are closed and whose sides are all line segments are called **polygons**. Common polygons include squares and quadrilaterals (e.g., rectangles, squares, parallelograms). A circle is not a polygon because it has no line segments.

Triangles and Their Properties

A **triangle** is a three-sided polygon. The point where two sides of a triangle meet is called a **vertex** (plural: vertices).

Triangles may be named according to their sides. A triangle in which no two sides are of equal length is called a **scalene triangle**. A triangle with two equal sides is called an **isosceles triangle**. The third side of an isosceles triangle is called the **base**, and the base angles (the angles opposite the equal sides) are equal. An **equilateral triangle** is one in which all three sides are equal. An equilateral triangle is also **equiangular**, with each angle measuring 60°.

Triangles may also be named according to their angles. A triangle with one obtuse angle (greater than 90°) is called an **obtuse triangle**. A triangle with three acute angles (less than 90°) is called an **acute triangle**. A triangle with a right angle is called a **right triangle**.

Figures 2.31 to 2.34 illustrate a few of these types of triangles.

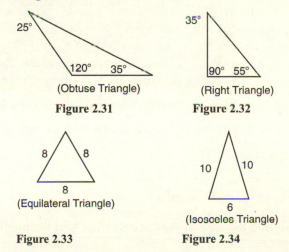

(Obtuse Triangle)	(Right Triangle)
Figure 2.31	**Figure 2.32**
(Equilateral Triangle)	(Isosceles Triangle)
Figure 2.33	**Figure 2.34**

Some problems may require you to determine the measure of an angle of a triangle. In this case, it is helpful to know that the sum of the measures of the angles of a triangle is 180°.

Right Triangles and the Pythagorean Theorem

Right triangles have a special relationship involving the length of the sides. In a right triangle, the side opposite the right angle is called the hypotenuse. The Pythagorean theorem, which shows a special relationship among the sides of a right triangle, states the following:

The square of the length of the hypotenuse equals the sum of the squares of the other two sides. Therefore, $a^2 + b^2 = c^2$, where a and b are the legs of the triangle, and c is the hypotenuse.

Therefore, any time that you know the lengths of two sides of a right triangle, use the Pythagorean theorem to find the length of the third side.

EXAMPLE 26

What is the length of the side designated as m in Figure 2.35?

Figure 2.35

SOLUTION

Using the Pythagorean theorem, we know that $a^2 + b^2 = c^2$. Then, by substitution, $6^2 + 8^2 = m^2$. Simplify to $36 + 64 = 100 = m^2$. Therefore, $m = \sqrt{100} = 10$ cm. (Note that the small box inside the triangle indicates that this angle is 90°.)

Area of a Triangle

To find the area of the triangle, first find the **height** or **altitude**. This is a line segment that extends from the vertex of the triangle perpendicular to the opposite side. The formula for the area of a triangle is $A = \frac{1}{2}bh$. In this formula, h represents the altitude and b is the base to which the altitude is drawn.

EXAMPLE 27

What is the area of ΔMNO shown in Figure 2.36?

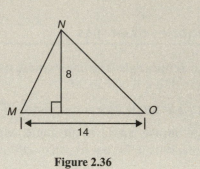

Figure 2.36

SOLUTION

By substitution into the formula for the area of a triangle, we get $A = (\frac{1}{2})(14)(8) = 56$ square units.

EXAMPLE 28

The area of a triangle is 42 square inches. If the base is 7 inches, what is the height?

SOLUTION

By substitution, $42 = (\frac{1}{2})(7)(h) = 3.5h$. Then $h = \frac{42}{3.5} = 12$ inches.

Quadrilaterals and Their Properties

Quadrilaterals are four-sided plane figures. One special property shared by all quadrilaterals is that the sum of the measures of the interior angles is 360°.

Parallelograms

The property that defines a parallelogram involves its sides, namely, that the opposite sides of a parallelogram are parallel. Given this definition, the following three statements can be proven:

(a) Opposite sides are congruent.

(b) Opposite angles are congruent.

(c) The diagonals bisect each other.

Figure 2.37 shows these properties for parallelogram $ABCD$, where $\overline{AB} \cong \overline{CD}$ and $\overline{AD} \cong \overline{BC}$.

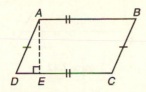

Figure 2.37

Consecutive angles are two angles that have their vertices at the endpoints of the same side of a parallelogram. In Figure 2.37, $\angle A$ and $\angle B$ are a pair of consecutive angles.

A perpendicular line segment that connects any point of a line on one side of a parallelogram to the line that is on the opposite side is called the **altitude** of the parallelogram. In Figure 2.37, $\overline{AE}$ is an altitude.

The area of a parallelogram is found by using the formula $A = bh$, where b is the base, and h is the height (altitude) drawn perpendicular to the base.

EXAMPLE 29

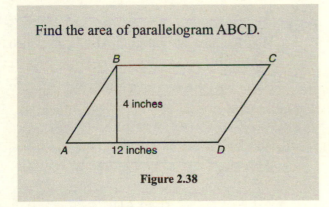

Find the area of parallelogram ABCD.

Figure 2.38

SOLUTION

Using the known values, $A = (\frac{1}{2})(12)(4) = 24$ square inches.

48

Rectangles

A **rectangle** is a parallelogram with right angles. Thus, a rectangle has the properties of a parallelogram plus an additional property that can be proven, namely, that the diagonals are congruent.

To find the area of a rectangle, use the formula $A = lw$, where l is the length and w is the width.

EXAMPLE 30

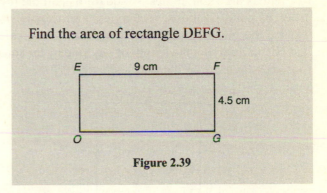

Find the area of rectangle DEFG.

Figure 2.39

SOLUTION

$A = (9)(4.5) = 40.5$ square centimeters.

Rhombi

A **rhombus** has all the properties of a parallelogram. In addition, all four sides are the same length. In actuality, any quadrilateral with four congruent sides is a rhombus. Similar to the parallelogram, the diagonals of a rhombus bisect each other. It can be proven that the diagonals are perpendicular to each other. Figure 2.40 illustrates rhombus $PQRS$.

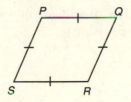

Figure 2.40

To find the area of a rhombus, use the formula $A = (\frac{1}{2})(d_1)(d_2)$, where d_1 and d_2 are the diagonals.

EXAMPLE 31

Find the area of a rhombus if the lengths of its diagonals are 8 and 12.

SOLUTION

$A = (\frac{1}{2})(8)(12) = 48$ square units.

Squares

A **square** is a quadrilateral whose sides are all the same length. Because the sides are equal, all of its interior angles are right angles. A square has all the properties of parallelograms, rectangles, and rhombi. In a square, the measure of either diagonal may be calculated by multiplying the length of any side by the square root of 2. Figure 2.41 illustrates square *TUVW*.

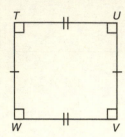

Figure 2.41

The area of a square may be found in two ways. One way is to use the formula $A = s^2$, where s is the length of the side of the square. A second way is to use the formula $A = (\frac{1}{2})(d^2)$, where d is the length of the diagonal.

EXAMPLE 32

Find the area of a square in which the diagonal measures 6 inches.

SOLUTION

Using the second formula from the paragraph above, $A = (\frac{1}{2})(6^2) = 18$ square inches.

Trapezoids

A **trapezoid** is a quadrilateral in which only two sides are parallel. These parallel sides are called bases. The median of a trapezoid is the line segment that joins the midpoints of the nonparallel sides. The median of a trapezoid is parallel to the two bases, and it is equal to one-half their sum. In Figure 2.42, *JKLM* is a trapezoid with bases $\overline{JK}$ and $\overline{ML}$. Also, $\overline{NP}$ is the median of *JKLM*.

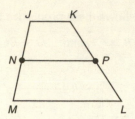

Figure 2.42

The perpendicular segment that connects any point on one of the bases to one point on the other base is called an altitude of the trapezoid.

To find the area of a trapezoid, use the formula $A = \frac{1}{2}(h)(b_1 + b_2)$, where h is the altitude and b_1 and b_2 are the lengths of the bases.

An **isosceles trapezoid** is one in which the nonparallel sides are congruent. The pair of angles that includes one of the parallel sides is called a pair of base angles. In an isosceles trapezoid, the base angles are congruent and the diagonals are congruent. The opposite angles of an isosceles trapezoid are supplementary.

EXAMPLE 33

Find the area of trapezoid ABCD, in which AD = 7 in.

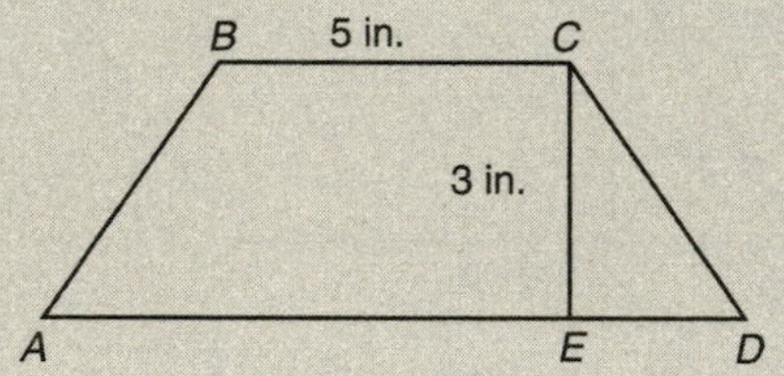

B   5 in.   C

3 in.

A   E   D

Figure 2.43

SOLUTION

By definition, $\overline{CE}$ represents an altitude of this trapezoid. By substitution, $A = (\frac{1}{2})(3)(5 + 7) = 18$ square inches.

(Note that the lengths of $\overline{AB}$ and $\overline{CD}$ are neither known nor are they needed to determine the area of *ABCD*.)

Circles

A **circle** is the set of all points at a fixed distance from a given point. Circles are not considered polygons because they do not have straight edges. However, they do have special properties, as shown in Figure 2.44.

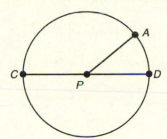

Figure 2.44

A circle is named by its **center** point, shown as P. A **radius** is a line segment whose endpoints are the center and a point on the circle. AP is an example of a radius (plural: radii). A **diameter** is a line segment whose endpoints are points on the circle and whose midpoint is the center. CD is an example of a diameter. We use the term *perimeter* in referring to the measurement around polygons. For circles, this same measurement is called the **circumference**. To find the circumference of a circle, use the formula $C = 2\pi r$, where r is the radius. Because $d = 2r$, where d is the diameter, you may also use the formula $C = \pi d$. This last formula reveals the definition of π, which is the ratio of the circumference to the diameter of any circle.

EXAMPLE 34

Olivia wants to line the outer edge of a circular flower garden with stones. The diameter of the flower garden is 6 feet. How many 1-foot stones will she need?

SOLUTION

We want the circumference of a circle for which the diameter is 6 feet. Then $C = (\pi)(6) \approx 18.85$ feet. Because the number of stones must be an integer, Olivia will need 18 stones (19 stones would be too many).

Sometimes you may be asked to find the **area** of a circle. In that case, use the formula $A = \pi r^2$, where r is the length of the radius.

EXAMPLE 35

The radius of a circle is 5 cm. What is the area?

SOLUTION

$A = (\pi)(5^2) = 25\pi \approx 78.54$ square centimeters.

Geometric Constructions

Often in geometry, constructions are made using a variety of tools. Two of these tools are the **compass** and the **straightedge**. When constructing geometric figures, we do not use instruments that are calibrated or scaled.

A compass is a tool that is used for drawing circles. Besides drawing circles, a compass can be used to copy segments and find the midpoints of segments. Compasses are also used to copy and bisect angles.

A straightedge is just what the name implies; it is any object that helps you draw a straight line segment. Strictly speaking, a ruler is a straightedge, but its measurement marks are not used to do geometric constructions.

Copying a Line Segment

Consider $\overline{CD}$ in Figure 2.45.

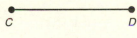

Figure 2.45

The first step is to use a straightedge to draw a line longer than $\overline{CD}$. Mark point E somewhere on that line. To copy $\overline{CD}$, set your compass to the length of $\overline{CD}$ by placing the compass point on point C and the marking end of the compass on point D. Then place the point of the compass on E and draw an arc that intersects the line. Label this point of intersection point F. Then $\overline{CD}$ is congruent to $\overline{EF}$, as shown in Figure 2.46. This is written as $\overline{CD} \cong \overline{EF}$.

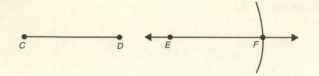

Figure 2.46

Finding the Midpoint of a Line Segment

We'll use the same line segment $\overline{CD}$ from Figure 2.45. Place the compass point on C and set the compass to reach more than half the length of $\overline{CD}$. Next, make an arc that is more than half a circle. Keep the compass at the same setting, and repeat the process with point D. Name the points at which the two arcs intersect E and F. Using the straightedge, draw a line that passes through points E and F. The intersection of $\overline{EF}$ and $\overline{CD}$ (call it point M) represents the midpoint of $\overline{CD}$. (It can be proven that M is also the midpoint of $\overline{EF}$.) Figure 2.47 shown below illustrates the construction.

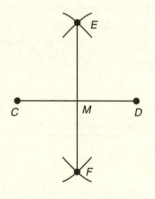

Figure 2.47

Copying an Angle

To construct an angle that is congruent to a given $\angle ABC$, draw any ray $\overrightarrow{NM}$, as shown in Figure 2.48.

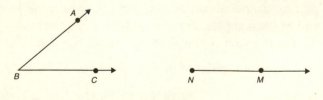

Figure 2.48

Next, place the point of the compass at point B and draw an arc whose endpoints lie on each ray of $\angle ABC$. Label these points D and E. Keeping the same setting of the compass, draw an arc from a point P on $\overrightarrow{NM}$ that is slightly larger than $\overset{\frown}{DE}$. These drawings are shown in Figure 2.49. (Note that $BE = BD = NP$.)

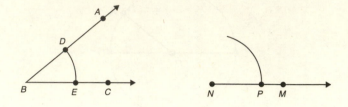

Figure 2.49

Now place the point of the compass at E and the marking end of the compass at D. Without changing this setting, place the compass point at P and make an arc that intersects the arc drawn in Figure 2.49. Call this point of intersection Q. Finally, draw $\overrightarrow{NQ}$. Then $\angle QNM$ is congruent to $\angle ABC$, as shown in Figure 2.50. This can be written as $\angle QNM \cong \angle ABC$.

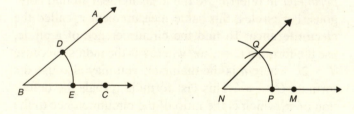

Figure 2.50

Bisecting an Angle

To bisect an angle (divide it in half), we start with angle K. Place the compass point on point K and construct an arc that intersects both rays of angle K. Name the two points where the arc intersects the rays as point J and point L, as shown in Figure 2.51.

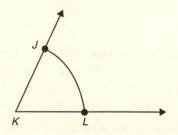

Figure 2.51

Next, place the point of the compass on L. Increase the span of the compass a bit and construct an arc. Keep the same setting on the compass, place the point of the compass on J, and construct an arc. The two arcs should intersect. Name that point M. Finally, use the straight-edge to draw a ray from point K through point M. Then $\overline{KM}$ bisects $\angle JKL$, as shown in Figure 2.52. This is equivalent to the statement $\angle JKM \cong \angle MKL$.

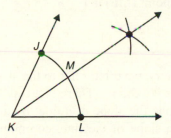

Figure 2.52

Coordinate Geometry

Coordinate geometry refers to the study of geometric figures through the use of algebraic principles. The basis for this branch of geometry is the **coordinate plane** (also called the Cartesian plane), which is created by drawing a set of perpendicular lines. The horizontal line is called the **x-axis** and the vertical line is called the **y-axis**. The point at which these lines intersect is called the **origin**.

The x-axis and y-axis divide the coordinate plane into four sections called **quadrants**. These are labeled with Roman numerals beginning with quadrant I on the top right. Moving counterclockwise, the top left section is quadrant II, the bottom left section is quadrant III, and the bottom right section is quadrant IV.

Figure 2.53 illustrates the location and naming of the four quadrants.

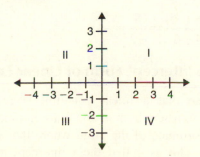

Figure 2.53

Ordered Pairs

The location of points on the coordinate plane is designated by a set of two numbers called an **ordered pair**, in the form (x, y). The ordered pair shows the x-coordinate (called the **abscissa**) and the y-coordinate (called the **ordinate**) of the point. As examples, $(1, 2)$ is the point whose x-coordinate is 1 and whose y-coordinate is 2; $(-1, 3)$ is the point whose x-coordinate is -1 and whose y-coordinate is 3. The origin is the "starting point" and is always labeled $(0, 0)$.

These three points are shown in Figure 2.54.

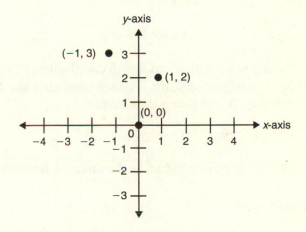

Figure 2.54

To plot a point on the graph when given the coordinates, draw perpendicular lines from the number-line coordinates to the point where the two lines intersect. To find the coordinates of a given point on the graph, draw perpendicular lines from the point to the coordinates on the number line. The x-coordinate is written before the y-coordinate, and a comma and a space are used to separate the two.

Distance

Consider the graph shown in Figure 2.55. In this graph, point A has the coordinates $(4, 2)$, and point B has the coordinates $(-3, -5)$.

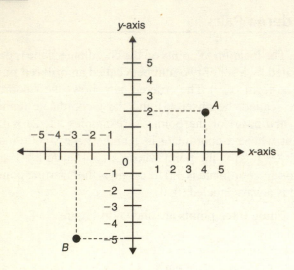

Figure 2.55

For any two points A and B with coordinates (x_A, y_A) and (x_B, y_B), respectively, the distance between A and B is determined by the following formula:

$$d = \sqrt{(x_A - x_B)^2 + (y_A - y_B)^2}$$

This is commonly known as the **distance formula**.

EXAMPLE 36

Find the distance between the points $(-3, 4)$ and $(1, 7)$.

SOLUTION

$$d = \sqrt{(-3-1)^2 + (4-7)^2} = \sqrt{16+9} = \sqrt{25} = 5.$$

Although we used the notation (x_A, y_A) and (x_B, y_B) to represent the coordinates of the two points A and B, we normally refer to the unknown coordinates of two given points as (x_1, y_1) and (x_2, y_2). This more common notation will be used for the remaining formulas.

Midpoint

Some problems require that you find the midpoint (MP) of a segment between two points. If the two points are (x_1, y_1) and (x_2, y_2), then the formula for the midpoint

is $MP = \left(\dfrac{x_1 + x_2}{2}, \dfrac{y_1 + y_2}{2} \right)$.

EXAMPLE 37

Find the midpoint of a line segment whose endpoints are $(-1, 2)$ and $(3, -6)$.

SOLUTION

The midpoint (MP) is $\left(\dfrac{-1+3}{2}, \dfrac{2-6}{2} \right) = (1, -2)$.

Slope

In geometry, we often refer to the slope of a line as the steepness it exhibits. There is a way to mathematically determine the slope of a line: by using points on the line. The slope of the line, commonly referred to as m, containing two points (x_1, y_1) and (x_2, y_2) is determined by the formula $m = \dfrac{y_2 - y_1}{x_2 - x_1}$. Following are some special cases of lines.

(a) All horizontal lines have a slope of zero.

(b) All vertical lines have a slope that is undefined.

(c) Parallel lines have equal slopes.

(d) Perpendicular lines have slopes that are negative reciprocals of each other.

Note that a negative reciprocal of any number n means $-\dfrac{1}{n}$.

EXAMPLE 38

Find the slope of the line that passes through the points $(6, -5)$ and $(4, 3)$.

SOLUTION

$$m = \frac{3 - (-5)}{4 - 6} = \frac{8}{-2} = -4.$$

Slope Intercept Form of Linear Equations

Suppose that a linear equation is in the form $y = mx + b$, where both m and b are numbers. Then b is the y-coordinate of the point where the line crosses the y-axis. This is called the y-intercept and can be expressed as $(0, b)$. Furthermore, m is the slope.

As an example, for the graph of $y = 3x + 4$, its slope is 3 and its y-intercept is 4. This means that the line crosses the y-axis at (0, 4).

To locate other points on this line, and plot it on the coordinate graph, simply substitute values for x and solve the equation for y. If $x = 1$, then $y = (3)(1) + 4 = 7$. Thus, one point on this line is (1, 7). If $x = -2$, then $y = (3)(-2) + 4 = -2$. Thus, a second point on this line is (-2, -2). To graph this line, plot the points at (1, 7) and (-2, -2), then connect them. Note that (0, 4) lies on this line.

EXAMPLE 39

Find the slope of the line that is represented by $6x + 2y = 18$.

SOLUTION

First, rewrite the equation as $2y = -6x + 18$. After division by 2, the equation becomes $y = -3x + 9$. Thus, the slope of the line represented by this equation is -3.

The Point-Slope Form of Linear Equations

The point-slope form of an equation for a line with slope m passing through a point P, designated by (x_1, y_1) is $y - y_1 = m(x - x_1)$. Use this form of the equation if the slope of a line is known and one point is given.

EXAMPLE 40

Find the equation of the line with a slope of 3 that passes through (2, 4).

SOLUTION

Using the point-slope formula and substituting known values, we get $y - 4 = 3(x - 2)$. This equation becomes $y - 4 = 3x - 6$. After further simplification, we get $y = 3x - 2$.

EXAMPLE 41

Find the equation of a line with a slope of -4 and passing through (1, 3).

SOLUTION

We begin with $y - 3 = -4(x - 1)$. Then $y - 3 = -4x + 4$, which simplifies to $y = -4x + 7$.

Transformational Geometry

Transformational geometry involves how two- and three-dimensional figures look when they are moved from their original place. One way that figures are moved is by sliding them (**translation**). In this case, every part of the figure (points, lines) slides in the same direction for the same distance. In Figure 2.56, a six-sided figure A is translated to the right. The translated figure is represented as A'.

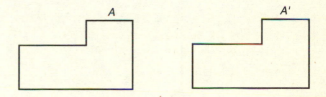

Figure 2.56

Note that a translation may involve a shift horizontally, vertically, or both.

A second way that figures are moved is by turning them (**rotation**). When a figure is rotated, it is turned about a single point. In Figure 2.57, a rectangle $PQRS$ is rotated 90° clockwise about the origin. The "new" rectangle is denoted as $P'Q'R'S'$.

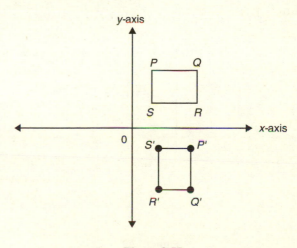

Figure 2.57

The third way that figures are moved is by flipping them (**reflection**). When a figure is reflected, it is "flipped" over a given line so that we see its reflection, as if the given line were a mirror. Each point in the reflected figure is the same distance from the line as the corresponding point in the figure in its original location. In Figure 2.58, ΔABC is reflected across the y-axis. The new triangle is denoted as $\Delta A'B'C'$.

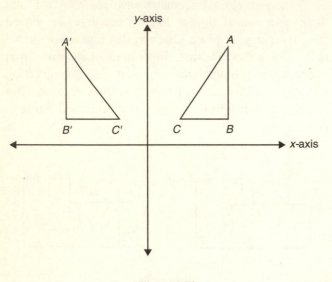

Figure 2.58

Symmetry

If a plane figure can be "folded" so that the two halves match exactly, then that figure has **reflectional symmetry**, and the "fold" line is called the **line of symmetry**. Figure 2.59 illustrates the letter H with one of its two lines of symmetry (identified as line l_1).

Figure 2.59

A figure has **rotational symmetry** if it can be turned (rotated) and still look the same at some point in the rotation. Figure 2.60 shows rectangle $ABCD$, which has been rotated 180° resulting in rectangle $A'B'C'D'$

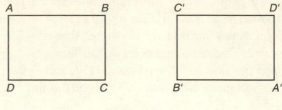

Figure 2.60

Dilations

A **dilation** is a type of transformation in which a figure is either reduced or enlarged. Thus, a dilated figure has the same shape as the original, but the size has changed.

There are two important properties about dilations. The first is the **scale factor**. This is the factor by which each side in the original figure is multiplied to obtain the dilated figure. If the scale factor is greater than 1, the image is enlarged. If the scale factor is less than 1, the image is reduced.

The second important property about dilation is the **center of dilation**. This is a fixed point—often the origin in the Cartesian plane (0, 0)—around which all of the points are reduced or enlarged.

In Figure 2.61, the scale factor is 2 and the center of dilation is (0, 0).

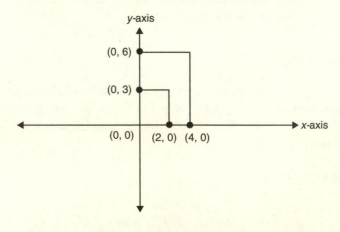

Figure 2.61

Plane figures may also be transformed into three-dimensional figures by rotating them in space. Suppose an isosceles triangle *ABC* is rotated about a line *S* that contains the altitude to its base; the result is a cone. The diameter of the base of the cone is equal to the length of the base of the triangle. Figure 2.62 illustrates this rotation.

Circle *O*, when rotated about a line *R*, is transformed into a sphere. The radius of the sphere is equal to the radius of circle *O*. This is illustrated in Figure 2.63.

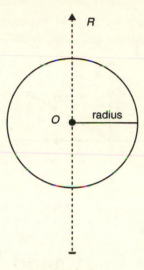

Figure 2.63

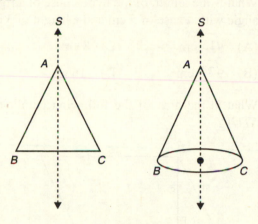

Figure 2.62

Chapter 2 Quiz

1. In the figure below, $\overrightarrow{BA}$ is perpendicular to $\overleftrightarrow{BC}$ and the measure of $\angle DBC$ is 38°.

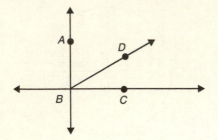

What is the measure of $\angle ABD$?

(A) 38°   (C) 52°

(B) 45°   (D) 58°

2. What is the volume of a pyramid that has a height of 8 inches and whose base has an area of 12 square inches?

(A) 32 cubic inches

(B) 42 cubic inches

(C) 45 cubic inches

(D) 95 cubic inches

3. What is the surface area of the figure shown below, to the nearest square unit?

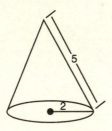

(A) 25   (C) 50

(B) 44   (D) 88

4. Given a rectangle whose area is 6 square inches and whose perimeter is 10 inches, dilate it by a scale factor of 2. What is the area of the new rectangle?

(A) 20 square inches

(B) 24 square inches

(C) 44 square inches

(D) 60 square inches

5. What is the length of the hypotenuse of a right triangle with a base of 5 cm and a height of 3 cm?

(A) $\sqrt{15}$ cm   (C) 8 cm

(B) $\sqrt{34}$ cm   (D) 15 cm

6. What is the area of the following parallelogram *STUV*?

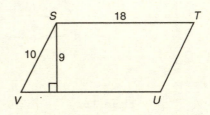

(A) 56 square units

(B) 90 square units

(C) 108 square units

(D) 162 square units

7. What is the measure of arc $\overarc{AXC}$ in circle *B*?

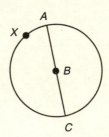

(A) 150°   (C) 180°

(B) 160°   (D) 270°

8. The area of a circle is 225π cm². What is the length of the diameter of this circle?

(A) 15 cm   (C) 30 cm

(B) 20 cm   (D) 40 cm

9. What transformation maps △*ABC* and △*DEF* in the figure below?

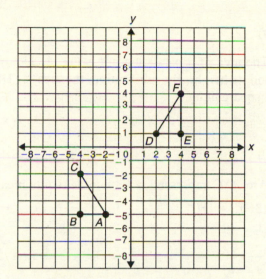

(A) Reflect △*ABC* over the *y*-axis and shift up six spaces.

(B) Reflect △*ABC* over the *x*-axis and shift up six spaces.

(C) Reflect △*ABC* over the *y*-axis and shift down six spaces.

(D) Reflect △*ABC* over the *y*-axis, reflect over the *x*-axis, and shift down four spaces.

10.

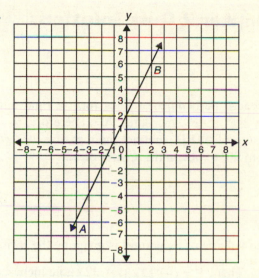

What is the slope of the line shown above?

(A) -2

(B) $-\dfrac{1}{2}$

(C) $\dfrac{1}{2}$

(D) 2

Chapter 2 Quiz Solutions

1. (C)

Because perpendicular lines form a right angle, we know that $\angle ABC$ measures 90°. Therefore, to find the measure of $\angle ABD$, subtract the measure of $\angle DBC$ (38°) from 90° to obtain the answer of 52°.

2. (A)

The volume of a pyramid is given by the formula $V = \frac{1}{3} Bh$. Then, $V = (\frac{1}{3})(12)(8) = 32$ cubic inches.

3. (B)

The surface area of a cone is given by the formula $SA = \pi r^2 + \pi r l$. Then $SA = \pi(2^2) + \pi(2)(5) = 14\pi \approx 44$ square inches.

4. (B)

We know the area of the smaller rectangle (6 square inches) and the scale factor, so we can determine the area of the larger rectangle by squaring the scale factor. Thus, the area of the rectangle after the dilation will be $(6)(2^2) = 24$ square inches.

5. (B)

The Pythagorean theorem indicates that $a^2 + b^2 = c^2$, where a and b are the base and height, and c is the hypotenuse. Thus, $c^2 = 3^2 + 5^2 = 34$. So $c = \sqrt{34}$ cm.

6. (D)

The area of a parallelogram is the product of its base and its height. By substitution, the area is $(18)(9) = 162$ square units.

7. (C)

Arc $\overparen{AXC}$ represents a semicircle, so its measure is $(\frac{1}{2})(360°) = 180°$.

8. (C)

Area $= 225\pi = \pi r^2$, so $r = \sqrt{225} = 15$. Thus, the diameter is $(2)(15) = 30$ cm.

9. (A)

By reflecting triangle ABC over the y-axis, each x-value will change to its opposite, but each y-value will remain the same. The vertices A, B, and C become $(2, -5)$, $(4, -5)$, and $(4, -2)$, respectively. When this reflected triangle is shifted up six spaces, each x-value remains the same, but each y-value increases by six. Thus, the vertices for A, B, and C now become $(2, 1)$, $(4, 1)$, and $(4, 4)$, respectively. This result is shown by triangle DEF.

10. (D)

Choose two points on the graph, for example, $(-1, 0)$ and $(0, 2)$. The slope equals the ratio of the change in y-values divided by the change in x-values, which equals $\frac{2-0}{0-(-1)} = \frac{2}{1} = 2$.

Patterns, Algebra, and Functions

Patterns

Algebra involves the study of patterns, which is a useful way to make predictions. We study a variety of patterns, which may be numerical, pictorial, recursive, or a combination of these.

Recursive Patterns

A **recursive** pattern is one in which the first number is given, and then a formula is used to generate each successive number. The Fibonacci sequence 1, 1, 2, 3, 5, 8, 13, . . . is a recursive pattern. In this sequence, we begin with the numbers 1 and 1. Then each successive number is generated by adding the two numbers that precede it.

Recursive patterns can be noted using algebraic expressions. In the previous example, the sequence of Fibonacci numbers (F_n), may be generated by using the following expression: $F_n = F_{n-1} + F_{n-2}$

Iterative Patterns

A pattern may also be categorized as **iterative**. An iterative pattern is repetitive, one that repeats an operation. Figure 3.1 is an example of an iterative pattern.

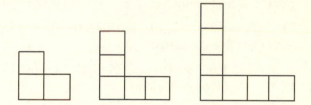

Figure 3.1

Each subsequent block in Figure 3.1 contains one more block on each side (the height and the base). These patterns may also be expressed algebraically. Suppose we want to know how many blocks we would need for a similar figure whose base was 8 blocks long. For this example, draw a chart like the one below.

Length of base	2	3	4	5	6	7	8
Number of blocks	3	5	7	9	11	13	15

From the chart, we can see that, as the length of each block in the base increases, the number of blocks increases by 2 from the previous number of blocks.

Algebraically, doubling the length of the base and subtracting 1 determines the number of blocks. Thus, if the length of the base is

2, then $(2)(2) - 1 = 3$ (3 blocks needed)

3, then $(2)(3) - 1 = 5$ (5 blocks needed)

4, then $(2)(4) - 1 = 7$ (7 blocks needed)

n, then $(2)(n) - 1 = b$, where b equals the number of blocks needed

Relations

A **relation** is simply a set (collection) of members that are ordered pairs. Members are also called elements. A set is indicated by braces and is normally assigned a capital letter. Here are some examples of relations:

$A = \{(5, 7), (9, -1)\}$. Set A has two elements, namely, $(5, 7)$ and $(9, -1)$.

$B = \{(p, 4), (\text{peach}, z), (0.8, \text{box})\}$. Set B has three elements, namely, $(p, 4)$, (peach, z), and $(0.8, \text{box})$.

$C = \{(\text{tree}, w), (6, 6), (\text{math}, \text{tree}), (\text{infinity}, \text{sun})\}$. Set C has four elements.

$D = \{(\text{shoe}, 3), (-2, 5), (\text{shoe}, 7), (c, d), (0, 17)\}$. Set D has five elements.

$E = \{(a, 10), (b, 10), (c, 11), (d, 12), (e, 13), (f, 10)\}$. Set E has six elements.

Look at set C. Notice that "tree" appears both as a first part of an element in (tree, w) and as a second part of an element in $(\text{math}, \text{tree})$. Also notice that one of the ordered pairs (elements), namely, $(6, 6)$, has the same first and second part.

Now look at set D. Notice that there are two ordered pairs that have the same first element, namely, $(\text{shoe}, 3)$ and $(\text{shoe}, 7)$. Set E, has three ordered pairs that have the same second element, namely, $(a, 10)$, $(b, 10)$, and $(f, 10)$.

In relations, where each element is an ordered pair, some elements may have a shared first part or a shared second part. We do *not* repeat any identical elements. Thus, if a relation consisted of $(1, 3)$ and $(1, 3)$, write this pair only once. However, if a relation consisted of $(1, 3)$ and $(3, 1)$, both would be included because they are <u>not</u> identical.

Domain and Range

The domain of a relation is the set of all first parts of each ordered pair, and the range is the set of all second

parts of each ordered pair. Let's explain these definitions as they apply to each of the sets, A, B, C, D, and E that we discussed earlier.

For set A, the domain is $\{5, 9\}$, and the range is $\{7, -1\}$.

For set B, the domain is $\{p, \text{peach}, 0.8\}$, and the range is $\{4, z, \text{box}\}$.

For set C, the domain is $\{\text{tree}, 6, \text{math}, \text{infinity}\}$, and the range is $\{w, 6, \text{tree}, \text{sun}\}$.

For set D, the domain is $\{\text{shoe}, 22, c, 0\}$, and the range is $\{3, 5, 7, d, 17\}$.

For set E, the domain is $\{a, b, c, d, e, f\}$, and the range is $\{10, 11, 12, 13\}$.

Functions

A **function** is a special type of relation. For each element of the domain in a function, there is exactly one assigned element in the range. The letter x is normally used to represent domain elements, and it is called the independent variable. The letter y is normally used to represent range elements, and it is called the dependent variable.

Let's look at each of the five relations mentioned above.

Set A has only two elements in its domain, and each of them has been assigned to only one element in its range. This is a function.

Set B has three elements in its domain. Each of them has been assigned to only one range element. This is a function.

Set C has four elements in its domain. Although the word *tree* appears as an element in both the domain and the range, each element in its domain is still assigned to only one element in the range. This is a function.

SPECIAL NOTE:

> The definition of a function does not prohibit a specific element from belonging to both the domain and the range.

Set D has four elements in its domain but has five elements in its range. Note that the element "shoe" is paired with each of 3 and 7. This situation violates the rule for a function. This is <u>not</u> a function.

Set E has six elements in its domain, and each of them is assigned to only one element in the range. Even though each of a, b, and f in the domain is assigned to the number 10 in the range, this does not violate the rule governing functions. This is a function.

Relations and functions may also be expressed algebraically and graphically.

EXAMPLE 1

Show algebraically why the relation $y^2 = x$ is not a function.

SOLUTION

Select a perfect square for x, such as 9. If $y^2 = 9$, then $y = 3$ or $y = -3$. Because both $(9,3)$ and $(9,-3)$ belong to this relation, we have two ordered pairs with identical domain values but two different range values. Thus, it cannot be a function.

EXAMPLE 2

What are the domain and range of $y^2 = x$?

SOLUTION

Below is a graph of this relation.

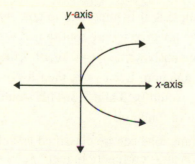

y-axis

x-axis

Figure 3.2

Because the graph lies to the right of the y-axis, except for the point $(0, 0)$, the value of x can never be negative. As x increases, we can see that the corre-

sponding positive y-value increases; also, the negative corresponding y-value decreases. Thus, the domain is all nonnegative numbers and the range is all numbers.

EXAMPLE 3

If $y = 5 - x^2$ and the domain is $\{0, -2, 3\}$, what is the range?

SOLUTION

Just substitute each value of x into the equation. If $x = 0$, $y = 5 - 0 = 5$. If $x = -2$, $y = 5 - (-2)^2 = 5 - 4 = 1$. If $x = 3$, $y = 5 - (3)^2 = 5 - 9 = -4$. Thus, the range is $\{5, 1, -4\}$.

Example 3 is an example of a function because, for any specific x-value, there will be only one y-value. When dealing with functions, symbols such as $f(x)$, $g(x)$, and $h(x)$ are commonly used in place of the letter y. So, in Example 3, we could have written $f(x) = 5 - x^2$. Furthermore, the expression $f(1)$ means to determine the value of y when $x = 1$. For the function $f(x) = 5 - x^2$, $f(1) = 5 - 1 = 4$.

As another example, consider the function $y = 4x + 6$. Using $g(x)$ to replace y, we can write $g(-3) = (4)(-3) + 6 = -6$.

Functions follow the rules of addition, subtraction, multiplication, and division, which means that (a) $(f + g)(x) = f(x) + g(x)$, (b) $(f - g)(x) = f(x) - g(x)$, (c) $(f \times g)(x) = f(x) \times g(x)$, and (d) $(\frac{f}{g})(x) = \frac{f(x)}{g(x)}$, provided that $g(x) \neq 0$.

EXAMPLE 4

If $f(x) = 2x^2 - 1$ and $g(x) = 3x + 5$, what are the simplified expressions for $(f - g)(x)$ and $(f \times g)(x)$?

SOLUTION

$(f - g)(x) = (2x^2 - 1) - (3x + 5) = 2x^2 - 3x - 6$.
$(f \times g)(x) = (2x^2 - 1)(3x + 5) = 6x^3 + 10x^2 - 3x - 5$.

The **composition** function $(f \circ g)(x) = f(g(x))$. This means that first we determine the expression for $g(x)$, then apply the rule for $f(x)$. In similar fashion, $(g \circ f)(x) = g(f(x))$. In general, $f(g(x)) \neq g(f(x))$.

EXAMPLE 5

Using the expressions for $f(x)$ and $g(x)$ in Example 4, determine the simplified expressions for $f(g(x))$ and $g(f(x))$.

SOLUTION

$f(g(x)) = f(3x + 5) = (2)[(3x + 5)^2] - 1 = (2)(9x^2 + 30x + 25) - 1 = 18x^2 + 60x + 49$.
$g(f(x)) = g(2x^2 - 1) = (3)(2x^2 - 1) = (3)(2x^2 - 1) + 5 = 6x^2 + 2$.

EXAMPLE 6

If $f(x) = x^2 + 3$ and $g(x) = 3x + 1$, what is the value of $(f \circ g)(2)$?

SOLUTION

First, we determine that $g(2) = (3)(2) + 1 = 7$. Then $f(7) = 7^2 + 3 = 52$.

The **inverse** of $f(x)$, written as $f^{-1}(x)$, is found by interchanging x and y, then solving for y. It can be shown that if $f^{-1}(x) = g(x)$, then $f(g(x)) = g(f(x)) = x$.

EXAMPLE 7

If $f(x) = 3x + 2$, what is the simplified expression for $f^{-1}(x)$?

SOLUTION

Start with $y = 3x + 2$. By interchanging variables, we get $x = 3y + 2$. Then subtracting 2 from each side yields $x - 2 = 3y$. Finally, dividing by 3, we get $y = \dfrac{x-2}{3}$. Thus, $f^{-1}(x) = \dfrac{x-2}{3}$.

Notice that $f(f^{-1}(x)) = f(\dfrac{x-2}{3}) = (3)(\dfrac{x-2}{3}) + 2 = x - 2 + 2 = x$ and that $f^{-1}(f(x)) = f^{-1}(3x + 2) = \dfrac{(3x+2) - 2}{3} = \dfrac{3x}{3} = x$.

Graphically, the inverse of a function represents the reflection about the line $y = x$. Figure 3.3 illustrates the graphs of $f(x) = 3x + 2$ and $f^{-1}(x) = \dfrac{x-2}{3}$.

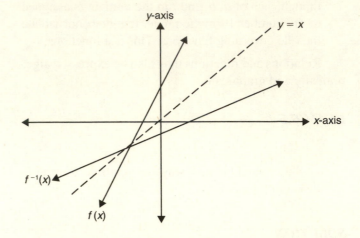

Figure 3.3

EXAMPLE 8

If $f(x) = x^2 - 3$, what is the simplified expression for $f^{-1}(x)$?

SOLUTION

Begin with $y = x^2 - 3$. Next, interchange the variables so that $x = y^2 - 3$. Adding 3 to each side yields $x + 3 = y^2$. Taking the positive square root of each side, we get $y = \sqrt{x+3}$. Thus, $f^{-1}(x) = \sqrt{x+3}$.

In Example 8, it is important to note that we could take only the *positive* square root to get $y = \sqrt{x+3}$. If we had erroneously written $y = \pm\sqrt{x+3}$, then we would not have a function. Let $x = 6$, then for $y = \pm\sqrt{x+3}$, the y values would be 3 and -3. This would contradict the meaning of function.

Some functions can be classified as either even or odd. If $f(x)$ is an **even** function, then $f(-x) = f(x)$ for all x values in the domain. If $f(x)$ is an **odd** function, then $f(-x) = -f(x)$ for all x values in the domain. An example of an even function is $f(x) = 3x^2$. An example of an odd function is $f(x) = x^3$. Many functions are neither even nor odd.

Another interesting property of functions is periodicity. A function $f(x)$ is periodic if there exists a positive real number p such that $f(x + p) = f(x)$ for all x in the domain. An example would be $f(x) = \sin x$. It can be shown that $\sin(x + 2\pi) = \sin x$, where x is measured in radians.

Direct and Inverse Proportional Relationships

A **ratio** is a comparison of two quantities. As an example, the ratio of 2 to 5 can be written as 2:5 or as the fraction $\frac{2}{5}$. A **proportion** represents two or more equivalent ratios. For example, the ratio of 2:5 is equivalent to the ratio of 4:10. In fractional form, we can write $\frac{2}{5} = \frac{4}{10}$. There are two major ways to describe proportions: direct and inverse.

A **direct proportion** exists if one variable always changes by the same factor as another. Suppose that you traveled 1,000 miles on a train, and the train went 100 miles per hour. This trip would take 10 hours. If you traveled 2,000 miles on this train that is traveling at 100 miles per hour, the trip would take 20 hours. Let x represent the time in hours and let y represent the distance in miles. We note that when x changes from 10 to 20, y changes from 1,000 to 2,000. Thus, each variable doubled. We could have also reduced the number of hours. If $x = 2$ hours, then $y = 200$ miles. When x changes from 10 to 2, y changes from 1,000 to 200. In this case, each variable was divided by 5.

For this train illustration, we can write $y = 100x$. The corresponding graph is shown in Figure 3.4.

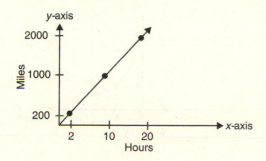

Figure 3.4

Note that the slope of this line is 100, which matches the value of k. Also, we note that the line contains the origin.

Another example of a direct proportion is shown by the formula $C = \pi d$, in which C is the circumference of a circle and d is the diameter. If we use 3.14 as the value of π, and if $d = 3$, then $C = 9.42$. If $d = 12$, then $C = 37.68$. Notice that both variables were multiplied by 4. In general, whenever there exists a direct proportion between x and y, we can express this relationship algebraically as $y = kx$. The constant k is called the **constant of proportionality**.

Two variables are said to have an **inverse proportion** if one variable increases, and the other variable decreases by the same factor. Here are some examples of inversely proportional relationships:

EXAMPLE 9

Julia has three friends over for dinner. A pizza that contains 12 slices is to be shared equally among the four of them. Unexpectedly, four more friends stop in. If the pizza is to be shared equally among everyone, how many fewer slices will each person get?

SOLUTION

Originally, each person would have received $\frac{12}{4} = 3$ slices. When four more friends come to Julia's house, there are a total of eight people. Then each person will get $\frac{12}{8} = 1\frac{1}{2}$ slices of pizza. Thus, each person received $1\frac{1}{2}$ fewer slices of pizza.

In Example 9, notice that the number of people doubled, but the amount of pizza for each person was halved.

EXAMPLE 10

Jason decides to paint his bedroom. The job would take him six hours to do alone. Jason then calls two of his friends to come over and help. How many hours would be required to paint the bedroom if all three are working together? (Assume that all three people are working at the same rate.)

SOLUTION

One person working alone needs six hours. This implies that a total of $(6)(1) = 6$ labor-hours are needed for this job. Because a total of three people will be doing this job, the number of hours now required is $\frac{6}{3} = 2$.

Note that in Example 10, the number of people tripled, but the number of hours needed became one-third of the original number of hours.

An inverse proportion can also be noted algebraically. If x is inversely proportional to y, then the formula is $x = k/y$ (or $xy = k$), again where k is the constant of proportionality.

Consider this equation: $y = \frac{20}{x}$. Here is a table of a few pairs of values for x and y:

x	y
2	10
4	5
8	2.5

In this case, y is inversely proportional to x. Whenever x is doubled, y is halved. This illustrates a key property of inverse proportions: If one variable is multiplied by a given factor, the other is divided by the same factor.

The graph for $y = \frac{20}{x}$ is shown in Figure 3.5 for positive x, y values.

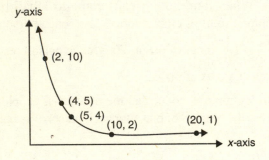

Figure 3.5

Lines of Symmetry

In plotting the graph of a function (or a relation), lines of symmetry (if they exist) can be used to facilitate the location of key points. Here are three basic rules of symmetry.

1. A graph is symmetric with respect to the x-axis if $(x, -y)$ is also on the graph whenever (x, y) is on the graph.

2. A graph is symmetric with respect to the y-axis if $(-x, y)$ is also on the graph whenever (x, y) is on the graph.

3. A graph is symmetric with respect to the origin if $(-x, -y)$ is also on the graph whenever (x, y) is on the graph.

Figures 3.6, 3.7, and 3.8 illustrate these symmetries, respectively. Note that Figure 3.6 does <u>not</u> represent a function.

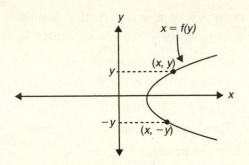

Figure 3.6

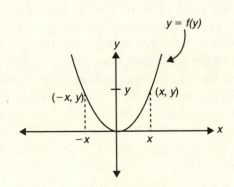

Figure 3.7

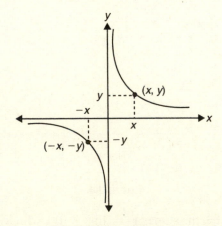

Figure 3.8

Representations of Nonlinear Functions

A polynomial function $P(x)$ has degree n, if it can be written in the form $P(x) = a_n x^n + a_{n-1} x^{n-1} + a_{n-2} x^{n-2} + \ldots + a_1 x + a_0$, where each of the a_i are real numbers and $a_n \neq 0$. Here are three special cases:

$P(x) = a_0$ is a constant function and has degree zero. Its graph is a horizontal line.

$P(x) = a_1 x + a_0$ is a linear function and has degree 1. Its graph is a slanted line with a slope of a_1.

$P(x) = a_2 x^2 + a_1 x + a_0$ is a quadratic function and has degree 2. Its graph is a parabola that opens upward if $a_2 > 0$; it opens downward if $a_2 < 0$.

It is more difficult to analyze the graph of a polynomial function with degree greater than 2, but here are a few hints that will help:

1. Find lines of symmetry.

2. Determine the x and y intercepts.

3. Investigate how the function changes as $|x|$ becomes larger.

EXAMPLE 11

> Determine the line(s) of symmetry, and the x- and y-intercepts for the graph of $y = x^4 - 5x^2 + 4$. Also, sketch the graph.

SOLUTION

We can determine that when x is replaced by $-x$, the value of y is unchanged. This implies that the function is even and therefore is symmetric about the y-axis. When $x = 0$, $y = 4$; thus, $(0, 4)$ is the y-intercept. We can write the function in factored form as $y = (x^2 - 4)(x^2 - 1) = (x - 2)(x + 2)(x - 1)(x + 1)$. Thus, the four x-intercepts are $(2, 0)$, $(-2, 0)$, $(1, 0)$, and $(-1, 0)$. As $|x|$ increases, the value of x^4 becomes larger. Figure 3.9 shows the general sketch of this function.

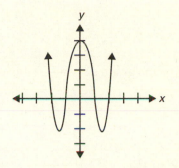

Figure 3.9

Rational Functions and Their Graphs

When $P(x)$ and $Q(x)$ are polynomials, $y = \dfrac{P(x)}{Q(x)}$ is called a rational function, provided that $Q(x)$ is not the zero function. The domain is the set of x-values for which $Q(x) \neq 0$. Let $P(x) = a_n x^n + a_{n-1} x^{n-1} + \ldots + a_1 x + a_0$ and $Q(x) = b_m x^m + b_{m-1} x^{m-1} + \ldots + b_1 x + b_0$. Here is a general procedure for graphing rational functions.

1. Determine lines of symmetry, if they exist.

2. Determine any intercepts. The y-intercept is $(0, \dfrac{a_0}{b_0})$ and the x-intercept(s) can be found at values of x where $P(x) = 0$.

3. Find vertical asymptotes. A line $x = c$ is called a **vertical asymptote** if $Q(c) = 0$ and $P(c) \neq 0$.

4. Find horizontal asymptotes. The line $y = b$ is called a horizontal asymptote if y approaches b as x approaches either $+\infty$ or ∞. There are three guidelines for finding horizontal asymptotes.

   (a) If $m = n$, then $y = \dfrac{a_n}{b_m}$ is the horizontal asymptote.

   (b) If $m > n$, then $y = 0$ is the horizontal asymptote.

   (c) If $m < n$, then there is no horizontal asymptote.

EXAMPLE 12

Describe the graph of $y = \dfrac{x}{(x-1)(x+3)}$.

SOLUTION

Let $x = 2$ so that $y = \dfrac{2}{(2-1)(2+3)} = \dfrac{2}{5}$. Then the point $(2, \frac{2}{5})$ lies on the graph. Because $(2, -\frac{2}{5})$ is not on this graph, we conclude that the graph is not symmetrical about the x-axis. Substitute $x = -2$ so that $y = \dfrac{-2}{(-2-1)(-2+3)} = \dfrac{2}{3}$. Then the point $(-2, \frac{2}{3})$ lies on the graph. Because neither $(-2, \frac{2}{5})$ nor $(-2, -\frac{2}{5})$ lies on the graph, we know that this graph is not symmetrical about the y-axis, and it is not symmetrical about $(0, 0)$.

When $x = 0$, $y = 0$, so both the x- and y-intercept are located at $(0, 0)$.

The vertical asymptotes are found by solving $x - 1 = 0$ and $x + 3 = 0$. So the vertical asymptotes are $x = 1$ and $x = -3$.

Finally, note that the denominator is actually $x^2 + 2x - 3$. This means that the degree of the denominator is 2, whereas the degree of the numerator is 1. Thus, $y = 0$ is the horizontal asymptote.

Figure 3.10 is a sketch of this function.

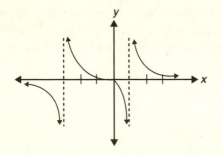

Figure 3.10

Algebraic Operations

When working with the basic operations of addition, subtraction, multiplication, and division involving algebra, it is helpful to know some standard vocabulary. Following are some terms used in this section of the chapter:

Variable: A placeholder that may take on any of several values at a given time. In algebra, letters are typically used to designate variables. These variables are used to represent numbers.

Constant: A symbol that takes on only one value.

Term: A constant, a variable, or a combination of constants and variables. 3.25, $7y$, ab^2, and $\dfrac{4x}{3}$ are all terms.

Coefficient: The constant portion of any term. In the term $4n^3$, the coefficient is 4. In the term a^2, the coefficient is 1.

Expression: A collection of one or more terms; 4, $3st$, $4x-1$, and $\dfrac{2}{3y+5}$ are all expressions.

Monomial: An algebraic expression that consists of only one term. $9xy$, 16, and $\frac{1}{3}z^3$ are all monomials.

Binomial: An algebraic expression that consists of two terms. $x^2 - 25$ and $xy - 8z$ are binomials.

Trinomial: An algebraic expression that consists of three terms. Examples of trinomials are $7a^2b^2 - 3ab + 4$ and $m - 34n + 3mn$.

Polynomial: A collective term for an algebraic expression consisting of two or more terms. This definition would include binomials, trinomials, and expressions such as $1 + x + xy + yz + a^3$.

Simplifying Algebraic Expressions

There are a number of ways to simplify algebraic expressions, including simplifying signs, using number properties (e.g., distributive property), and simplifying exponents. In all simplification processes, remember to clear out the parentheses or other grouping symbols first, then clear exponents, and combine like terms.

When adding only positive number or only negative numbers, it helps to use the absolute value of the terms. To add two positive numbers (e.g., 24 + 32), add the absolute values, and keep the positive sign (in this case, 56). To add two negative numbers (e.g., $-24 + -32$), add the absolute values, and keep the negative sign (in this case, -56). (Note that a positive number need not have the plus sign preceding it.)

Subtracting with negative numbers may be easier if you think that subtracting a negative number is the same as adding its opposite. That is, $-5 - (-3)$ is the same as $-5 + 3$.

When multiplying and dividing numbers with positive or negative signs, remember the following:

Positive times positive = positive ($4 \times 3 = 12$)

Positive divided by positive = positive ($\frac{24}{3} = 8$)

Negative times negative = positive ($-4 \times -3 = 12$)

Negative divided by negative = positive ($\frac{-24}{-3} = 8$)

The only way to get a negative result with the multiplication and division operations is when the signs are mixed; that is, when you have one positive number and one negative number. Examples are $4 \times -3 = -12$ and $\frac{-24}{3} = -8$.

When simplifying expressions, it is important to remember to perform computations in the order of operations. First, do any computations inside the parentheses or other grouping symbols, for example, $(3n^2 + 2n + 14 - n^2 + 4n - 3) = 2n^2 + 6n + 11$. Then, use the distributive property of multiplication over addition to eliminate parentheses: $5m^2(3m^2n + 2mn + n^2) = 15m^4n + 10m^3n + 5n^2$. Finally, perform all multiplication and division, then addition and subtraction.

Simplifying Exponents

When a number is multiplied by itself a specific number of times, it is said to be **raised to a power**. The way it is written is $a^n = b$, where a is the number or **base**, n is the **exponent** or **power** that indicates the number of times the base is to be multiplied by itself, and b is the product of this multiplication. For example, in the expression 2^4, 2 is the base and 4 is the exponent. This means that 2 is multiplied by itself 4 times ($2 \times 2 \times 2 \times 2 = 16$).

Any negative number raised to an even power results in a positive number, for example, $(-2)^4 = 16$. Any negative number raised to an odd power results in a negative number. So $(-2)^3 = -8$. Be careful with an expression such as -2^4. The exponent applies to the number 2, but _not_ to the negative sign. Thus, $-2^4 = -(2^4) = -16$.

Here are several general rules related to exponents, with numerical examples:

1. $a^p a^q = a^{p+q}$

   $(3^2)(3^3) = 3^{2+3} = 3^5 = 243$.

2. $(a^p)^q = a^{pq}$

   $(2^2)^3 = 2^6 = 64$.

3. $\dfrac{a^p}{a^q} = a^{p-q}, \ a \neq 0$.

   $\dfrac{2^5}{2^2} = 2^3 = 8$.

4. $(ab)^p = a^p b^p$

   $(4 \times 3)^2 = 4^2 \times 3^2 = (16)(9) = 144$

5. $\left(\dfrac{a}{b}\right)^p = \dfrac{a^p}{b^p}, \ b \neq 0$.

   $\left(\dfrac{2}{5}\right)^3 = \dfrac{2^3}{5^3} = \dfrac{8}{125}$.

An exponent may take several forms. It may be positive, negative, zero, or a fraction. A negative exponent involves fractions. Here are a couple more exponent rules:

6. $a^{-n} = \dfrac{1}{a^n}, \ a \neq 0$.

   $2^{-3} = \dfrac{1}{2^3} = \dfrac{1}{8}$.

When a number has an exponent of zero, the result is 1, as long as the base is not equal to zero:

7. $a^0 = 1, \ a \neq 0$.

   $4^0 = 1$.

An exponent that is in fraction form involves roots. If m and n are positive integers, $n > 1$, $a^{\frac{m}{n}} = \sqrt[n]{a^m}$. The numerator becomes the exponent of a, and the denominator tells what root to take. As examples, $4^{\frac{3}{2}} = \sqrt{4^3} = \sqrt{64} = 8$ and $8^{\frac{7}{3}} = \sqrt[3]{8^7} = \sqrt[3]{2,097,152} = 128$. Note that when $n = 2$, it need not be written as the index.

SPECIAL NOTE:

$\sqrt[3]{2,097,152}$ is a rather cumbersome number to evaluate (although calculators simplify the process). Another way to evaluate $\sqrt[3]{8^7}$ is to first write it as $(\sqrt[3]{8})^7 = 2^7 = 128$. Note that expanding 2^7 is much quicker than evaluating $\sqrt[3]{2,097,152}$.

If a fractional exponent were negative, apply both rules. The same operation takes place, but the result would be a fraction, for example, $27^{-\frac{2}{3}} = \dfrac{1}{27^{\frac{2}{3}}} = \dfrac{1}{\sqrt[3]{27^2}} = \dfrac{1}{\sqrt[3]{729}} = \dfrac{1}{9}$. Be aware that we could have evaluated $\sqrt[3]{27^2}$ by taking the cube root first. Thus, $(\sqrt[3]{27})^2 = 3^2 = 9$.

EXAMPLE 13

What is the value of -4^{-3}?

SOLUTION

$-4^{-3} = -\dfrac{1}{4^3} = -\dfrac{1}{64}$.

EXAMPLE 14

What is the value of $\dfrac{-2}{3^{-1}}$?

SOLUTION

$\dfrac{-2}{3^{-1}} = \dfrac{-2}{\frac{1}{3}} = (-2)(\frac{3}{1}) = -6$.

EXAMPLE 15

What is the value of $\dfrac{5^{22}}{5^{20}}$?

SOLUTION

The "path of least resistance" is to write the example as $5^{22-20} = 5^2 = 25$.

EXAMPLE 16

What is the simplified expression for $n^8 \times n^{-4}$?

SOLUTION

We only need to use the first rule. $n^8 \times n^{-4} = n^{8+(-4)} = n^4$.

EXAMPLE 17

What is the value of $49^{-\frac{5}{2}}$?

SOLUTION

$49^{-\frac{5}{2}} = \dfrac{1}{49^{\frac{5}{2}}} = \dfrac{1}{(\sqrt{49})^5} = \dfrac{1}{7^5} = \dfrac{1}{16,807}$.

Evaluating Polynomials

Evaluating a polynomial means to simplify it to a single numerical value. When you are asked to evaluate a polynomial, the expression will be provided, as well as a numerical value to substitute for each variable.

EXAMPLE 18

Evaluate: $x^2 - \dfrac{y}{2} + xy$, if $x = 3$ and $y = 2$.

SOLUTION

Substitute the value 3 for each x and the value 2 for each y. Then $(3)^2 - \dfrac{2}{2} + (3)(2) = 9 - 1 + 6 = 14$.

EXAMPLE 19

Evaluate $n^3 + 3n^2 + 4n + 6$, if $n = -2$.

SOLUTION

Substitute the value -2 for each n. Be careful to use parentheses because they help when working with negative numbers. Then $(-2)^3 + (3)(-2)^2 + 4(-2) + 6 = (-2)(-2)(-2) + (3)(-2)(-2) + 4(-2) + 6 = (-8) + 12 + (-8) + 6 = -16 + 18 = 2$.

Performing Operations on Polynomials

When adding or subtracting polynomials, combine like terms, that it, those that differ only in their numerical coefficients. In subtraction, make sure that you first change the sign of each term in the second expression—the one that is being subtracted—and then follow the rules of addition.

EXAMPLE 20

What is the simplified expression for $(3n^2 + 2n + np) + (4n^2 + 5n + 3)$?

SOLUTION

We can group the terms as follows: $3n^2 + 4n^2 + 2n + 5n + np + 3$. Now combine like terms to get the answer of $7n^2 + 7n + np + 3$.

EXAMPLE 21

What is the simplified expression for $(4n^3 - 3q^2) - (6n^3 - 2q^2 + 4)$?

SOLUTION

First, change the sign of the terms in the second expression. The example now reads $4n^3 - 3q^2 - 6n^3 + 2q^2 - 4$. Then, rearrange as $4n^3 - 6n^3 - 3q^2 + 2q^2 - 4$ so that like terms appear together. The answer is $-2n^3 - q^2 - 4$.

When multiplying polynomials, it is vital to know the laws of exponents. Most important, when multiplying expressions that contain exponents, remember to add the exponents. Start by multiplying the coefficients, then multiply the variables (adding exponents as needed).

To multiply a polynomial by a monomial, use the distributive property. Multiply each term of the polynomial by the monomial, then combine the results.

To multiply two polynomials, multiple each of the terms of the first polynomial with each of the terms of the second polynomial, then combine the results.

EXAMPLE 22

What is the simplified product for $(3)(a^3)(5)(a^2)(2)(ab)(b^2)$?

SOLUTION

$(3)(5)(2) = 30$, $(a^3)(a^2)(ab)(b^2) = a^6b^3$. Thus, the final answer is $30a^6b^3$.

EXAMPLE 23

What is the simplified product for $(3xz^3)(4x^2 + 2y)$?

SOLUTION

Using the distributive property, $(3xz^3)(4x^2 + 2y) = (3xz^3)(4x^2) + (3xz^3)(2y) = 12x^3z^3 + 6xyz^3$.

EXAMPLE 24

What is the simplified product for $(2m^2 + n)(3m + 2n + 5)$?

SOLUTION

We use the distributive property by writing $[(2m^2)(3m) + (2m^2)(2n) + (2m^2)(5)] + [(n)(3m) + (n)(2n) + (n)(5)] = (6m^3 + 4m^2n + 10m^2) + (3mn + 2n^2 + 5n) = 6m^3 + 4m^2n + 10m^2 + 3mn + 2n^2 + 5n$.

Division of a monomial by a monomial is achieved by first dividing the constant coefficients and the variable factors separately, then multiplying the quotients.

EXAMPLE 25

What is the quotient of $6xyz^2$ divided by $2y^2z$?

SOLUTION

Write the example as $(\frac{6}{2})(\frac{x}{1})(\frac{y}{y^2})(\frac{z^2}{z})$. Then the answer becomes $3xy^{-1}z = \frac{3xz}{y}$.

Division of a polynomial by a polynomial is achieved by the following procedure, called long division:

Step 1: The terms of both the polynomials are arranged in order of ascending or descending powers of one variable.

Step 2: The first term of the dividend is divided by the first term of the divisor, which gives the first term of the quotient.

Step 3: The first term of the quotient is multiplied by the entire divisor, and the result is subtracted from the dividend.

Step 4: Using the remainder obtained from Step 3 as the new dividend, Steps 2 and 3 are repeated until the remainder is zero or the degree of the remainder is less than the degree of the divisor.

Step 5: The result is written in the following format: Dividend ÷ divisor = quotient + remainder ÷ divisor.

EXAMPLE 26

What is the simplified form for $\dfrac{2x^2 + x + 6}{x + 1}$?

SOLUTION

$$
\begin{array}{r}
2x - 1 \\
x + 1 \overline{) 2x^2 + x + 6} \\
-(2x^2 + 2x) \\
\hline
-x + 6 \\
-(-x - 1) \\
\hline
7
\end{array}
$$

Thus, the answer is $2x - 1 + \dfrac{7}{x + 1}$.

Factoring Algebraic Expressions

Factoring a polynomial (or any algebraic expression) means writing it as a product of its prime factors. There are several concepts to keep in mind while factoring:

1. A prime factor is a polynomial with no factors other than itself and 1. The least common multiple (LCM) for a set of numbers is the smallest quantity divisible by every number of the set. For algebraic expressions, the least common numerical coefficients for each of the given expressions will be a factor.

2. The greatest common factor (GCF) for a set of numbers is the largest factor that is common to all members of the set.

3. For algebraic expressions, the greatest common factor is the polynomial of the highest degree and the largest numerical coefficient that is a factor of all the given expressions.

The following formulas are helpful when multiplying certain common types polynomials:

1. $a(c + d) = ac + ad$
2. $(a + b)(a - b) = a^2 - b^2$
3. $(a + b)(a + b) = (a + b)^2 = a^2 + 2ab + b^2$
4. $(a - b)(a - b) = (a - b)^2 = a^2 - 2ab + b^2$
5. $(x + a)(x + b) = x^2 + (a + b)x + ab$
6. $(ax + b)(cx + d) = acx^2 + (ad + bc)x + bd$
7. $(a + b)(a + b)(a + b) = (a + b)^3 = a^3 + 3a^2b + 3ab^2 + b^3$
8. $(a - b)(a - b)(a - b) = (a - b)^3 = a^3 - 3a^2b + 3ab^2 - b^3$
9. $(a - b)(a^2 + ab + b^2) = a^3 - b^3$
10. $(a + b)(a^2 - ab + b^2) = a^3 + b^3$
11. $(a + b + c)^2 = a^2 + b^2 + c^2 + 2ab + 2ac + 2bc$
12. $(a - b)(a^3 + a^2b + ab^2 + b^3) = a^4 - b^4$
13. $(a - b)(a^{n-1} + a^{n-2}b + a^{n-3}b^2 + \ldots + ab^{n-2} + b^{n-1}) = a^n - b^n$, where n is any positive integer
14. $(a + b)(a^{n-1} - a^{n-2}b + a^{n-3}b^2 - \ldots - ab^{n-2} + b^{n-1}) = a^b + b^n$, where n is any positive odd integer.

The general procedure for factoring a polynomial is to first identify common factors. Then continue factoring using the "reverse" method of any of the products formulas shown above.

EXAMPLE 27

Express $16n^2 + 40n - 24$ in factored form.

SOLUTION

The greatest common factor of the three terms is 8. Then divide 8 into each term, to get $8(2n^2 + 5n - 3)$. We now seek to check formulas #5 or #6 for any further factoring that is possible. $2n^2 + 5n - 3$ can be factored further. Use the FOIL method. FOIL is the acronym for

First-Outer-Inner-Last. To determine the first term in each set of parentheses, consider the factors that make up $2n^2$. The only factors could be $2n$ and n. For the last number in each set of parentheses, consider the factors that make up the last term in the expression, in this case 3. The only possible factors are 1 and 3. Finally, to determine the location of the 1 and 3, place them inside the parentheses, then check by multiplying the outer terms and inner terms to see that, when combined, they make the middle term of the original expression. We find that $(2n^2 + 5n - 3) = (2n - 1)(n + 3)$. (This can be verified by actually doing the four multiplications.) Thus, the final answer is $8(2n-1)(n+3)$.

EXAMPLE 28

Factor the expression $4a^2 + 12a + 9$.

SOLUTION

First, determine whether there is a common factor in each term. In this case, there is no common factor. So, factor the expression into its two prime factors, using the FOIL method.

There are two possible ways to factor the first term, $4a \times a$, and $2a \times 2a$. The next step is to "guess and check." Begin with $(2a+)(2a+)$.

Then, consider the possible factors for the last term, in this case 1×9, and 3×3. Again, guess and check. If we try the factors $(2a + 3)(2a + 3)$, then we employ the FOIL method.

$2a \times 2a = 4a^2$ (the first term of the original expression)

$3 \times 3 = 9$ (the last term of the original expression)

$(2a \times 3) + (2a \times 3) = 12a$ (the middle term of the original expression).

Each part checks correctly, so that the answer is $(2a + 3)(2a + 3)$.

EXAMPLE 29

Factor this expression:
$36n^2 - 49m^2$.

SOLUTION

It is very helpful to be able to recognize numbers and variables that are perfect squares. This example illustrates the "difference of two squares." The formula for factoring such expressions is: $a^2 - b^2 = (a + b)(a - b)$.

Now designate the values represented by a^2 and b^2 in the problem. a stands for $6n$ and b stands for $7m$. Then, write the factors as demonstrated in the difference of two squares formula. Thus, the answer becomes $(6n + 7m)(6n - 7m)$. Sometimes a polynomial can be factored by the grouping method. There are two clues that indicate this might be the way to factor. The first clue is if the polynomial has no factor that is common to all terms. The second clue is if the polynomial has an even number of terms.

To solve by grouping, pair the terms of the polynomial into separate groups by terms that share a common factor.

EXAMPLE 30

Factor the expression $2mn + 3m + 10n + 15$.

SOLUTION

Group the first two terms together, since they share the common factor of m. Group the last two terms together because they share a factor of 5. This leads to $(2mn + 3m) + (10n + 15)$. Then, factor each set of terms to get $m(2n + 3) + 5(2n + 3)$. The two groups now share a common factor of $(2n + 3)$, so the polynomial factors into $(2n + 3)(m + 5)$.

NOTE:

When grouping a polynomial for factoring, it is acceptable to move terms around so that groups suitable for factoring are formed. Consider the following polynomial:

EXAMPLE 31

Factor the expression $4c^3 - 3c + 20c^2 - 15$.

SOLUTION

Rearrange the terms to make groups that share a common factor. Rewrite as $(4c^3 + 20c^2) - (3c + 15)$. Next, factor each set of terms to get $4c^2(c + 5) - 3(c + 5)$. The two groups now share a common factor of $(c + 5)$, so the polynomial factors as $(c + 5)(4c^2 - 3)$.

EXAMPLE 32

Factor the polynomial: $4pr + 2qr - 2ps - qs$.

SOLUTION

First, group the terms according to common factors to get $(4pr + 2qr) - (2ps + qs)$ (Note: When a negative sign is placed in front of the second set of parentheses, it changes the signs of the terms within the parentheses.)

Next, factor out the common factors from each set of parentheses. This yields $2r(2p + q) - s(2p + q)$. Finally, since the common binomial is $2p + q$, the complete factoring becomes $(2p + q)(2r - s)$.

Solving Linear equations

Linear equations with one variable can be put into the form $ax + b = 0$, where a and b are constants, and $a \neq 0$. To solve a linear equation means to transform it into the form $x = \dfrac{-b}{a}$. To solve any algebraic equation, first simplify each side of the equation, combining like terms, and following the order of operations. Then, you may need to add, subtract, multiply, or divide the same number and/or variable from each side of the equation. If an equation has a variable on both sides of the equal sign, it is convenient to put similar terms on the same sides. While the process really involves adding, subtracting, multiplying, or dividing a value or a variable from each side of the equation, many students learned to solve equations by "moving" terms to opposite sides of the equal sign in order to have similar terms on the same side. In that case, be sure to change the sign of any terms that "move across" the equal sign.

EXAMPLE 33

Solve for x: $9x - 4 = 5x + 8$.

SOLUTION

First, move the $5x$ to the left side of the equation and change its sign. This results in $9x - 5x - 4 = 8$. Then, move the -4 to the right side of the equation and change its sign. Now the equation reads as $9x - 5x = 8 + 4$. Combining like terms, we get $4x = 12$. Thus, the answer is $x = \dfrac{12}{4} = 3$.

Sometimes a linear equation appears in fractional form. In these problems, first eliminate the fractions by using cross-multiplication, and then solve the equation as usual.

EXAMPLE 34

Solve for n: $\dfrac{2n - 4}{3} = \dfrac{n - 1}{6}$.

SOLUTION

By using cross-multiplication, we get $6(2n - 4) = 3(n - 1)$. This is equivalent to $12n - 24 = 3n - 3$. Next, move like terms to the same side of the equal sign, changing the signs of the terms you move, then solve for the variable. Then we get $12n - 3n = 24 - 3$, followed by $9n = 21$. Thus, the answer is $\dfrac{21}{9} = \dfrac{7}{3}$.

Occasionally, there may be radicals in the equation. In these problems, it is necessary to square both sides to eliminate the radical before solving. Since it is possible to get extraneous solutions in this type of equation, it is very important to check all answers.

EXAMPLE 35

Solve for x: $\sqrt{3x + 1} = 5$.

SOLUTION

The first step is to square both sides of the equation. Then $(\sqrt{3x + 1})^2 = 5^2$, which becomes $3x + 1 = 25$. Then $3x = 24$, and thus $x = 8$.

Note that the answer of 8 does check the original equation.

EXAMPLE 36

Solve for x: $\sqrt{1-3x}+3=1$.

SOLUTION

First, subtract 3 from each side to get $\sqrt{1-3x}=-2$. By squaring both sides, the equation will read $1-3x=4$. Then $-3x=3$, so $x=-1$. But wait! We need to check this answer. By substituting -1 for x, the expression under the square root sign has a value of $1-(3)(-1)=4$. However, $\sqrt{4}+3=2+3\neq1$. Therefore, the answer of -1 is extraneous. This means that there is no solution.

Reminder: Even though $(-2)^2=2^2=4$, the symbol $\sqrt{4}$ always means 2. Similarly, the symbol $-\sqrt{4}$ means -2.

Solving Absolute Value Equations

You may also be asked to solve equations involving absolute value. The absolute value of a, written as $|a|$, is defined as follows:

$|a|=a$ when $a>0$, $|a|=-a$ when $a<0$, and $|a|=0$ when $a=0$.

When the definition of absolute value is applied to an equation, the quantity inside the absolute value symbol is considered to have two values. This value can be either positive or negative before the absolute value is taken. As a result, each absolute value equation actually contains two separate equations.

EXAMPLE 37

Solve for x:

$|3x+5|=17$.

SOLUTION

The given equation is true if either $3x+5=17$ or $3x+5=-17$.

For the first equation, subtract 5 to get $3x=12$. Thus, $x=4$.

For the second equation, subtract 5 to get $3x=-22$. Thus, $x=-\dfrac{22}{3}$. Therefore, the solution set is $\{4,\ -\dfrac{22}{3}\}$.

Remember that the absolute value of a number cannot be negative. So, for the equation $|2x-4|=-10$, for example, there would be no solution. Similarly, given an equation such as $|x+4|=0$, the only answer would be $x=-4$.

Problem solving with algebraic expressions

The first step to solving word problems is to translate the problem from words into an algebraic equation. For example, the phrase "the sum of 7 and y" can be translated to $7+y$. It may be helpful to remember some key words that indicate which operation to use.

Addition:	and, more than, sum, increased by
Subtraction:	less than, difference, decreased by, reduced by
Multiplication:	times, product of
Division:	quotient, ratio
Equals:	is, yields, the result

EXAMPLE 38

Using the variable n, write the following in algebraic symbols.

"When 3 is added to 4 times a number, the result is 31."

SOLUTION

"4 times a number" translates to $4n$. Then "3 is added to" translates to $4n+3$. "The result is 31" means $=31$. Thus, the answer is $4n+3=31$.

In some problems, it is necessary to represent two quantities using the same variable.

EXAMPLE 39

In a physics class, students made model cars out of different materials, and tested how far they would travel. The first car traveled the shortest distance, and the second car traveled 36 inches farther than the first car. The sum of the distances was 128 inches. Using the variable s, write an equation for which the solution will represent the distance (in inches) traveled by the first car. Also, determine the distance that each car traveled.

SOLUTION

Let the first car's distance in inches be represented by s. Then the second car's distance in inches is $s + 36$, since it traveled 36 inches farther than the first car. The total distance traveled is 128 inches, so the equation become $s + s + 36 = 128$. Then $2s + 36 = 128$, which simplifies to $2s = 92$. We find that $s = 46$, which is the number of inches traveled by the first car. The distance traveled by the second car is represented by $s + 36$ inches, and this value is 82 inches.

Ratio and Proportion

The **ratio** of two numbers x and y, written as $x : y$, is the fraction $\frac{x}{y}$, where $y \neq 0$. A **proportion** is an equality of two ratios. An example of a proportion is $\frac{8}{10} = \frac{12}{15}$. Each of these fractions can be reduced to $\frac{4}{5}$.

Given the proportion $\frac{a}{b} = \frac{c}{d}$, there are several equivalent statements that follow:

1. $ad = bc$

2. $\frac{b}{a} = \frac{d}{c}$

3. $\frac{a}{c} = \frac{b}{d}$

EXAMPLE 40

What is the value of y in the proportion $\frac{9}{y} = \frac{5}{16}$?

SOLUTION

Cross-multiplying yields $5y = (9)(16) = 144$. Then $y = \frac{144}{5} = 28.8$.

EXAMPLE 41

What is the value of x in the proportion $\frac{x+1}{4} = \frac{15}{12}$?

SOLUTION

Cross-multiplying yields $12(x + 1) = 60$, which simplifies to $12x + 12 = 60$. Then $12x = 48$, so $x = 4$.

EXAMPLE 42

Given that $\frac{a}{b} = \frac{c}{d}$, if $a + b = 60$, $c = 3$, and $d = 2$, what is the value of b?

SOLUTION

Don't hit the panic button! Since $a + b = 60$, we can write $a = 60 - b$. Then $\frac{60-b}{b} = \frac{3}{2}$. Cross-multiply to get $3b = 120 - 2b$. Adding $2b$ to both sides leads to $5b = 120$. Thus, $b = 24$.

Variation

Assume that when x_1 is the value of x, the corresponding value of y is y_1. Likewise, when x_2 is the value of x, then y_2 is the value of y.

If x **varies directly** as y, then $\frac{x_1}{x_2} = \frac{y_1}{y_2}$. If x **varies inversely** as y, then $\frac{x_1}{x_2} = \frac{y_2}{y_1}$.

Now suppose that when $x = x_1$, $y = y_1$, and $z = z_1$. If x **varies jointly** as y and z, then $\dfrac{x_1}{x_2} = \dfrac{y_1 z_1}{y_2 z_2}$.

EXAMPLE 43

> x varies directly as y. When $y = 15$, $x = 2$. What is the value of x when $y = 20$?

SOLUTION

Using the proportion $\dfrac{x_1}{x_2} = \dfrac{y_1}{y_2}$, we have $\dfrac{2}{x_2} = \dfrac{15}{20}$.

Then $15x_2 = 40$, so $x_2 = 2\dfrac{2}{3}$.

EXAMPLE 44

> The number of workers needed to complete a project varies inversely as the number of hours. If five workers can complete the project in 12 days, how many workers are required in order to complete the project in 10 days?

SOLUTION

Let the x's represent the number of workers and let the y's represent the number of days. We'll use the proportion $\dfrac{x_1}{x_2} = \dfrac{y_2}{y_1}$. In this example, $x_1 = 5$, $y_1 = 12$, and $y_2 = 10$. So $\dfrac{5}{x_2} = \dfrac{10}{12}$. Cross-multiply to get $10x_2 = 60$; thus $x_2 = 6$.

EXAMPLE 45

> It is known that x varies jointly as y and z. When $y = 8$ and $z = 6$, $x = 72$. What is the value of x when $y = 9$ and $z = 4$?

SOLUTION

Use the proportion $\dfrac{x_1}{x_2} = \dfrac{y_1 z_1}{y_2 z_2}$. Then $\dfrac{72}{x_2} = \dfrac{(8)(6)}{(9)(4)}$.

The proportion simplifies to $\dfrac{72}{x_2} = \dfrac{48}{36}$. Now $48x_2 = (72)(36) = 2592$. Thus, $x_2 = 54$.

In Chapter 2, we discussed the general form of a linear equation. As an extension, we may be given two linear equations in x and y in which we must solve for each variable. Often, the equations will be written in the form $ax + by = c$, where a, b, c are constants, with a, $b \neq 0$. If there is a unique solution for x and y, then the graphs of the two lines intersect at one point.

EXAMPLE 46

> Solve algebraically for x and y: $\begin{cases} x + y = 3 \\ 3x - 2y = 14 \end{cases}$

SOLUTION

One approach that works quite well is the substitution method. In the first equation, we can write $y = 3 - x$. Now substitute this expression for y in the second equation, which will read as $3x - 2(3-x) = 14$. Then we remove the parentheses to get $3x - 6 + 2x = 14$. After combining similar terms and adding 6 to both sides, the equation simplifies to $5x = 20$. Thus, $x = 4$. Return to the first equation and replace this value for x. So, $4 + y = 3$, which means that $y = -1$. This pair of numbers will also check the second original equation, since $(3)(4) - (2)(-1) = 14$.

Graphically, the solution to Example 46 means that the lines representing these two equations will intersect at the point $(4, -1)$. In order to graph each line, we only need two points.

For the graph of $y = 3 - x$, let $x = 0$. Then $y = 3$. If $x = 1$, $y = 2$. So, the points $(0, 3)$ and $(1, 2)$ determine the graph of the first equation.

For the graph of $3x - 2y = 14$, let's choose $x = 0$. Then $0 - 2y = 14$, so $y = -7$. As a second point, let's choose $x = 2$. Then $6 - 2y = 14$. This simplifies to $-2y = 8$, so $y = -4$. So, the points $(0, -7)$ and $(2, -4)$ determine the graph of the second equation.

Figure 3.11 shows the graphs of these two lines, as well as the point of intersection.

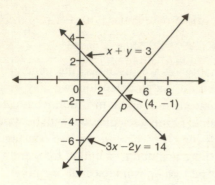

Figure 3.11

EXAMPLE 47

Solve algebraically for x and y: $\begin{cases} 2x + 3y = 6 \\ 4x + 6y = 9 \end{cases}$

SOLUTION

An easy approach would be to multiply the first equation by -2. This will create the equivalent equation $-4x - 6y = -12$. If we add this equivalent equation to the original second equation, the result is $0x + 0y = -5$. Of course, the left side is always zero for any values of x and y. The statement $0 = -5$ is automatically false, so there is no solution.

Graphically, we can show that the lines representing these two equations are parallel to each other. For the first equation, let's use the points $(0, 2)$ and $(3, 0)$. For the second equation, we'll use the points $(0, 1.5)$ and $(2.25, 0)$.

Figure 3.12 shows that the graphs of these lines are parallel. Thus, there is no point of intersection.

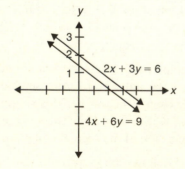

Figure 3.12

EXAMPLE 48

Solve algebraically for x and y: $\begin{cases} 2x + y = 8 \\ 4x + 2y = 16 \end{cases}$

SOLUTION

Multiply the first equation by -2 to get $-4x - 2y = -16$. If we add this equation to the second original equation, the result reads as $0 = 0$. Since $0 = 0$ is always true, we conclude that any pair of values of x and y that satisfy $2x + y = 8$ will also satisfy $4x + 2y = 16$. The graph for these equations is simply one line.

Inequalities

An **inequality** is a statement that compares two quantities that have different values. The symbols for inequality are: $>$ (greater than), $\geq$ (greater than or equal, $<$ (less than), $\leq$ (less than or equal), and $\neq$ (not equal). The symbols $\geq$ and $\leq$ actually imply that one of two conditions are given. Thus, by writing $x \geq 4$, we are stating that either x equals 4 or that x is greater than 4. Similarly, the statement $y \leq -2$ means that y is either equal to -2 or that y is less than -2.

An **absolute inequality** refers to one that is <u>always</u> true. Examples are $2 < 6$, $10 \geq 10$, and $x + 4 < x + 8$.

A **conditional inequality** refers to one that is true only in certain cases. For example, $x + 5 < 11$ is true for values of x less than 6.

Graphing an Inequality in One Variable

The graph of an inequality in one variable can be any of the following:

a) A ray including its endpoint

b) A ray without its endpoint

c) A line segment with its endpoints

d) A line segment without one or both endpoints

EXAMPLE 49

Graph the inequality $x > 2$.

SOLUTION

On a number line, place an open circle on 2 and darken all numbers to the right of 2. The result will be a ray facing to the right, without its endpoint. Figure 3.13 shows the graph.

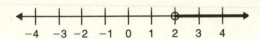

Figure 3.13

EXAMPLE 50

Graph the inequality $x \leq 1$.

SOLUTION

On a number line, place a dot on 1 and darken all numbers to the left of 1. The result is a ray facing to the left, with its endpoint. Figure 3.14 shows the graph.

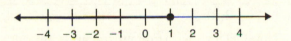

Figure 3.14

EXAMPLE 51

Graph the inequality $5 > x \geq 2$.

SOLUTION

On a number line, place an open circle on 5, a dot on 2, and darken all numbers between 2 and 5. The result is a line segment with only one endpoint. Figure 3.15 shows the graph.

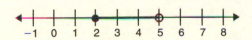

Figure 3.15

An example of a line segment with both endpoints would be the graph of $-1 \leq x \leq 6$.

An example of a line segment with neither endpoint would be the graph of $5 < x < 12$.

Solving Inequalities Algebraically in One Variable

The rules for solving inequalities are nearly the same as those used for solving equations, with one exception. Whenever the inequality is multiplied or divided by a negative quantity, the order of the inequality is reversed.

As a numerical example, consider the inequality $4 < 6$. If we multiply both sides by -3, the left side becomes -12 and the right side becomes -18. But since -12 is larger than -18, the inequality changes order (direction) so that it reads $-12 > -18$. Similarly, if we divide both sides of $4 < 6$ by -2, the left side becomes -2 and the right side becomes -3.

Since -2 is the larger number, we write $-2 > -3$.

Note that this rule applies equally to negative numbers. If we start with $-5 < 3$ and multiply both sides by -4, the result is $20 > -12$. If we divide both sides of $-5 < 3$ by $-\frac{1}{2}$, the inequality changes to $10 > -6$. (Remember that dividing by $-\frac{1}{2}$ is equivalent to multiplying by -2.)

EXAMPLE 53

Solve for x: $3x + 2 < -7$.

SOLUTION

Subtract 2 from each side to get $3x < -9$. Just divide both sides by 3 to get the answer of $x < -3$. (Do not change the order of the inequality, since we are dividing by a <u>positive</u> number.)

EXAMPLE 54

Solve for m: $-4m + 5 \leq m + 7$.

SOLUTION

Subtract m from each side to get $-5m + 5 \leq 7$. Next, subtract 5 from each side. The resulting inequality is $-5m \leq 2$. Finally, divide both sides by -5 (and reverse the order of the inequality). The answer is $m \geq -\dfrac{2}{5}$.

EXAMPLE 55

Solve for y: $-5 < \dfrac{2}{3}y + 1 < 9$.

SOLUTION

Subtract 1 from each of the three parts to get $-6 < \dfrac{2}{3}y < 8$. The last step is to multiply all parts by $\dfrac{3}{2}$ to get the answer of $-9 < y < 12$.

Quadratic Equations

Let a, b, and c be real numbers. An equation in the form $ax^2 + bx + c = 0$, with $a \neq 0$, is called a **quadratic equation in x**. There are three basic methods in solving this type of equation.

If $b = 0$, the easiest method is to simply isolate x and take the square root of each side of the equation.

EXAMPLE 56

Solve for x: $4x^2 - 3 = 17$.

SOLUTION

Add 3 to each side to get $4x^2 = 20$. Now divide by 4 to get $x^2 = 5$. By taking the square root of each side, the two answers are $x = \sqrt{5}$ or $x = -\sqrt{5}$.

Sometimes, the given equation can be factored. Recall that if a product of two (or more) quantities is zero, then at least one of these quantities must equal zero. This is commonly known as the product rule for zero.

EXAMPLE 57

Solve for x: $2x^2 + x - 2 = 1$.

SOLUTION

First, subtract 1 from both sides so that the equation has all nonzero terms on one side. Then $2x^2 + x - 3 = 0$. We can factor the left side so that $(2x + 3)(x - 1) = 0$.

Now, either $2x + 3 = 0$ or $x - 1 = 0$. The two answers are $x = -\dfrac{3}{2}$ or $x = 1$.

A third approach, which actually works for <u>all</u> quadratic equations, is the Quadratic formula. The solution to $ax^2 + bx + c = 0$ is always given by

$$x = \frac{-b \pm \sqrt{b^2 - 4ac}}{2a}.$$

(Note that this equation represents <u>two</u> answers, namely $\dfrac{-b + \sqrt{b^2 - 4ac}}{2a}$ and $\dfrac{-b - \sqrt{b^2 - 4ac}}{2a}$.)

EXAMPLE 58

Solve for x: $2x^2 + 9x + 5 = 0$.

SOLUTION

We identify $a = 2$, $b = 9$, and $c = 5$. Then

$$x = \frac{-9 \pm \sqrt{9^2 - 4(2)(5)}}{2(2)} = \frac{-9 \pm \sqrt{81 - 40}}{4} = \frac{-9 \pm \sqrt{41}}{4}.$$

Note that if we wish to approximate the two answers, we could write $\sqrt{41} \approx 6.4$. Then

$$\frac{-9 + \sqrt{41}}{4} \approx \frac{-9 + 6.4}{4} = -0.65. \text{ Similarly,}$$

$$\frac{-9 - \sqrt{41}}{4} \approx \frac{-9 - 6.4}{4} = -3.85.$$

We can also check the answers for Examples 56 and 57 by using the Quadratic formula.

In Example 56, we write the equation as $4x^2 - 20 = 0$. Note that $b = 0$. Then

$$x = \frac{-0 \pm \sqrt{0^2 - (4)(4)(-20)}}{(2)(4)} = \frac{\pm \sqrt{320}}{8}$$

$$= \frac{\pm (\sqrt{64})(\sqrt{5})}{8} = \pm \sqrt{5}.$$

This matches our answer to Example 56.

The Discriminant of a Quadratic Equation

The answers to any quadratic equation are commonly referred to as **roots**. Not all quadratic equations have two real roots. Consider the equation $x^2 - 6x + 9 = 0$. By factoring, we have $(x - 3)(x - 3) = 0$. Thus, the only root is 3.

By contrast, consider the equation $x^2 - 4x + 9 = 0$. Using the Quadratic formula, the roots are

$$\frac{-(-4) \pm \sqrt{(-4)^2 - (4)(1)(9)}}{2(1)} = \frac{4 \pm \sqrt{16 - 36}}{2} = \frac{4 \pm \sqrt{-20}}{2}.$$

However, $\sqrt{-20}$ is not a real number. Thus, this equation has no real roots. (There are actually two complex roots, but this is beyond the scope of this book and the test you'll be taking.)

The number of real roots of any quadratic equation is determined by the value of $b^2 - 4ac$, which is called the **discriminant**. If $b^2 - 4ac < 0$, there are no real roots.

If $b^2 - 4ac = 0$, there is one real root. If $b^2 - 4ac > 0$, there are two real roots.

Furthermore, if $b^2 - 4ac$ is a perfect square, then both roots are rational.

EXAMPLE 59

How many real roots are there for the equation $10x^2 - x - 2 = 0$?

SOLUTION

$a = 10$, $b = -1$ and $c = -2$. Then $b^2 - 4ac = (-1)^2 - 4(10)(-2) = 1 + 80 = 81 > 0$. Therefore, there are two real roots. (Both are rational, since 81 is a perfect square.)

EXAMPLE 60

The equation $3x^2 - 11x + k = 0$ has exactly one real root. What is the value of k?

SOLUTION

We must have $b^2 - 4ac = 0$. By substitution, $(-11)^2 - 4(3)(k) = 0$. This equation simplifies to $121 - 12k = 0$, so $k = \frac{121}{12}$.

Chapter 3 Quiz

1. What is the simplified expression for $3ac^2 + 2b^2c + 7ac^2 + 2ac^2 + b^2c$?

   (A) $12ac^2 + 3b^2c$ (C) $11ac^2 + 4ab^2c$

   (B) $14ab^2c^2$ (D) $15ab^2c^2$

2. What is the simplified expression for $(2a + b)(3a^2 + ab + b^2)$?

   (A) $6a^3 + 5a^2b + 3ab^2 + b^3$

   (B) $5a^3 + 3ab + b^3$

   (C) $6a^3 + 2a^2b + 2ab^2$

   (D) $3a^2 + 2a + ab + b + b^2$

3. What is the quotient for $(m^2 + m - 14) \div (m + 4)$?

   (A) $m - 2$

   (B) $m - 3 + \dfrac{-2}{m + 4}$

   (C) $m - 3 + \dfrac{4}{m + 4}$

   (D) $m - 3$

4. What is the factored form of $2c^2 + 5cd - 3d^2$?

   (A) $(2c - 3d)(c + d)$

   (B) $(2c - d)(c + 3d)$

   (C) $(2c + 3d)(c - d)$

   (D) $(2c + d)(c - 3d)$

5. At a factory, three out of every 1000 parts are defective. In a day, the factory produces 25,000 parts. How many of these parts would be defective?

   (A) 7500   (C) 75

   (B) 750   (D) 70

6. What is the solution for p in the inequality $-3p + 1 \geq 16$?

   (A) $p \geq -5$ (C) $p \leq -\dfrac{17}{3}$

   (B) $p \geq -\dfrac{17}{3}$ (D) $p \leq -5$

7. What are the solutions for x in the equation $|5x| - 12 = -2$?

   (A) $\dfrac{14}{5}$ or $-\dfrac{14}{5}$

   (B) $\dfrac{14}{5}$ or 2

   (C) 2 or -2

   (D) No solution

8. What are the solutions for x in the equation $4x^2 + 5x - 6 = 0$?

   (A) $\dfrac{3}{4}$ or -2

   (B) $-\dfrac{3}{4}$ or 2

   (C) $-\dfrac{3}{2}$ or 1

   (D) $\dfrac{3}{2}$ or -1

9. If $f(x) = \dfrac{3x - 2}{5}$, which of the following represents the inverse function $f^{-1}(x)$?

   (A) $\dfrac{5}{3x - 2}$

   (B) $\dfrac{5x + 2}{3}$

   (C) $\dfrac{3}{2x + 5}$

   D) $\dfrac{2x - 3}{5}$

10. Which one of the following systems of equations has no solution?

   (A) $2x - 3y = 10$ (C) $3x + 4y = 5$
        $2x + 3y = 10$ $4x + 3y = -5$

   (B) $2x - y = 10$ (D) $3x + y = 4$
        $4x - 2y = 20$ $9x + 3y = 8$

Chapter 3 Quiz Solutions

1. (A)

Rearrange the terms so that all like terms appear together. The expression can be written as $(3ac^2 + 7ac^2 + 2ac^2) + (2b^2c + 1b^2c)$. Now add the coefficients within each set of parentheses to get the answer of $12ac^2 + 3b^2c$.

2. (A)

By performing the six separate multiplications of monomials, we get $(2a)(3a^2)+(2a)(ab)+(2a)(b^2)+(b)(3a^2)+(b)(ab)+(b)(b^2) = 6a^3 + 2a^2b + 2ab^2 + 3a^2b + ab^2 + b^3 = 6a^3 + 5a^2b + 3ab^2 + b^3$.

3. (B)

$$(m^2 + m - 14) \div (m + 4) = m + 4 \overline{\smash{\big)}\ m^2 + m - 14}$$

$$\begin{array}{r} m \quad -3 \\ m+4\overline{\smash{\big)}m^2 + m - 14} \\ \underline{-(m^2 + 4m)} \\ -3m - 14 \\ \underline{-(-3m - 12)} \\ -2 \end{array}$$

The answer is $m - 3 + \dfrac{-2}{m + 4}$

4. (B)

$(2c-d)(c+3d) = (2c)(c)+(2c)(3d)+(-d)(c)+(-d)(3d)$

$= 2c^2 + 6cd - cd - 3d^2 = 2c^2 + 5cd - 3d^2$.

5. (C)

Let x represent the number of defective parts. Then $\dfrac{3}{x} = \dfrac{1000}{25,000}$. We can simplify the ratio on the right side to $\dfrac{1}{25}$. Using the proportion $\dfrac{3}{x} = \dfrac{1}{25}$, cross-multiply to get $x = (3)(25) = 75$.

6. (D)

Subtract 1 from each side of the inequality to get $-3p \geq 15$. Next, divide by -3 and reverse the order of the inequality. Then $\dfrac{-3p}{-3} \leq \dfrac{15}{-3}$, so $p \leq -5$.

7. (C)

Add 12 to both sides of the equation to get $|5x| = 10$. Then either $5x = 10$ or $5x = -10$. Therefore, $x = 2$ or -2.

8. (A)

Factoring the left side of the equation, we get $(4x - 3)(x + 2) = 0$. Then either $4x - 3 = 0$ or $x + 2 = 0$. Therefore, $x = \dfrac{3}{4}$ or -2.

9. (B)

To find the inverse of $f(x)$, replace $f(x)$ with x and replace x with y. Now y will represent $f^{-1}(x)$. Then $x = \dfrac{3y - 2}{5}$. Now proceed to solve this equation for y. Multiply by 5 to get $5x = 3y - 2$. Adding 2 to each side, we get $5x + 2 = 3y$. Finally, divide the equation by 3. Thus, $y = f^{-1}(x) = \dfrac{5x + 2}{3}$.

10. (D)

Multiply the first equation by 3 to get $9x + 3y = 12$. By subtracting the second equation, $9x + 3y = 8$, the result is $0 = 4$. This means that there is no solution for x and y. For answer choice (A), the solution is $(5, 0)$. For answer choice (B), there are an infinite number of pairs of solutions. For answer choice (C), the solution is $(-5, 5)$.

CHAPTER 4

Data Analysis and Probability

Data Collection Concepts

To make important decisions, we often use statistics based on data that someone has collected, analyzed, and interpreted. The data collection process is much like the scientific method; a researcher poses a question, collects data, displays the data, interprets it, and draws conclusions.

There are several basic concepts related to data collection, including sampling and the most common way to collect quantitative data—surveys.

We define a **population** as the complete set of people or events that a researcher would like to study. In some cases, it is possible to collect data from an entire population (e.g., surveying all females in a college algebra course). In most cases, however, surveying an entire population is impossible for a variety of reasons. Therefore, researchers collect data from a **sample**. A sample is a selected subset of the population. Based on the results obtained from the sample, we can generalize the results as representative of the entire population.

We collect data in order to answer questions for which the answers are not immediately obvious. One effective way of collecting data is through the use of surveys. A **survey** provides a numerical depiction of the characteristics, preferences, opinions, and/or attitudes of the sample. Surveys are often designed using a **Likert scale**, which allows the participants to rate the degree to which the questions or statements apply to them. This scale usually contains the following five levels of satisfaction: (a) Strongly disagree, (b) Disagree, (c) Neither agree nor disagree, (d) Agree, and (e) Strongly agree.

When collecting quantitative data, it is important to remember that the larger the sample size, the more we can be confident that our results can be generalized to the population of interest. For example, if you wanted to determine what percentage of teachers have an advanced degree, a sample size of 500 teachers would make the results more reliable than a sample size of 10 teachers.

Many factors affect the selection of sample size, including (a) the degree of precision required, (b) the availability of necessary resources, and (c) the expected time for responses.

Random Sampling

A sample may be selected in a variety of ways, the most common of which is random sampling. In **random sampling**, each individual in the population has an equal chance of being selected to participate in a survey. This type of sampling makes it most likely that the sample we have selected is representative of the population under study.

One way of obtaining a random sample is to assign a number to each member of the population. The population becomes a set of numbers. Then, using the random number table, we can choose a sample of the desired size. For example, suppose 1,000 voters are registered and eligible to vote in an upcoming election. To conduct a poll, you need a sample of 50 people, so to each voter, you assign a number between 1 and 1,000. Then, using the random number table or a computer program, you choose 50 numbers randomly. This selection, which will represent the 50 voters, becomes your required sample.

Organizing, Displaying, and Analyzing Data

Repeated measurements yield data, which should be organized in such a way that each observation can belong to one (and only one) category. The most popular graphical displays include pie graphs, bar graphs, time series line graphs, histograms, scatter plots, and box-and-whisker plots. Non-graphical displays include frequency distributions and stem-and-leaf plots.

Pie Graphs

This type of graph is best used to show the percentage (or fractional) contribution of the component parts of one category. In a pie graph, each component is assigned to a percent, which then becomes a sector of the circle containing all the component parts.

EXAMPLE 1

The mayor of the town of Peoplefine has mailed a survey to each adult resident, who was asked to rate the quality of the mayor's ability to govern the town. The five ratings given were (a) excellent, (b) very good, (c) average, (d) below average, and (e) poor. The results showed that $\frac{2}{5}$ of the population ranked the mayor as "excellent," $\frac{1}{3}$ ranked him as "very good," $\frac{1}{10}$ ranked him as "average," $\frac{1}{12}$ ranked him as "below average," and $\frac{1}{12}$ ranked him as "poor." Create an appropriate pie graph.

SOLUTION

You recall that a circle contains $360°$, so we need to convert each fraction to degrees. For example, $\frac{2}{5}$ corresponds to $(\frac{2}{5})(360°) = 144°$. Following this procedure, here are the conversions for the other given fractions: $\frac{1}{3}$ corresponds to $120°$, $\frac{1}{10}$ corresponds to $36°$, and $\frac{1}{12}$ corresponds to $30°$. The last step is to partition a circle into sectors with the appropriate central angles. Each sector is labeled with a category. Figure 4.1 shows the completed pie graph.

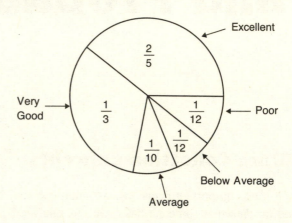

Figure 4.1

Bar Graphs

In this type of graph, the categories are listed and spaced evenly along a horizontal axis. Each category is represented by a rectangle, all of which have the same width. The number representing the category's frequency determines the height of each rectangle. By convention, the vertical axis begins with zero. Along the horizontal axis, each rectangle is labeled with its associated category. The frequencies are listed in numerical order along the vertical axis.

EXAMPLE 2

Twenty students are foreign language majors at a small university. Seven of them are majoring in German, three are majoring in Russian, five are majoring in Spanish, three are majoring in French, and two are majoring in Italian. Create a bar graph.

SOLUTION

We will have five rectangles, each of the same width. Each rectangle will be labeled with the appropriate foreign language. On the vertical axis, we will use the numbers 0 through 7 because seven represents the highest frequency of any category. Figure 4.2 shows the completed bar graph.

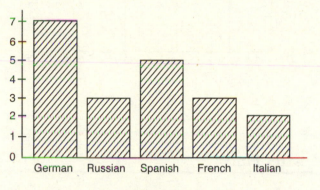

Figure 4.2

Time Series Line Graphs

This type of graph is extremely useful when we wish to show a trend of a single quantity over a specified period of time. The units of time (for example months, days, years) are evenly spaced along the horizontal axis and the frequencies are placed on the vertical axis. Dots are used to identify a specific unit of time with its associated frequency. As with bar graphs, these frequencies must show an arithmetic pattern. Finally, line segments will be used to connect the dots in sequence.

EXAMPLE 3

During the first six months of this year, Amanda kept track of how many different projects she was assigned at work. Here are her results: January, 28; February, 22; March, 52; April, 8; May, 12; June, 40. Construct a time series line graph.

SOLUTION

The months will be placed on the horizontal axis, beginning with January and ending with June. The vertical axis will begin at zero and will be scaled in

units of 4. Note that, because the highest frequency is 52, it would be very cumbersome to use a scaling unit of 1. A scaling of 4 would be convenient, even though one of the numbers (22) does not divide evenly by 4. Figure 4.3 shows the completed graph.

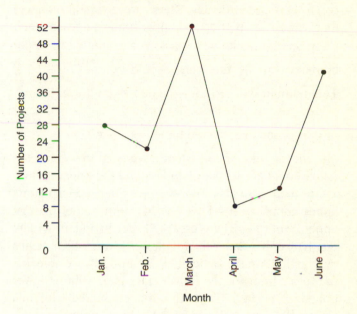

Figure 4.3

Histograms

This type of graphical display of data is very similar to a bar graph. The major differences are that (a) the rectangles must be connected, and (b) the horizontal axis must be labeled numerically at the left side of the first rectangle and to the right side of the last rectangle. Each rectangle will be composed of a group of data, called a **class**.

Before constructing a histogram, we need some definitions. Suppose that a teacher has a class of twenty students. Each student lists his or her height in inches, the results of which are tabulated.

Instead of listing each height separately, however, the heights are listed in groups of data (classes). The height of the shortest student is 60 inches and the height of the tallest student is 79 inches. The teacher decides to use the following four groups of heights:

Group I: 60−64 inches, Group II: 65−69 inches, Group III: 70−74 inches, Group IV: 75−79 inches. The results then show that five students are in Group I, seven students are in Group II, six students are in Group III, and two students are in Group IV.

For the first class, the number 60 is called the **lower limit** and the number 64 is called the **upper limit**. Each of these four classes has both a lower and an upper limit. However, we want to eventually connect the rectangles that represent these classes. To accomplish this goal, we create **class boundaries**. These are artificial numbers that lie midway between an upper limit of one class and a lower limit of the next class. For example, the upper boundary of the first class would be $\frac{64+65}{2} = 64.5$. This number will also be assigned as the lower boundary of the second class. Similarly, the upper boundary of the second class would be $\frac{69+70}{2} = 69.5$.

For the sake of consistency, we need to identify the lower boundary of the first class and the upper boundary of the fourth class. For the first class, notice that its upper boundary (64.5) is one half unit higher than its upper limit (64). Therefore, the lower boundary will be one half unit smaller than its lower limit, which means that it will have the value of 59.5. Similarly, we note that the lower limit for the fourth class is 75, but its lower boundary is 74.5. Thus, the upper boundary for this class will be one half unit higher than its upper limit. So the upper boundary for the fourth class is 79.5.

As a summary, here is a list of each class, its lower and upper boundaries, and its frequency:

Group I	59.5 − 64.5	5
Group II	64.5 − 69.5	7
Group III	69.5 − 74.5	6
Group IV	74.5 − 79.5	2

EXAMPLE 4

Construct a histogram for the data shown above.

SOLUTION

The highest frequency is 7, so our vertical axis will be scaled in units of 1, from 0 to 7. Figure 4.4 shows the completed histogram.

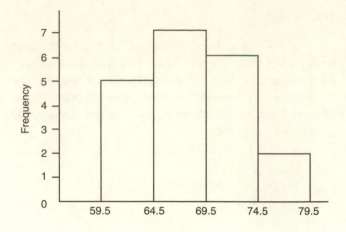

Figure 4.4

Scatter Plots

A **scatter plot** is a method of showing the relationship of two different numerical quantities by using an *xy*-coordinate plane. We will restrict our values to positive numbers for each of the quantities.

EXAMPLE 5

In a small class of 9 students, the teacher was interested in comparing the number of absences during the school year with each student's final numerical grade. Here are the results in tabular form:

Number of
absences: 0 5 3 9 1 7 3 2 6

Final grade: 98 80 90 60 93 55 85 90 75

Draw a scatter plot of these results.

SOLUTION

The positive *x*-axis will be labeled "Number of Absences" and the positive *y*-axis will be labeled "Final Grade." For each number of absences, a dot will be placed to indicate the associated final grade. Figure 4.5 shows the scatter plot.

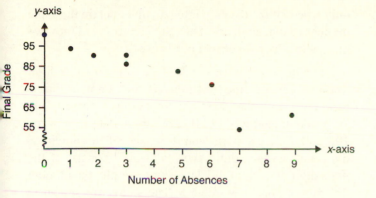

Figure 4.5

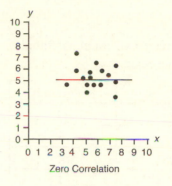

Zero Correlation

Figure 4.7

Because the grades range from 55 to 98, a squiggle line is shown between 0 and 55. This indicates that there are no values between 0 and 55. The teacher could draw the conclusion that the number of absences negatively affect students' final grade.

A statistic called **correlation** describes the numerical relationship between two variables. A scatter plot is one graphical way of viewing the type of correlation between two given quantities. There are basically three types of correlation: positive, zero, and negative.

With **positive** correlation, as one variable increases, the other variable also increases. And as one variable decreases, so does the other variable decrease.

With **zero** correlation, the change in either variable is not related to the change in the other variable.

With **negative** correlation, as one variable increases, the other variable decreases. Conversely, as one variable decreases, the other variable increases.

Figures 4.6, 4.7, and 4.8 illustrate these three types of correlation. (The calculation of a numerical value for the correlation between two variables is beyond the scope of this book and the test.)

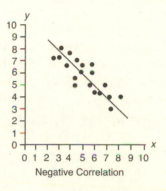

Negative Correlation

Figure 4.8

Frequency Distributions

A **frequency distribution** is a method by which the given data is classified by a type or label. For each label, its frequency in the distribution is recorded. We'll show two examples, one of which is nonnumerical and one of which is numerical.

EXAMPLE 6

At a gathering of 30 people, each person was asked to write his or her eye color. Here are the data:

brown	amber	amber	blue	blue
hazel	hazel	blue	amber	hazel
brown	blue	amber	brown	amber
hazel	brown	hazel	amber	amber
hazel	amber	blue	blue	blue
amber	blue	amber	hazel	amber

Write a frequency distribution for these four eye colors.

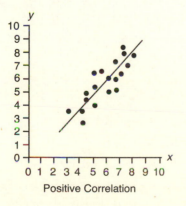

Positive Correlation

Figure 4.6

SOLUTION

We just create two columns. Simply count the number of each eye color!

Eye Color	Frequency
Amber	11
Blue	8
Brown	4
Hazel	7

EXAMPLE 7

The record low temperatures of last year for twenty-five cities were collected. Here are the twenty-five temperatures (note that there are some repetitions):

13°, 37°, 20°, 19°, 21°, 17°, 24°, 9°, 14°, 20°, 23°, 20°, 21°, 26°, 26°, 17°, 14°, 36°, 10°, 25°, 15°, 4°, 30°, 5°, and 28°. Use the following five classes (3°−9°, 10°−16°, 17°−23°, 24°−30°, and 31°−37°) to construct a frequency distribution.

SOLUTION

When we arrange the data in ascending order, they appear as follows:

4°, 5°, 9°, 10°, 13°, 14°, 14°, 15°, 17°, 17°, 19°, 20°, 20°, 20°, 21°, 21°, 23°, 24°, 25°, 26°, 26°, 28°, 30°, 36°, and 37°. The next step is simply to count the number of data in each class. Here is the completed frequency distribution.

Class	Frequency
3° − 9°	3
10° − 16°	5
17° − 23°	9
24° − 30°	6
31° − 37°	2

Stem-and-Leaf Plots

The **stem-and-leaf plot** method requires that the data be arranged in ascending order. It should be used only when all the data are integers that contain the same number of placeholders. The data are arranged into two groups in which a vertical bar is used.

The stem consists of all digits, except the units digit. The leaf contains the unit digit of each number that is associated with that stem. As an example, the number 76 would appear as 7 | 6. If each of the data is between 100 and 999, the stem would consist of the hundreds digit and the tens digit; the leaf would consist of the units digit of each of the data. For example, the number 235 would appear as 23 | 5. The stems are shown in ascending order in a vertical column, and the leaves for each stem are written horizontally in ascending order.

EXAMPLE 8

Ken is an avid bowler. He has kept track of his bowling scores for the 30 most recent games. As a tribute to his consistency, his lowest score was 160 and his highest score was 219. (He hopes to bowl 300 someday!) His results were as follows: 189, 209, 195, 162, 175, 189, 202, 218, 213, 210, 192, 178, 176, 163, 196, 160, 188, 182, 195, 212, 168, 197, 219, 210, 210, 184, 198, 161, 169, and 192. Construct a stem-and-leaf plot.

SOLUTION

Because each number has three digits, the first two digits appear on the left side of the vertical bar. The right side of the vertical bar (i.e., the leaf part) must contain only single digits. Arranged in ascending order, the data appears as follows: 160, 161, 162, 163, 168, 169, 175, 176, 178, 182, 184, 188, 189, 189, 192, 192, 195, 195, 196, 197, 198, 202, 209, 210, 210, 210, 212, 213, 218, and 219. The completed stem-and-leaf plot is as follows:

```
16 | 0  1  2  3  8  9
17 | 5  6  8
18 | 2  4  8  9  9
19 | 2  2  5  5  6  7  8
20 | 2  9
21 | 0  0  0  2  3  8  9
```

Before we cover the topic of box-and-whisker plots, we must discuss several statistical concepts.

Measures of Central Tendency and Dispersion

Sometimes we need only a summary of the information for a data set. One such statistic is called the **range**, which is simply the difference between the highest and the lowest numbers. For example, if the highest grade in a test is 90 and the lowest grade is 60, the range is 30. This number has limited value because it tells us nothing about the nature of the individual data.

The following quantities are often called measures of **central tendency** because they reveal how the data are distributed. We will discuss the three most popular measures of central tendency, identified as the **mean**, **median**, and **mode**. Each of these concepts will be applied both to individual data and to grouped data.

Arithmetic Mean

The **arithmetic mean** (usually referred to simply as the mean) of a list of individual data is found by adding the numbers, then dividing by the total frequency. The commonly used symbol for a mean is $\bar{x}$. Mathematically, given the n numbers x_1, x_2, x_3, ..., x_n, $\bar{x} = \dfrac{\sum\limits_{1}^{n} x_i}{n}$.

Note that $\sum\limits_{1}^{n} x_i$ is equivalent to $x_1 + x_2 + x_3 + \ldots + x_n$.

EXAMPLE 9

What is the mean for the numbers 24, 18, 50, 22, and 18?

SOLUTION

The sum of these five numbers is 132, so that $\bar{x} = \dfrac{132}{5} = 26.4$.

Sometimes, we need to calculate a **weighted average**, which assigns "weights" to each different value in the list of data. These weights often represent the frequencies of the different values.

Suppose the frequencies of $x_1, x_2, x_3, \ldots, x_n$ are given by $f_1, f_2, f_3, \ldots, f_n$, respectively. Then $\bar{x} = \dfrac{\sum\limits_{1}^{n} f_i x_i}{\sum\limits_{1}^{n} f_i}$.

EXAMPLE 10

In a group of 27 data, the number 3 occurs three times, the number 7 occurs twice, the number 2 occurs once, the number 8 occurs five times, the number 0 occurs ten times, and the number 4 occurs six times. What is the mean?

SOLUTION

Using the formula $\bar{x} = \dfrac{\sum\limits_{1}^{n} f_i x_i}{\sum\limits_{1}^{n} f_i}$, the mean is evaluated

as $\dfrac{(3)(3)+(2)(7)+(1)(2)+(5)(8)+(10)(0)+(6)(4)}{3+2+1+5+10+6}$

$= \dfrac{89}{27} \approx 3.3$.

To calculate the mean for grouped data (that is, data that appears in classes), the midpoint of each class is used. Then each midpoint is multiplied by the class frequency. After adding these products, the sum is divided by the total frequency.

EXAMPLE 11

What is the mean for the following grouped frequency distribution?

Class	Frequency
3° − 9°	3
10° − 16°	5
17° − 23°	9
24° − 30°	6
31° − 37°	2

SOLUTION

This is the frequency distribution that we saw in Example 7. The midpoints of the five classes are 6°, 13°, 20°, 27°, and 34°. Thus, the mean is

$$\frac{(3)(6)+(5)(13)+(9)(20)+(6)(27)+(2)(34)}{25}$$

$$=\frac{493}{25}=19.72°.$$

Median

The second measure of central tendency that we will discuss is the median. First, the data must be arranged in ascending order. (Arrangement in descending order, though less common, would also be acceptable.)

The **median** of a list of individual data is the middle value of all the data. There are actually two distinct situations: an odd number of data or an even number of data. Let n represent the number of data values, where n is an odd number. Then the position of the median is given as $(n + 1) \div 2$.

If n represents the number of data, where n is an even number, then the median is defined as the mean of the two middle numbers. The position of the median is still given as $(n + 1) \div 2$.

EXAMPLE 12

What is the median for the numbers 26, 22, 16, 11, 27, 26, 20, 20, and 15?

SOLUTION

In ascending order, the numbers appear as 11, 15, 16, 20, 20, 22, 26, 26, and 27. Because $n = 9$, the position of the median is given by $\frac{9+1}{2}$ = 5. The fifth number is 20.

EXAMPLE 13

What is the median for the numbers 44, 38, 19, 6, 31, and 37?

SOLUTION

In ascending order, the numbers appear as 6, 19, 31, 37, 38, and 44. The position of the median is $\frac{6+1}{2}$ = 3.5. This implies that the median is the average of the third and fourth numbers, which is $\frac{31+37}{2}$ = 34.

We are about to explore the technique for calculating the median for grouped data.

Let's first mention that, with grouped data, the position of the median for n data is always $n \div 2$, regardless of whether the number of data is odd or even.

EXAMPLE 14

What is the median for the following grouped data?

Class	Frequency
3° − 9°	3
10° − 16°	5
17° − 23°	9
24° − 30°	6
31° − 37°	2

SOLUTION

This is a replica of the data in Example 11. We need three key definitions. For any given class, the two numbers shown are the **lower and upper limits**. Thus, for the first class, the lower limit is 3° and the upper limit is 9°. Each given class also has a **lower and upper boundary**. These numbers are determined by subtracting one-half unit from the lower limit and adding one-half unit to the upper boundary, respectively. Thus, for the first class, the lower boundary is 3 − 0.5 = 2.5 and the upper boundary is 9 + 0.5 = 9.5. The **width** of any class is the difference between the upper and lower boundaries. (This will be a constant within any single example of grouped data.)

Because there are 25 numbers, the position of the median is 12.5. We note that the first two classes contain 3 + 5 = 8 numbers. The next nine numbers are included within the third class, which means that, through the first three classes, 8 + 9 = 17 numbers are included.

This implies that the 12.5th number lies in the third class. Eight numbers were included in the first two classes, so we need the $12.5 - 8 = 4.5^{th}$ number in the third class. The next step is to write the fraction $\frac{4.5}{9}$, which reduces to $\frac{1}{2}$. The width of the third class is $23.5 - 16.5 = 7$, so we multiply $\frac{1}{2}$ by 7 to get 3.5. Finally, add 3.5 to the lower boundary of the third class. The answer is $16.5 + 3.5 = 20$.

The actual formula for determining the median for any grouped data is:

$$M = L + \left[\frac{\frac{N}{2} - C}{F} \right](W)$$

In this formula, M = the median, L = the lower boundary of the class that contains the median, N = the total number of data, C = the cumulative frequency up to (but not including) the class that contains the median, F = the frequency of the class that contains the median, and W = the common width of each class. A mnemonic to remember this imposing formula is the phrase **My Lucky Number Comes From Wishing**. However, you must remember to divide N by 2. Let's check our solution to Example 14.

$$M = 16.5 + \left[\frac{\frac{25}{2} - 8}{9} \right](7) = 16.5 + \left(\frac{4.5}{9} \right)(7) = 20.$$

EXAMPLE 15

What is the median for the following grouped data distribution?

Class	Frequency
58 – 62	6
63 – 67	9
68 – 72	11
73 – 77	6
78 – 82	3
83 – 87	1

SOLUTION

Let's use the formula:

$$M = L + \left[\frac{\frac{N}{2} - C}{F} \right](W)$$

Because there are 36 numbers, the median position is 18. Through the first two classes, there are a total of 15 numbers. The next eleven numbers are located in the third class, so the eighteenth number will be found in this class. The lower boundary of the third class is 67.5, and the width of this class equals $72.5 - 67.5 = 5$. So $L = 67.5$, $N = 36$, $C = 15$, $F = 11$, and $W = 5$. By direct substitution, we get

$$M = 67.5 + \left[\frac{\frac{36}{2} - 15}{11} \right](5) = 67.5 + (\frac{3}{11})(5) \approx 68.86.$$

Mode

The third measure of central tendency is the mode. The **mode**, when it exists, is the number(s) that occur(s) most frequently. The only situation for which a mode does *not* exist is when each of the given data has a frequency of 1. Thus, the set of data 3, 8, 19, 20, and 90 has no mode. Here are some groups of data, with the mode(s) identified.

Group A: 15, 16, 18, 5, 12, 5. The mode is 5 because it occurs twice.

Group B: 7, 7, 7, 2, 2, 1, 2, 7, 10, 10, 10. The mode is 7 because it occurs four times, which is more frequent than any of the other numbers.

Group C: 2, 4, 2, 4, 2, 4, 6, 3, 3. The modes are 2 and 4; they both occur three times.

Group D: 1, 5, 8, 8, 5, 1. The modes are 1, 5, and 8; each number occurs twice.

NOTE:

For grouped data distributions, we use the term *modal class*. This refers to the class with the highest frequency. In Example 14, the modal class would be the third class.

Skewness

Skewness refers to the lack of symmetry in the appearance of a graph for grouped data. If a graph is **symmetrical**, then the mean, median, and mode all coincide. If a graph is **negatively skewed** (also known as skewed to the left), then the mean is less than the median, which is less than the mode. If a graph is **positively skewed** (also known as skewed to the right), then the mode is less than the median, which is less than the mean. Figures 4.9, 4.10, and 4.11 illustrate these three situations.

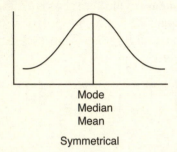

Mode
Median
Mean

Symmetrical

Figure 4.9

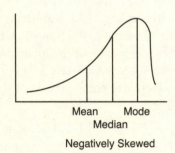

Mean   Mode
Median

Negatively Skewed

Figure 4.10

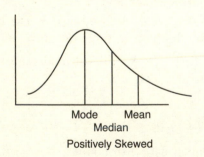

Mode   Mean
Median

Positively Skewed

Figure 4.11

Measures of Variability

We have already mentioned that the range is the difference between the highest and lowest values of a group of data. Each number in a given distribution of data corresponds to a **percentile**, which indicates how high (or low) its value is when compared to all other numbers. For example, if you scored 90 on an exam, your percentile would depend on the scores of the rest of the class. If the class mean were only 70, then a score of 90 would correspond to a relatively high percentile. However, if the class mean were 95, then a score of 90 would correspond to a relatively low percentile.

The actual percentile assigned to an individual score indicates the approximate percentage of scores that lie at or below it. Thus, if your score of 90 were ranked as the 80th percentile, it means that approximately 80% of the other scores were at or below 90.

In general, the nth percentile of a group of numbers, arranged in ascending order, is that value for which n% of the numbers are equal to or less than that value. Thus, $(100 - n)$% of the numbers lie above that value. In Figure 4.12, X represents the 70th percentile of a group of numbers.

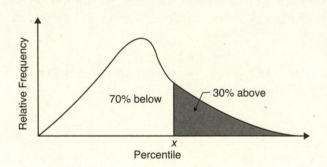

70% below   30% above

x
Percentile

Figure 4.12

The most common percentiles are the 25th, 59th, and 75th percentiles. These are also known as the lower (or first) quartile, median, and upper (or third) quartiles, respectively. The symbols used to represent the 25th, 59th, and 75th percentiles are Q_1, Q_2, and Q_3, respectively. The **interquartile range**, abbreviated as the IQR, is the difference between the upper quartile and the lower quartile. So IQR $= Q_3 - Q_1$.

EXAMPLE 16

> In a list of individual data, the 75th percentile is 23 and the IQR is 10. Which number represents the 25th percentile?

SOLUTION

Let x represent the 25th percentile. By substitution, $10 = 23 - x$. Then $x = 13$.

Box-and-Whisker Plots

The final graphical display we will discuss are **box-and-whisker plots.** This type of graph shows the following five values of a distribution of data: the lowest value, the first quartile (25th percentile), the median (50th percentile), the third quartile (75th percentile), and the highest value. (The actual mathematical procedure for finding the first and third quartile is beyond the scope of this book.)

EXAMPLE 17

> In a distribution of individual data, the lowest value is 2, $Q_1 = 7.5$, the median is 16.5, $Q_3 = 25$, and the highest value is 32. Construct a box-and-whisker plot.

SOLUTION

We choose a convenient scale, such as 0 to 35, in intervals of 5. The two "whiskers" connect the lowest value with Q_1 and the highest value with Q_3. Figure 4.13 shows the diagram thus far.

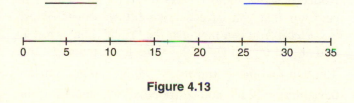

Figure 4.13

Now draw a rectangular box between Q_1 and Q_3, so that the vertical sides of the box contain these quartiles.

Now draw a vertical bar inside the box that matches the value of the median.

Figure 4.14 shows the box-and-whisker plot up to this point.

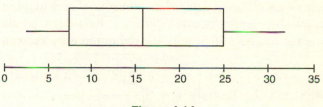

Figure 4.14

The last set of directions is to label these five values, as shown in Figure 4.15. The box-and-whisker plot is now complete.

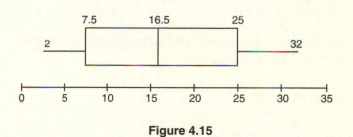

Figure 4.15

Standard Deviation and Variance

When we are interested in learning more about the variability of the data in any distribution (individual or grouped) with respect to the mean, the **standard deviation** is the most commonly used statistic. The (nonnegative) number associated with the standard deviation reveals the extent to which the data are dispersed about the mean. The higher this value, the more spread out are the actual data. For lower values, the data tend to lie closer to the mean. A standard deviation of zero can occur only if all the data are equal. We will consider each distribution of data as a sample.

For a distribution of individual data, the sample standard deviation, denoted as s, is defined as

$$s = \sqrt{\frac{\sum_{1}^{n}(X_i - \overline{X})^2}{n-1}}$$. In this formula, X represents each

individual data value, $\overline{X}$ the mean, and n represents the number of data. Another variation of this formula is

$s = \sqrt{\dfrac{\sum_1^n f_i(X_i - \overline{X})^2}{n-1}}$, for which f represents the frequency of each underlined value in the data and X represents each underlined data value. Note that if each number in the distribution occurs only once, then this formula and the one identified with the definition are identical.

We'll use the formula $s = \sqrt{\dfrac{\sum_1^n f_i(X_i - \overline{X})^2}{n-1}}$ in our computations when at least one of the data occurs more than once. The **sample variance**, denoted as s^2, is simply the square of the sample standard deviation. Thus,

$$s^2 = \frac{\sum_1^n (X_i - \overline{X})^2}{n-1} \text{ or } s^2 = \frac{\sum_1^n f_i(X_i - \overline{X})^2}{n-1}.$$ Note that

the data need not be arranged in order but that doing so will facilitate the computation.

EXAMPLE 18

What are the sample variance and standard deviation for the following data: 12, 3, 8, 6, 16, and 15?

SOLUTION

The sum of these six numbers is 60, so the mean is 10. Then the variance is

$$(12-10)^2 + (3-10)^2 + (8-10)^2 + (6-10)^2$$
$$\frac{+ (16-10)^2 + (15-10)^2}{5}$$
$$= \frac{4+49+4+16+36+25}{5} = 26.8.$$ Thus, the standard

deviation is $\sqrt{26.8}$, which is approximately 5.18.

EXAMPLE 19

A sample consists of five 13s, two 21s, one 33, and seven 40s. What are the sample variance and standard deviation of this sample?

SOLUTION

If you need to write this sample as individual numbers, it would appear as follows: 13, 13, 13, 13, 13, 21, 21, 33, 40, 40, 40, 40, 40, 40, 40. The mean is
$$\frac{(5)(13) + (2)(21) + (1)(33) + (7)(40)}{15} = \frac{420}{15} = 28. \text{ Then}$$
the variance is computed as
$$\frac{(5)(13-28)^2 + (2)(21-28)^2 + (33-28)^2 + (7)(40-28)^2}{14}$$
$$= \frac{1125 + 98 + 25 + 1008}{14} \approx 161.14. \text{ Thus, the standard}$$
deviation is $\sqrt{161.14} \approx 12.69$.

Note that your TI 30X calculator does have a built-in feature for calculating the sample variance and standard deviation. We'll show this feature for Example 19. Press "2nd," "STAT," "1-VAR." Your screen will display a blinking black grid on the left. When you press "DATA" the screen will read "$X_1 = $," for which you enter 13. Now press the blue "down" arrow so that "FRQ=1" appears. Because the number 13' occurs five times, enter 5. Press the "down" arrow so that "$X_2 =$" appears on the screen. Enter 21, press the "down" arrow so that "FRQ=1" appears.

We know that the data group consists of two 21's, so enter 2. Press the "down" blue arrow and enter 33 when you see "$X_3 =$." Now press the "down" arrow; because "FRQ=1" is the actual frequency for 33, just press the "down" arrow. Now your screen will display "$X_4 =$."

Enter 40, press the "down" arrow, and enter 7 when you see "FRQ=1." At this time, you have entered all the data, with their corresponding frequencies. Press "Enter" and you will see the number 7 in the lower right corner of the screen. This just verifies the last entry for frequency.

Finally, press "STATVAR" and four statistical symbols will appear at the top, with a cursor under "M." Notice that the number 15 is on the lower right. This confirms that you have entered fifteen values (which is correct). You can now use the "right" blue arrow to find any of the values of the statistics listed at the top. You will find that $\overline{x}$ (mean) = 28, S_x (sample standard deviation) ≈ 12.69, and σ_x (population standard deviation, pronounced as "sigma sub x") ≈ 12.26. The answer of 12.69, which represents S_x, matches our computation in Example 19.

It is worth noting that, if each data has a frequency of 1, then simply press the "down" arrow every time that "FRQ=1" appears on your screen. Another point to mention is that when you entered the last frequency for Example 19, you could have simply pressed the "down" arrow instead of pressing "Enter." Then when "$X_5 =$" appears, press "STATVAR." Because you are not entering any number for "$X_5 =$", your calculator recognizes that you have entered all the data.

To erase all the data you have entered, press "2nd," "EXIT STAT," then press "Y."

For a grouped frequency distribution, the formulas for variance and standard deviation are nearly identical. The key difference is that the class marks become the respective values of the X_i s. We'll use the TI-30X feature to do our calculations.

EXAMPLE 20

Miss Trigg gave her class of 20 students an exam, and the results are shown in the following grouped data frequency table. (All students scored at least 64, but no one scored 100.) What are the variance and standard deviation?

Class	Frequency
64 – 72	4
73 – 81	7
82 – 90	3
91 – 99	6

SOLUTION

$V = (sd)^2$

First, be sure that you have cleared all statistical data from Example 19. Now, identify the class marks as 68, 77, 86, and 95. Press "2nd," "STAT," and "1-VAR." For the value of X_1, enter 68 followed by a frequency of 4. For X_2, enter 77 followed by a frequency of 7. For X_3, enter 86 followed by a frequency of 3. For X_4, enter 95 followed by a frequency of 6. After pressing "STATVAR," you can scroll to "S_x" to show a value of approximately 10.31. Then the variance = $(10.31)^2 \approx 106.3$.

Note that we could have solved Example 18 by using the standard formulas, but you would first need to calculate the mean. In addition, the quantities $f_i(X_i - \overline{X})^2$ become rather large and cumbersome.

Drawing Conclusions from Data

After data have been collected, displayed, and analyzed, it is time to draw conclusions about whether any new knowledge was gained. The process of drawing conclusions occurs when a researcher attempts to explain what the data represents and what the analysis shows. For example, suppose a survey is conducted among 500 mathematics teachers about the type of computer they prefer. Data analysis revealed that 80% of the teachers preferred Computer Type A. There are several conclusions that might be drawn from this result. Perhaps Computer Type A is more user-friendly, or perhaps it provides the same programs for a cheaper price than other computer types. Maybe the 80% of teachers that preferred Computer Type A had been trained to use it, so they feel most comfortable with that type.

Conclusions may also be drawn by observing **trends**. Trends are often documented through data collection, such as through a census. An effective way to identify trends is to plot data into graphs that represent change over time, like a line graph. We may use trends in data to predict outcomes that go beyond the range of data that were collected. This process is called **extrapolation**.

Concepts of Set Theory

A collection of objects is called a **set**, which is usually denoted by a capital letter. If S represents a set, then its objects are called **elements**. Sets are designated with braces, and a set's elements are separated by commas. When we write $x \in S$, we mean that x is an element of S. Likewise, $x \notin S$ means that x is not an element of S. Thus, if $S = \{1, 3, 5, 7\}$, we can write $1 \in S$ and $4 \notin S$.

Suppose S and T are two different sets such that every element of S is also an element of T. Then S is called a **proper subset** of T, which is expressed as $S \subset T$. As an example, $S = \{2, 4, 6\}$ and $T =$ (all positive even numbers}.

If S and T contain exactly the same elements, then these sets are **equal**. This is written as $S = T$. S is called an **improper subset** of T. We could also state that T is an improper subset of S. The elements need not be written in the same order. As an example, we can write $\{1, 2, 3\} = \{2, 3, 1\}$.

The symbol $\subseteq$ is used when one set is either equal to or a subset of a second set. Thus, if $S \subseteq T$, we can conclude that either $S \subset T$ or $S = T$.

The set with no elements is called the **empty set**, denoted as $\varnothing$. By convention, the empty set is a proper subset of all other nonempty sets. Be sure you do *not* confuse this symbol with the set consisting of zero, which is denoted as $\{0\}$.

The **universal set**, denoted as U, is used to specify the set for which all other sets under consideration are subsets. As an example, $U = \{$all natural numbers$\}$, $A = \{2, 5, 8, 13\}$, $B = \{3, 5, 13, 15, 23, 25\}$, and $C = \{10, 100, 1000\}$. Then each of A, B, and C is a proper subset of U.

For the following four definitions, $S = \{3, 4, 7, 8\}$ and $T = \{4, 6, 8, 9, 11\}$.

The **union** of two sets, symbolized as $\cup$, is the set that consists of elements that exist in either or in both sets. Thus $S \cup T = \{3, 4, 6, 7, 8, 9, 11\}$. Note that $S \cup T = T \cup S$.

The **intersection** of two sets, symbolized as $\cap$, is the set that consists of only elements that are common to both sets. Thus, $S \cap T = \{4, 8\}$. Note that $S \cap T = T \cap S$. In addition, if two sets do not share any common elements, then their intersection is written as the empty set. If $V = \{100, 200\}$, then $S \cap V = \varnothing$.

The **difference** of two sets S and T, written as $S - T$, is the set that consists of elements that exist in S but do not exist in T. Thus, $S - T = \{3, 7\}$. Note that the difference of sets T and S, expressed as $T - S$, is $\{6, 9, 11\}$. In general, $T - S \neq S - T$.

Suppose that the universal set $U = \{1, 2, 3, 4, 5, 6, 7, 8, 9, 10, 11\}$. The **complement** of a set S, written as S', is the set of all elements in U that are <u>not</u> found in S. Thus, $S' = \{1, 2, 5, 6, 9, 10, 11\}$.

Venn diagrams are pictorial ways to represent sets. Figures 4.16, 4.17, 4.18, and 4.19 illustrate the concepts union, intersection, difference, and complement of sets, respectively. In each figure, the shaded region represents the solution; U = universal set.

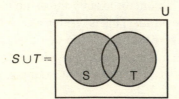

Figure 4.16

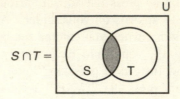

Figure 4.17

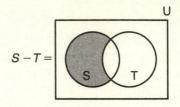

Figure 4.18

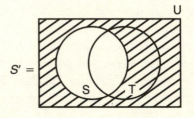

Figure 4.19

Sample Spaces

We introduce the concept of a **probability experiment**, which is simply a series of actions from which we can ascertain the likelihood of a particular action occurring. For example, suppose we toss a penny twice. There are four different results, known formally as **outcomes**, that may occur. Letting H = heads and T = tails, the four outcomes are HH, HT, TH, and TT. Note that there are two parts to each outcome. Also note that the outcome HT is different from the outcome TH.

A **sample space**, usually denoted as S, is the set of all possible outcomes of a probability experiment. In the example mentioned above, we can write S = {HH, HT, TH, TT}.

EXAMPLE 21

> A probability experiment consists of rolling an ordinary die once. What is the complete sample space?

SOLUTION

Because the only possible outcomes are 1, 2, 3, 4, 5, and 6, the sample space is {1, 2, 3, 4, 5, 6}.

EXAMPLE 22

> A five-sided solid figure is numbered 1, 2, 3, 4, and 5 on each of its faces. If this figure is rolled twice, how many outcomes are in its sample space?

SOLUTION

Any of the numbers 1, 2, 3, 4, or 5 may appear on either the first roll or the second roll. Thus, there are (5)(5) = 25 different outcomes that can occur.

For Example 22, (2, 4), (5, 5), and (3, 2) are three examples of the outcomes. Here, (2, 4) means "2" is the number on the first roll and "4" is the number on the number on the second roll. Note that the outcome (2, 4) is not equivalent to the outcome (4, 2) because (4, 2) means "4" is the result of the first roll and "2" is the result of the second roll.

EXAMPLE 23

> An experiment consists of drawing three cards in succession from a deck of 52 cards. Each of the second and third cards are drawn without replacement. How many outcomes are there in the sample space?

SOLUTION

Each outcome consists of three parts. For the first draw, there are 52 possibilities; however, because each of the remaining two cards are drawn without any replacement, there are 51 and 50 possibilities, respectively, for these two draws. Thus, there are (52)(51)(50) = 132,600 outcomes.

One of the outcomes of Example 23 might appear as $A_s 2_D Q_H$, where A_s means ace of spades, 2_D means two of diamonds, and Q_H means queen of hearts. In Example 23, if the selections were made with a replacement, then we could have the same card appear twice or even three times. For this experiment, there would be $(52)^3 = 140,608$ outcomes.

Any collection of outcomes is called an **event**, usually denoted by a capital letter. However, an event may consist of just one outcome. In Example 21, if event A consists of outcomes that are even numbers, then $A = \{2, 4, 6\}$. In Example 22, if event B consists of outcomes in which the same number appears twice, then $B = \{(1, 1), (2, 2), (3, 3), (4, 4), (5, 5)\}$. Likewise, in Example 23, if event C consists of outcomes in which the first draw is the jack of diamonds, the second draw is the ace of clubs, and the third draw is the 5 of hearts, then $C = \{J_D A_C 5_H\}$.

Basic Probability

Probability is defined as the chance of an event occurring. If A represents an event, then P(A) represents the probability of A occurring. If an event is certain to occur, then P(A) = 1. As you can imagine, very few events contain absolute certainty. As an example, if A represents the event that it is raining today somewhere, then we can be sure that P(A) = 1.

If an event cannot possibly occur, then its probability is zero. Let B represent the event that a person can run a mile in one minute. Even the fastest of horses cannot approach this speed, so we can state that no human can run this fast. Thus, P(B) = 0.

Most of the probability questions you will face will have values between 0 and 1. Be aware that we cannot have a probability value of less than zero or greater than 1. This means that for any event A, $0 \leq P(A) \leq 1$.

The **complement** of event A, denoted as A', represents the event that A does not occur. For any event A, $P(A') = 1 - P(A)$.

Classical Probability

Classical probability refers to the determination of probability values based on a sample space. The most common sample spaces involve (a) coins, (b) dice, and (c) cards. In each sample space, all outcomes are assumed to be equally likely to occur. The probability of any event occurring is the number of outcomes in the particular event divided by the number of outcomes in the sample space. The next six examples involve classical probability.

EXAMPLE 24

A penny and a nickel are each tossed once. What is the probability that both land as heads?

SOLUTION

Let the penny be tossed first. The sample space is {HH, HT, TH, TT}. Out of the four possible outcomes, only the outcome HH shows both heads. Therefore the required probability is $\frac{1}{4}$.

EXAMPLE 25

A penny, a nickel, and a dime are tossed once, in that order. What is the probability that the coins all land as heads or they all land as tails?

SOLUTION

There are eight outcomes in this sample space, namely, HHH, HHT, HTH, HTT, THH, THT, TTH, and TTT. Of these, only two outcomes show that the coins all land the same, namely, HHH and TTT. Thus, the required probability is $\frac{2}{8} = \frac{1}{4}$.

EXAMPLE 26

An ordinary die is rolled once. What is the probability that the die will show a number greater than 2?

SOLUTION

The outcomes in this event are 3, 4, 5, and 6. The sample space consists of six outcomes. Thus, the required probability is $\frac{4}{6}$, which reduces to $\frac{2}{3}$.

EXAMPLE 27

An ordinary die is rolled twice. What is the probability that the sum of the two rolls is 4?

SOLUTION

We first recognize that there are (6)(6) = 36 outcomes in the sample space. Because the lowest number possible for either roll of the die is 1, we need to examine only the outcomes in which each roll shows a number less than 4.

If the first roll shows 1, then the only result for the second roll is 3. This leads to (1, 3). Continuing in this fashion, the other two possibilities are (2, 2) and (3, 1). Thus, the required probability is $\frac{3}{36}$, which reduces to $\frac{1}{12}$.

Before we do the next two examples, let's do a quick review of the 52 cards in an ordinary deck. There are 13 cards of each suit, which are clubs, diamonds, hearts, and spades. The clubs and spades are black, whereas the diamonds and hearts are red. The cards of each suit are identified as ace, 2, 3, 4, . . . , 10, jack, queen, king. The jacks, queens, and kings are considered picture cards.

EXAMPLE 28

In drawing one card from a deck of cards, what is the probability of getting a red jack?

SOLUTION

The sample space consists of 52 outcomes. The two red jacks are the jack of diamonds and the jack of hearts. Thus, the required probability is $\dfrac{2}{52}$, which reduces to $\dfrac{1}{26}$.

EXAMPLE 29

In drawing one card from a deck of cards, what is the probability of not getting a club?

SOLUTION

There are a total of 13 clubs, so the probability of drawing a club is $\dfrac{13}{52} = \dfrac{1}{4}$. Therefore, the probability of not drawing a club is $1 - \dfrac{1}{4} = \dfrac{3}{4}$.

Empirical Probability

Empirical probability refers to the determination of probability values based on observations or historical data. If A represents an event, its empirical probability is simply the ratio of its frequency and the total frequency of all observations (or data).

EXAMPLE 30

A particular die is rolled 1,800 times and the results of the frequency of each outcome is as follows:

Outcome	Frequency
1	120
2	140
3	250
4	450
5	300
6	540

Based on this chart, what is the probability that, in rolling this die, it will land on a 3 or a 4?

SOLUTION

The number of times in which this die has landed on 3 or 4 is $250 + 450 = 700$. Because this die was rolled 1,800 times, the required probability is $\dfrac{700}{1,800} = \dfrac{7}{18}$.

EXAMPLE 31

A random group of 90 people were asked to select their favorite ice cream flavor. The choice of flavors was limited to vanilla, chocolate, strawberry, butter pecan, and cherry. Here are the results:

Flavor	Frequency
Vanilla	32
Chocolate	24
Strawberry	16
Butter pecan	10
Cherry	8

Based on this chart, what is the probability that a person selected from this group had chosen either vanilla or chocolate as his or her favorite flavor?

SOLUTION

A total of $32 + 24 = 56$ people chose one of these two flavors. Thus, the required probability is $\dfrac{56}{90}$, which reduces to $\dfrac{28}{45}$.

Comparing Classical Probability with Empirical Probability

In tossing a fair coin once, we know that the classical probability that the coin will land as tails is $\dfrac{1}{2}$. This means that if we toss this coin 20 times, the expected number of times that it will land as tails is $(\dfrac{1}{2})(20) = 10$.

Suppose that a person actually tosses this coin 20 times, and the result is tails 12 times. We then state that the empirical probability of getting tails, based on this actual coin tossing, is $\frac{12}{20} = \frac{3}{5}$. Although the two types of probability do not yield the same result, there is no contradiction. If the experiment of tossing this coin were to consist of many trials, say 100,000, then we would expect that the classical and empirical probabilities would be extremely close. The higher the number of trials, the more likely the two types of probability will result in the same value.

Compound Events

Any event that consists of two or more actions is considered a **compound event**. Examples are (a) rolling a die twice; (b) tossing a coin three times; and (c) selecting two cards from a deck, one at a time, with replacement of the first card.

Independent Events

Two events are **independent** if the probability of one event occurring has no effect on the probability of the other event occurring. The probability that both occur is the product of the probability for each event to occur. In symbols, the probability for both events A and B to occur is denoted as $P(A \cap B)$. If A and B are independent events, we can write $P(A \cap B) = P(A) \cdot P(B)$.

EXAMPLE 32

An ordinary die is rolled twice. What is the probability that the first roll will land on an even number and the second roll will land on a number greater than 4?

SOLUTION

Let A represent the event of getting an even number on the first roll and let B represent the event of getting a number greater than 4 on the second roll. By just using the sample space for a single roll of the die, we can see that $P(A) = \frac{3}{6} = \frac{1}{2}$ and $P(B) = \frac{2}{6} = \frac{1}{3}$. These events are independent, so $P(A \cap B) = \frac{1}{2} \cdot \frac{1}{3} = \frac{1}{6}$.

NOTE:

An alternative approach would be to identify the sample space of rolling a die twice, which consists of 36 outcomes. We would then count the number of outcomes that satisfy the given conditions. We would find six outcomes, namely, (2, 5), (2, 6), (4, 5), (4, 6), (6, 5), and (6, 6). The required probability is $\frac{6}{36}$, which reduces to $\frac{1}{6}$.

EXAMPLE 33

In drawing two cards from a deck of cards, one card at a time, with the replacement of the first card prior to drawing the second card, what is the probability that the first card is an ace and the second card is a black picture card?

SOLUTION

Let A represent the event of getting an ace on the first draw and let B represent the event of getting a black picture card on the second draw. Because the first card is replaced before the second one is drawn, these events are independent. $P(A) = \frac{4}{52} = \frac{1}{13}$ and $P(B) = \frac{6}{52} = \frac{3}{26}$. Thus, $P(A \cap B) = \frac{1}{13} \cdot \frac{3}{26} = \frac{3}{338}$.

Dependent Events

Events A and B are called **dependent** if the occurrence of one event affects the probability of the occurrence of another event. Many examples in real life illustrate the dependence of events. As an example, reading this book will definitely affect the probability that you will do well on your math teacher certification exam. As a second example, leaving on time for work affects the probability that you will arrive at work on time.

We now introduce the symbol $P(A \mid B)$. This notation shows the probability that event A occurs, given that event B has occurred. This is generally *not* equivalent in meaning to $P(B\,|\,A)$, which shows the probability that event B occurs, given that event A has occurred. Note that if $P(A\,|\,B) = 0$, then event A <u>cannot</u> occur if event B has already occurred. Similarly, if $P(A\,|\,B) = 1$, then event A *must* occur if event B has occurred. When A and B are dependent events, the formula to use for $P(A \cap B)$ is as follows: $P(A \cap B) = P(A) \cdot P(B\,|\,A)$, which is equivalent to $P(A \cap B) = P(B) \cdot P(A\,|\,B)$.

EXAMPLE 34

> If you are drawing two cards from a deck of cards, one card at a time, without replacing the first card prior to drawing the second card, what is the probability that the first card is an ace and the second card is a black picture card?

SOLUTION

At first glance, you might think that you are looking at an instant replay of Example 33. However, there is a key difference. In Example 33, the second card was drawn <u>after</u> replacing the first card. In this example, we will draw the second card <u>without</u> replacing the first card. This example illustrates dependent events because we will have only 51 cards available (not 52) when we draw the second card. Use A and B to represent the two events, respectively. Then $P(A) = \dfrac{1}{13}$, which matches P(A) in Example 33. However, because there are only 51 cards available for the second draw, $P(B\,|\,A) = \dfrac{6}{51} = \dfrac{2}{17}$.

Finally, $P(A \cap B) = P(A) \cdot P(B\,|\,A) = \dfrac{1}{13} \cdot \dfrac{2}{17} = \dfrac{2}{221}$.

EXAMPLE 35

> A box contains 6 red balls, 4 green balls, and 5 purple balls. Two balls are drawn from this box, one at a time, with no replacement of the first ball prior to drawing the second ball. What is the probability of drawing a red ball, followed by a purple ball?

SOLUTION

Let A represent the first event and let B represent the second event. Because there are a total of 15 balls, of which 6 are red, $P(A) = \dfrac{6}{15} = \dfrac{2}{5}$. After the first ball is drawn, there are now 14 balls, of which 5 are purple, $P(B\,|\,A) = \dfrac{5}{14}$. Thus, $P(A \cap B) = \dfrac{2}{5} \cdot \dfrac{5}{14} = \dfrac{1}{7}$.

NOTE:

> If we are given two events A and B in which they are actually independent, then $P(B\,|\,A) = P(B)$. This would imply that the occurrence of event A has no effect on the probability that event B will occur.

Mutually Exclusive Events

Two events A and B are called **mutually exclusive** if they cannot both occur at the same time. Here are a few examples of mutually exclusive events.

In drawing one card from a deck, event C represents getting an ace, and event D represents getting a queen.

(a) In rolling a die once, event E represents getting an even number, and event F represents getting a 3.

(b) In tossing a penny twice, event G represents getting two tails, and event H represents getting two heads.

Note that we can use capital letters other than A and B to represent events.

If A and B are any two mutually exclusive events, then $P(A \cap B) = 0$. This is a natural conclusion because the two events cannot both occur at the same time. It is also possible that neither event actually occurs. Using example (a) from the list above, it is possible to draw a card that is neither an ace nor a queen. Similarly, in example (b) from the list above, it is possible to roll a die and get a 5; in such a case, neither event E nor event F has occurred. Each of $P(A\,|\,B)$ and $P(B\,|\,A)$ must equal zero because the occurrence of one of these events automatically prevents the occurrence of the other event. For this reason, mutually exclusive events *must* be dependent events.

The Addition Rule of Probability for Two Events

We introduce the symbol $P(A \cup B)$, which means the probability that <u>at least one</u> of events A and B occurs. This is equivalent to stating that event A occurs, or event B occurs, or both A and B occur. The associated formula is:

$$P(A \cup B) = P(A) + P(B) - P(A \cap B)$$

If events A and B are mutually exclusive, then we know that $P(A \cap B) = 0$. Therefore, we can shorten the addition rule to $P(A \cup B) = P(A) + P(B)$.

EXAMPLE 36

A die is rolled twice. What is the probability of getting a sum of 3 or a sum of 8?

SOLUTION

Let C represent the event of getting a sum of 3, and let D represent the event of getting a sum of 8. (Remember that we can use any capital letters to represent events.) You recall that there are a total of 36 outcomes in the sample space. The only outcomes for which a sum of 3 is possible are $(1, 2)$ and $(2, 1)$, so $P(C) = \dfrac{2}{36} = \dfrac{1}{18}$. The outcomes for which a sum of 8 is possible are $(2, 6)$, $(3, 5)$, $(4, 4)$, $(5, 3)$, and $(6, 2)$. So $P(D) = \dfrac{5}{36}$. Because these events are mutually exclusive, $P(C \cup D) = \dfrac{1}{18} + \dfrac{5}{36} = \dfrac{7}{36}$.

EXAMPLE 37

One card is drawn from a deck of cards. What is the probability of drawing a picture card or a 2?

SOLUTION

Let G represent the event of drawing a picture card, and let H represent the event of drawing a 2. There are 12 picture cards and four 2s, so $P(G) = \dfrac{12}{52} = \dfrac{3}{13}$ and $P(H) = \dfrac{4}{52} = \dfrac{1}{13}$. Events G and H are mutually exclusive, so $P(G \cup H) = \dfrac{4}{13}$.

EXAMPLE 38

One card is drawn from a deck of cards. What is the probability of getting a queen or a spade?

SOLUTION

These events are not mutually exclusive because the queen of spades fits both conditions. Let Q represent the event of getting a queen and let S represent the event of getting a spade. Then $P(Q) = \dfrac{4}{52} = \dfrac{1}{13}$, $P(S) = \dfrac{13}{52} = \dfrac{1}{4}$, and $P(Q \cap S) = \dfrac{1}{52}$. Thus, $P(Q \cup S)$ $\dfrac{1}{13} + \dfrac{1}{4} - \dfrac{1}{52} = \dfrac{16}{52} = \dfrac{4}{13}$.

EXAMPLE 39

In a bag of 40 marbles, 15 are white, 20 are yellow, and the rest are purple. Two marbles will be drawn randomly, one at a time, with replacement. What is the probability that at least one of these marbles is white?

SOLUTION

Let V represent the event that the first marble is white, and let W represent the event that the second marble is white. We note that these events are not mutually exclusive. In addition, $P(V) = P(W) = \dfrac{15}{40} = \dfrac{3}{8}$ because the first marble is replaced before the second marble is drawn. Also, $P(V \cap W) = (\dfrac{3}{8})(\dfrac{3}{8}) = \dfrac{9}{64}$. Thus, $P(V \cup W)$ $= \dfrac{3}{8} + \dfrac{3}{8} - \dfrac{9}{64} = \dfrac{39}{64}$.

The Fundamental Counting Principle

This principle states that given a sequence of independent events, the total number of possibilities is the product of the possibilities of each event.

EXAMPLE 40

Suppose that Kyle has four ways to travel from Baltimore to Chicago, three ways to travel from Chicago to Denver, and six ways to travel from Denver to San Francisco. In how many different ways can Kyle travel from Baltimore to San Francisco, by way of Chicago and Denver?

SOLUTION

The total number of possibilities is simply the product of the ways in which each separate event can occur. Thus, the answer is $(4)(3)(6) = 72$.

A **tree diagram** is a convenient method for showing all possible results of a sequence of events, even when the events are dependent. Each event is shown as a branch, and the events are listed from left to right. This method is effective only when the total number of possibilities is relatively small.

EXAMPLE 41

Charlene is buying an ice cream cone with three scoops of ice cream, one of vanilla, one of chocolate, and one of strawberry. In how many different ways can these scoops appear on her ice cream cone?

SOLUTION

Figure 4.20 shows a tree diagram for the three scoops; V = vanilla, C = chocolate, and S = strawberry.

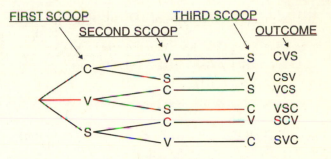

Figure 4.20

There are three different flavors to choose for the first scoop, two different flavors to choose for the second scoop, and just one flavor to choose for the third scoop. Thus, there is a total of $(3)(2)(1) = 6$ different ways to place the three scoops of ice cream on the cone. Note that the last column labeled "Outcome" does show the six ways.

A special case of the fundamental counting principle deals with the concept of **factorial numbers**, which are defined as follows. Let n represent a positive integer. Then n factorial, written as $n!$, is the product of all the positive integers less than or equal to n. Mathematically, we can write $n! = (n)(n - 1)(n - 2)(\ldots)(3)(2)(1)$. As examples, $4! = (4)(3)(2)(1) = 24$ and $10! = (10)(9)(8)(\ldots)(3)(2)(1) = 3,628,800$. Note that this definition does not apply to decimals or negative numbers. Thus $(\frac{1}{3})!$ and $(-2)!$ have no meaning.

It is easy to see that $1! = 1$ and $2! = 2$, but what about $0!$? Most books state that $0! = 1$ by definition, but there really is a logical explanation. We can verify the following identities: $4! \div 4 = 3!$ $3! \div 3 = 2!$ $2! \div 2 = 1!$ Based on this pattern, $1! \div 1$ be $0!$. But $1! \div 1 = 1$, so this implies that $0! = 1$. Your TI-30X calculator has a factorial button. To calculate $19!$, press in sequence, "19", "PRB", scroll to "!", and press "Enter." Your screen should display $19!$. Press "Enter" to get the result of approximately 1.216×10^{17}.

Permutations

A **permutation** is an arrangement of a set of objects. The number of permutations of n objects taken r at a time is given by the symbol $_nP_r$. Its value is $\dfrac{n!}{(n-r)!}$

$= \dfrac{(n)(n-1)(n-2)(\ldots)(n-r)(n-r-1)(\ldots)(1)}{(n-r)(n-r-1)(\ldots)(1)} = (n)(n-1)$

$(n-2)(\ldots)(n-r+1)$.

Note that if $n = r$, then $_nP_n = \dfrac{n!}{(n-n)!} = \dfrac{n!}{0!} = n!$

Your TI-30X calculator does have a feature for permutations. To calculate $_8P_3$, press 8 and "PRB." The screen will have the cursor under "nPr." Press "Enter," and the screen will display "8 nPr." Finally, press 3 followed by "Enter." The answer of 336 should appear in the lower right corner.

EXAMPLE 42

The Jackson family has won 11 trophies in tennis. They would like to display all of them on a shelf in the living room. Unfortunately, there is room for only 5 of them on the shelf. In how many ways can they select and arrange any 5 of these 11 trophies?

SOLUTION

Because this example illustrates an arrangement of 11 objects taken 5 at a time, the answer is $_{11}P_5 = 55,440$.

Another approach to the solution is as follows. From left to right, any one of the 11 trophies can be placed first, any one of 10 trophies can be placed second, any one of 9 trophies can be placed third, and so forth. You can see that, by the time the Jackson family reaches the fifth (last) open place on the shelf, the selection narrows down to one of 7 trophies. The answer can be calculated as $11 \times 10 \times 9 \times 8 \times 7 = 55,440$.

Combinations

A **combination** is an arrangement of objects <u>without</u> regard to their order. Commonly used synonyms for <u>combination</u> are <u>group</u>, <u>team</u>, and <u>committee</u>. The number of combinations of n objects taken r at a time is given by the symbol $_nC_r$. Its value is $\dfrac{n!}{(n-r)! \times r!} = \dfrac{_nP_r}{r!}$. This fraction is also equivalent to $\dfrac{(n)(n-1)(n-2)(\cdots)(n-r+1)}{r!}$.

Note the following two identities:

(a) $_nC_n = \dfrac{_nP_n}{n!} = \dfrac{n!}{n!} = 1$ and (b) $_nC_r = {_nC_{n-r}}$. You may be surprised by the identity mentioned in part (b). As an example, if $n = 20$ and $r = 3$, then $_{20}C_3 = {_{20}C_{17}}$. We can verify that both combinations have a value of 1,140. The explanation is that, for every group of 3 from 20 that is selected, there is a corresponding group of 17 that is not selected. Because each group of 3 is unique, so is each group of 17.

Your TI-30X calculator does have a feature for combinations. Follow the same procedure as for permutations, with one exception. After pressing "PRB," move the cursor to "nCr" instead of "nPr."

EXAMPLE 43

Given a conference of 11 women and 7 men, a committee of three people is selected. How many different committees are possible?

SOLUTION

The number of people of each gender is immaterial. There are a total of 18 people, from which a committee of three is to be selected. Therefore, the answer is $_{18}C_3 = 816$. On your TI-30X, the sequence of steps is: 18, "PRB," "nCr," 3, "Enter."

Chapter 4 Quiz

1. The following graph illustrates the relationship between temperature and the sale of jackets in $1,000 units.

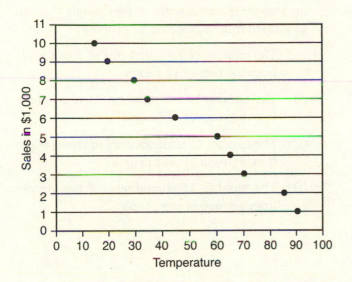

Which statement does this graph support?

(A) As temperature decreases, the sale of jackets increases.

(B) The sale of jackets is unchanged by temperature.

(C) As temperature increases, the sale of jackets increases.

(D) There is no relationship between temperature and the sale of jackets.

2. To the nearest ten thousandth, what is the probability of drawing an ace from a well-shuffled deck of 52 cards?

(A) 0.0192   (C) 0.0385

(B) 0.0196   (D) 0.0769

3. For which one of the following box-and-whisker plots is the value of the median one-half the sum of the values of the first and third quartiles?

(A)
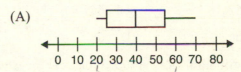

(B)
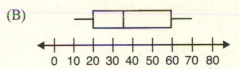

(C)
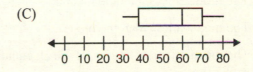

(D)
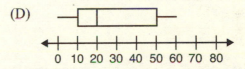

4. How many batting orders are possible for the nine players on a baseball team?

(A) 9   (C) 362,880

(B) 81   (D) 387,420,489

5. If two fair dice are thrown, what is the probability that the sum shown is 7 or 12?

(A) $\dfrac{5}{36}$ (C) $\dfrac{11}{36}$

(B) $\dfrac{7}{36}$ (D) $\dfrac{19}{36}$

6. The mean of a group of twenty numbers is 9. One of these numbers is removed, and the mean of the remaining numbers is 7. What is the value of the removed number?

(A) 16   (C) 40

(B) 25   (D) 47

7. Consider the following stem-and-leaf plot.

5 | 0 2 5 8
6 | 1 3 5
7 | 1 5 6
8 | 2 9

What is the value of the median?

(A) 62   (C) 66

(B) 64   (D) 68

8. A distribution for grouped data is negatively skewed. Which one of the following statements is correct?

(A) The median is less than the mean.

(B) The mode is less than the median.

(C) The mean is less than the mode.

(D) The mean, median, and mode are all equal to each other.

9. The numbers 4, 2, 7, and 9 occur with frequencies 2, 3, 11, and 4, respectively. Find the arithmetic mean.

(A) 7.25   (C) 6

(B) 6.35   (D) 5

10. Which one of the following has the same value as the number of committees of four people that can be formed from a group of 12 people?

(A) The number of arrangements of four people from a group of 12 people

(B) The number of committees of eight people from a group of 12 people

(C) The number of arrangements of three people from a group of nine people

(D) The number of committees of two people from a group of ten people

Chapter 4 Quiz Solutions

1. **(A)**

Draw a line through the set of data points. Notice that high temperature values are associated with low sale values. Similarly, low temperatures are associated with high sales.

2. **(D)**

In a deck of 52 cards, there are four aces. Thus, the required probability is $\frac{4}{52} \approx 0.0769$.

3. **(A)**

The median corresponds to the vertical segment inside the box, which is 40. The leftmost vertical segment and the rightmost vertical segment represent the first and third quartiles, respectively. For answer choice (A), these numbers are 25 and 55. We note that $40 = (\frac{1}{2})(25 + 55)$. This relationship does not exist for the other answer choices.

4. **(C)**

The number of batting orders is equivalent to the number of arrangements of nine players, which is given by 9! = 362,880.

5. (B)

Of the 36 outcomes in the sample space for two dice, the seven outcomes that produce a sum of 7 or 12 are (1, 6), (2, 5), (3, 4), (4, 3), (5, 2), (6, 1), and (6, 6). Thus, the required probability is $\frac{7}{36}$.

6. (D)

The sum of the original group of numbers is $(20)(9) = 180$. After one number is removed, the sum of the remaining 19 numbers is $(19)(7) = 133$. Thus, the number that was removed is $180 - 133 = 47$.

7. (B)

There are 12 numbers, so the value of the median is midway between the sixth and seventh numbers. Thus, the median is $\frac{1}{2}(63 + 65) = 64$.

8. (C)

In a negatively skewed distribution, the mean is less than the median, which is less than the mode.

9. (B)

To find the mean, multiply each number by its frequency, add these products, then divide by the total frequency. Thus, the mean equals

$$\frac{(4)(2)+(2)(3)+(7)(11)+(9)(4)}{2+3+11+4} = \frac{127}{20} = 6.35.$$

10. (B)

The number of committees that can be formed with four people from a group of 12 is $_{12}C_4 = 495$. The number of committees of eight people that can be formed from a group of 12 is $_{12}C_8 = 495$. For any values of n and r, $_{n}C_r = {_{n}C_{n-r}}$. In this example, $n = 12$ and $r = 4$.

Mathematical Processes and Perspectives

Communicating Mathematical Ideas

A teacher must have knowledge of the nature of mathematics as a form of communication and be able to apply this knowledge to provide meaningful instruction to students. The skills that a teacher need include but are not limited to, the ability to

(a) identify statements that correctly communicate mathematical definitions and /or concepts.

(b) interpret written presentations of mathematics.

(c) select appropriate examples, pictorial illustrations, or symbolic representations to develop mathematical concepts.

As with any language, mathematics has its own syntax and grammar. Symbols can be translated into nouns and verbs, whereas equations can be translated into sentences. Mathematics is much more than words, for it includes pictures, graphs, proofs, and abstractions. Teachers must be able to use all these tools to convey mathematical concepts.

One very important skill that a mathematics teacher should possess is the ability to define objects and concepts with the utmost clarity. As an example, let's compare three different definitions of a square.

Definition 1: A square is a shape with a right angle.

Definition 2: A square is a four-sided quadrilateral with opposite sides parallel and congruent, four right angles, and congruent diagonals.

Definition 3: A square is a quadrilateral with four congruent sides and four right angles.

Definition 1 is woefully inadequate. We are not told how many sides there are and we are only assured of one right angle. There is an infinite number of geometrical figures that could fit this definition, including figures that have curved arcs as segments.

Definition 2 presents too much information. This definition extends beyond the basic information by describing additional properties of the square that can be proved using theorems.

Definition 3 is a concise and accurate description of the basic property of a square. We are told that there are four congruent sides, which means that the figure is a rhombus or a square. The definition contains the information that there are four right angles; thus only a square can satisfy these requirements.

Words that are used in mathematical contexts may be quite different from their usage in everyday language. In fact, the same word may have a different meaning when used in a different mathematical context. As an example, consider the word "range." In everyday usage, this word usually refers to the extent to which something can vary. However "range" can also be associated with an area for target practice, as well as an appliance in the kitchen.

With respect to mathematics, "range" can be used in statistics to represent the difference between the lowest and highest numbers in a group of numerical data. But, we can also use "range" to represent the set of values of a dependent variable of a function.

Another instance in which precision is highly important is in the usage of mathematical symbols. Consider the inverse sine function of an angle. If θ is a given angle, then both $\sin^{-1}\theta$ and $\arcsin\theta$ are acceptable symbols. Most math books would tend to use the $\arcsin\theta$ symbol, because the exponent of -1 is most commonly used to represent the reciprocal of a quantity. As such, we would recognize that $3^{-1} = \dfrac{1}{3^1} = \dfrac{1}{3}$. But, the inherent danger of using the symbol $\sin^{-1}\theta$ is that the interpretation could be either $\arcsin\theta$ or $\dfrac{1}{\sin\theta}$. The good news is that the exponent -1 is rarely used to represent the reciprocal of a trigonometric function.

Two other illustrations of the difference between common everyday words and their usage in mathematical contexts would be the words "between" and "some." If a person says, "the distance separating two cities is between 10 and 12 miles," we interpret this statement to mean that the numbers 10 and 12 are included in this estimate. However, when used in a mathematical context, the phrase "between 10 and 12" excludes both 10 and 12. The only way to be sure that 10 and 12 are included is to say "between 10 and 12, inclusive."

The word "some" is generally equivalent to "few" or "several." If a person says that she invited some people for dinner, we would assume that perhaps four or five people were invited. In mathematical logic, the word "some" means "at least one and possibly all." Thus, the phrase "some numbers in set R are integers" would mean that at least one number in R is an integer, but possibly all the numbers are integers.

Many advocates of educational reform, including the National Council of Teachers of Mathematics, suggest that teachers introduce mathematical words at the time when students need this information to solve a particular problem. This idea would be in contrast to providing students with a list of words and definitions at the start of each new chapter or section. However, regardless of the instructional strategy, mathematics teachers need to ensure that students have a thorough understanding of the definitions they are learning.

The Use of Notation in Presenting Mathematical Ideas

Although there are many instances in which mathematical notation is utilized, we will focus on two specific concepts, namely sets and intervals.

A set is a collection of objects called **elements**. Typically, sets are denoted with a capital letter and the elements are enclosed in braces. For example, if set A contains the elements 1, 3, 5, 7, and 9, we would write $A = \{1, 3, 5, 7, 9\}$. Alternatively, the elements in a set may be written in a descriptive form, if it is well defined. Thus, we could write $A = \{$positive odd integers less than 10$\}$. However, we would not use a descriptive form for $B = \{101, 5, 16, 3, 27, 32\}$ because there is no simple description of the elements in B.

The symbol $\in$ is used to illustrate that an element belongs to a set. For example, $3 \in A$ and $27 \in B$. The symbol $\notin$ is used to show that an element does not belong to a set. Thus, we can write $2 \notin A$ and $8 \notin B$.

Sets can also be related to one another. If all of the elements of one set belong to a second set, then the first set is considered a **subset** of the second set. For example, if set D is $\{2, 4, 6\}$, and set E is $\{0, 2, 4, 6, 8\}$, then set D is a subset of set E, and the symbol $\subset$ is used to represent this relationship. In this case, we can write $D \subset E$.

The **union** of two sets is a set that consists of all the elements that belong to at least one of the given sets. The symbol for union is $\cup$; thus, we can write $A \cup B = \{1, 3, 5, 7, 9, 16, 27, 32, 101\}$ and $D \cup E = \{0, 2, 4, 6, 8\}$.

NOTE:

Repeating elements are only listed once.

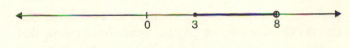

Figure 5.3

Occasionally, we want to identify elements that are common between sets. This is called the **intersection** of sets, which is denoted by the symbol ∩. Consider the following sets: $C = \{1, 2, 3, 5, 8, 13, 21, 34\}$ and $F = \{3, 5, 7, 9, 11, 13\ 15, 17\}$. The intersection of these sets includes the elements that are common to both, so $C \cap F = \{3, 5, 13\}$. In the previous examples, $A \cap B = \{3, 5\}$ and $D \cap E = \{2, 4, 6\}$.

There are occasions when two sets do not share any common elements. Their intersection is considered to be the **empty set** or **null set**, denoted as $\varnothing$. As an example, if $F = \{4, 6, 9, 10\}$ and $H = \{7, 8, 20\}$, then $F \cap H = \varnothing$.

We often use interval notation to describe a set of numbers. Typically, we use this notation to describe a certain span of numbers along a number line (or the x-axis). Consider the set of all numbers greater than 7. We could write this as an inequality: $x > 7$. Using interval notation, we would write this inequality as $(7, +\infty)$. The left parenthesis indicates that the number 7 is excluded from this set. The symbol $+\infty$ means "positive infinity." Since positive infinity is larger than any given number, a parenthesis must follow it. Figure 5.1 shows the graph of $x > 7$.

Figure 5.1

Now consider the set of all numbers greater than or equal to 9. This inequality can be written as $n \geq 9$. In interval notation, this would be written as: $[9, +\infty)$. The square bracket indicates that 9 is included in this set. (But remember that $+\infty$ must be followed by a parenthesis.) Figure 5.2 shows the graph of $n \geq 9$.

Figure 5.2

Sometimes we want to represent numbers that are found between two given values. Consider the set of all numbers that are between 3 and 8, including 3 (but not 8). This inequality can be written as $3 \leq p < 8$. In interval notation, we would write $[3, 8)$. We are showing that 3 is included in this set, while 8 is not included. Figure 5.3 shows the appropriate graph.

Mathematical Connections

In addition to using concise and precise mathematical language, a skilled mathematics teacher is able to use analogies and concrete examples to illustrate ideas and concepts. Here are a few examples that demonstrate this ability.

Teachers may refer to a flight of stairs or the inclination of a hill to help explain the concept of slope. Students are familiar with these physical models; thus the concept of steepness becomes more understandable. Pictorial representations are also an effective teaching tool. Leonardo da Vinci's anatomical sketch *Vitruvian Man* is an excellent way for students to understand proportions and the golden mean.

Teachers can show that multiplication is an extension of the process of repeated addition. For example, if a worker earns $200 per week, then we can calculate the earnings over an eight-week period by either adding eight $200 or simply multiplying 8 by $200. In a similar way, teachers can underline the importance of division by showing that it represents repeated subtraction. As an example, suppose a person has $300 in a bank and decides to withdraw $50 each week. We can determine the number of weeks needed in order to withdraw the entire $300 by subtracting $50 each week until the balance is $0. A quicker way is to divide $300 by $50.

As a third example, suppose that a teacher is presenting a lesson on linear relationships. In order to make the lesson more effective, the students can be assigned to collect and organize the data with a chart, table, or graph. Subsequently, the students should develop a linear model of their data and explore its usefulness in projecting values beyond the domain and range of the given values.

As a fourth example, let's consider the value of algebra tiles. Teachers of elementary mathematics have used base ten blocks, multiplication rectangles, and pictograms to assist students in learning the basic addition, subtraction, multiplication, and division operations. The use of algebra tiles can strengthen a student's understanding of the product of two binomials. As an example, we can use these tiles to show that $(x + 3)(x + 1) = x^2 + 4x + 3$. Figure 5.4 illustrates this multiplication process.

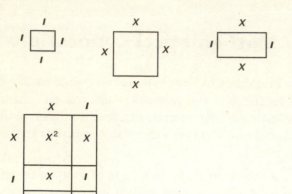

Figure 5.4

Note that these tiles would be equally effective in illustrating factoring and division. In this way, students would better understand not only the product of two binomials, but also the factoring division processes.

Mathematical Reasoning and Proof

We begin with the basics of **logic**. Logic is concerned with declarative unambiguous statements that must be either true or false. Examples of a declarative statement are:

(a) Judith is studying for her math exam.

(b) Chicago is in Illinois.

(c) All numbers are integers.

For statement (a), we don't automatically know whether it is true or false (but we can find out). Statement (b) is true, while statement (c) is clearly false.

An **argument** is simply a set of sentences in which all but the final one are called **premises**. The final sentence is called the **conclusion**.

A **valid** argument is one that satisfies the following condition: If all the premises are true, then the conclusion must be true. Thus, if any of the premises are false, we cannot infer any information concerning the truth (or falsity) of the conclusion. An **invalid** argument is one in which each premise is true and the conclusion is false.

Here is an example of a valid argument:

Premise 1: Each fraction can be written as a quotient of two integers.

Premise 2: One-half is a fraction.

Conclusion: One-half can be written as a quotient of two integers.

Note that both premises and the conclusion are true.

Here is an example of an invalid argument:

Premise 1: All cats have four legs.

Premise 2: The British Prime Minister is a cat.

Conclusion: The British Prime Minister has four legs.

We note that Premise 2 is false, which leads to a false conclusion.

Logical Equivalence of Sentences

Two sentences are **logically equivalent** if they are either both true or both false. Here is a list of commonly used symbols.

Word(s)	Symbol
Logically equivalent	<=>
And	∧
Or	∨
Not	~

Here are some basic sets of logically equivalent statements. In each case, P and Q are statements.

1. $P \wedge Q <=> Q \wedge P$.

2. $P \vee Q <=> Q \vee P$.

3. $\sim(\sim P) <=> P$

4. If P, then $Q <=>$ If $\sim Q$, then $\sim P$. The statement "If $\sim Q$, then $\sim P$" is called the **contrapositive** of the statement "If P, then Q."

NOTE:

The statement "If P, then Q" can be written in symbols as $P{\rightarrow}Q$. Similarly, "If $\sim Q$, then $\sim P$" can be written as $\sim Q{\rightarrow}\sim P$. The statement $Q{\rightarrow}P$ is called the **converse** of the statement $P{\rightarrow}Q$. The statement $\sim P{\rightarrow}\sim Q$ is called the **inverse** of the statement $P{\rightarrow}Q$. Neither the inverse nor the converse of a statement is logically equivalent to the original statement. However, the inverse and the converse <u>are</u> logically equivalent to each other.

EXAMPLE 1

Write the converse of the statement "If it rains, then I am going to the movies."

SOLUTION

Simply reverse the two parts of this sentence. The answer is "If I am going to the movies, then it rains."

EXAMPLE 2

Write the contrapositive of the statement "If a figure has four sides, then it is a rectangle."

SOLUTION

The contrapositive is found by negating both parts of this sentence and switching the order. The answer is " If it is not a rectangle, then the figure does not have four sides."

Note that in Example 2, <u>both </u>the statement and the contrapositive are <u>false</u>.

EXAMPLE 3

Write the inverse of "If I go to the bank, then I will not withdraw $100."

SOLUTION

To find the inverse, we negate both parts of the sentence, but retain the original order. The answer is "If I do not go to the bank, then I will withdraw $100."

Deductive Reasoning

Deductive reasoning is basically an extension of a valid argument, in which there are many premises from which a valid conclusion can be drawn. We begin with a valid statement that applies to a general class of examples and then apply it to a specific case.

EXAMPLE 4

The sum of the lengths of any two sides of a triangle must exceed the length of the third side. Look at Figure 5.5, in which $XY = 8$ and $YZ = 6$.

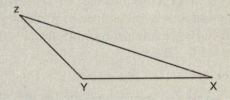

Figure 5.5

If $\overline{XZ}$ is the largest side, use deductive reasoning to find the restrictions on the length of $\overline{XZ}$.

SOLUTION

Since $XZ > XY$ and $XZ > YZ$, we know that $XZ > 8$. In addition, $XY + YZ > XZ$, which means that $14 > XZ$. By deductive reasoning, we conclude that $8 < XZ < 14$.

Inductive Reasoning

Inductive reasoning is essentially the reverse of deductive reasoning. Based on a numerical pattern of specific cases, we attempt to draw a more general conclusion.

We start with a proposition $P(n)$. The specific guidelines that are used for inductive reasoning are listed as follows:

(a) Verify that $P(1)$ is true.

(b) Assume that $P(k)$ is true for some $k > 1$.

(c) Verify that if both (a) and (b) are true, demonstrate that $P(k + 1)$ must also be true.

EXAMPLE 5

> Prove by mathematical induction that $1 + 3 + 5 + 7 + \ldots + (2n - 1) = n^2$.

SOLUTION

Let $P(n) = 1 + 3 + 5 + 7 + \ldots + (2n - 1)$. The statement is true for $n = 1$, since $P(1) = 1 = 1^2$. Next, we assume that $P(k) = k^2$. We are planning to prove that $P(k + 1) = (k + 1)^2$.

By definition, $P(k + 1)$ must be equivalent to the sum of the first k terms plus the $(k + 1)^{st}$ term. The sum of the first k terms is represented by $P(k)$ and is assumed to equal k^2. By the original formula, the $(k + 1)^{st}$ term is represented by $(2[k + 1] - 1) = 2k + 1$.

Then $P(k + 1) = k^2 + (2k + 1) = k^2 + 2k + 1$. But we know that $k^2 + 2k + 1$ can be factored as $(k + 1)(k + 1) = (k + 1)^2$. Thus, we have $P(k + 1) = (k + 1)^2$. Therefore, by mathematical induction, we have proven the original statement is true for all n.

Indirect Proof

For this type of proof, we consider two possible outcomes, namely the result we are trying to prove and its negative. We then assume the negative and show that a contradiction of known postulates, theorems, or definitions is reached by this assumption. In this way, we eliminate the negative of the result we are trying to prove. Thus, our original result must be true.

EXAMPLE 6

> Using an indirect proof, prove that the bisector of an angle of a scalene triangle cannot be perpendicular to the opposite side.

SOLUTION

We start with the negative of what we are trying to prove. This means that we will assume that the bisector of an angle of a scalene triangle is perpendicular to the opposite side. Look at Figure 5.6.

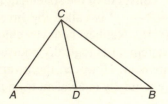

Figure 5.6

We are given that $\triangle ABC$ is scalene and that $\angle ACD \cong \angle BCD$. If we make the assumption that CD is perpendicular to AB, then each of $\angle ACD$ and $\angle BCD$ has a measure of 90°. Since $CD = CD$ by the identity postulate, this would lead to $\triangle ACD \cong \triangle BCD$ by the Angle-Side-Angle theorem. Furthermore, we would find that $AC = BC$ because they would be corresponding sides of congruent triangles. But we started with a scalene triangle ABC, which means that all three sides are a different length. Thus, we have a contradiction, and therefore the original result must be true. We conclude that the angle bisector CD cannot be perpendicular to AB.

Problem-Solving Strategies

The instruction of problem-solving strategies involves engaging students to use their existing knowledge to assist them in acquiring new knowledge. This process can be difficult if students do not have appropriate problem-solving skills. At the start of the problem-solving process, teachers can provide the students with some basic background information and perhaps show the students how to reduce a complex problem into simpler parts. Teachers may need to guide the students in helping to isolate the pertinent information of what is given, what is assumed, and what needs to be proven. Characteristics of the actual problem, such as the number of possible solutions, may indicate that one particular strategy is the best choice for solving the problem.

Once a strategy has been used successfully to solving the problem, teachers should direct the students to determine whether the solution makes sense within the context of the problem. As an example, if the problem requires finding the length of a side of a triangle, then any negative number solution would have to be discarded. Similarly, if a problem involves rational solutions, then an answer of $\sqrt{2}$ could not be acceptable.

Reasonableness and Estimation

Throughout the problem solving process, students should ask whether the results of the steps that are used actually make sense. In particular, students must be able to recognize if a quantity is either exceptionally large or exceptionally small. As an example, if an investment of $1000 is split by placing it into two separate accounts, it would be impossible for one account to contain $1500. By asking students to estimate the answer to either part of a problem or the entire problem, students will become better mathematical thinkers. For example, if $100 is to be given to three people A, B, and C in the ratio of $1 : 2 : 7$ respectively, the student must recognize that C will receive more money than either A or B. The ability to estimate an answer is an excellent assessment of the students' comprehension and readiness for more advanced problems.

Constructing a Table

When a problem provides a data set that can be organized by specific characteristics or groups, constructing tables of values will assist students to recognize patterns inherent in the data. For example, suppose the student has collected the following data for two variables, x and y.

x	1	2	3	4	5	6	7
y	0	3	8	15	24	35	48

Figure 5.6a

At first glance, it may appear that there is no relationship between the values of x and y.

However, if a student does some "experimenting" by squaring the x values, the corresponding squared values will be 1, 4, 9, 16, 25, 36, and 49. Hopefully, the student recognizes that each y value is 1 less than the square of its corresponding x value. Thus, the relationship can be expressed as $y = x^2 - 1$. The construction

of a table has the advantage of organizing the information into a form that can facilitate finding a solution.

Guess-and-Check

Although it may seem unusual, guessing is a valid problem-solving strategy that should be used when there are a relatively small number of possible solutions or when the list of potential solutions can be tested easily. As an example, suppose that it is known that the solution to the equation $3^x + 5x^2 - x^3 = 693$ is a positive integer less than 10. Since this would be a difficult equation to solve by algebraic techniques, a suggestion would be to simply guess, using an integer from 1 to 9. The student can readily see that the value of 1 could not possibly be a solution. Suppose the student decides to use the value of 5. Then, $3^5 + 5(5)^2 - 5^3 = 243 + 125 - 125 = 243$, which is too low. At this point, the student might believe that the number 7 is the correct solution. This leads to $3^7 + 5(7)^2 - 7^3 = 2187 + 245 - 343 = 2089$, which is too large. The only choice left is to select 6. Then $3^6 + 5(6)^2 - 6^3 = 729 + 180 - 216 = 693$, which is the correct answer.

Working Backwards

This is a strategy that works best when the solution is already known, and thus we need to provide the steps that lead to the solution. As an example, suppose that the student is asked to factor completely the polynomial $x^4 + 2x^3 + 2x^2 + x - 6$. The student decides to graph $y = x^4 + 2x^3 + 2x^2 + x - 6$, and finds that the points $(1, 0)$ and $(-2, 0)$ lie on the graph. Hopefully, the student recognizes that this means that both $(x - 1)$ and $(x + 2)$ must be factors of $x^4 + 2x^3 + 2x^2 + x - 6$. In order to determine the other factor(s), the student should divide the product of $(x - 1)$ and $(x + 2)$ into $x^4 + 2x^3 + 2x^2 + x - 6$. Now $(x - 1)(x + 2) = x^2 + x - 2$, and by long division, $(x^4 + 2x^3 + 2x^2 + x - 6) \div (x^2 + x - 2) = x^2 + x + 3$. It becomes fairly easy to check that $x^2 + x + 3$ cannot be factored, so the complete factoring is $(x - 1)(x + 2)(x^2 + x + 3)$.

Using a Diagram

The use of a diagram can never be overemphasized. Consider the following mixture problem, which is typically found in a second year algebra textbook.

A solution of 10 quarts of alcohol and water contains 20% alcohol. How many quarts of a solution of alcohol and water that contains 30% alcohol should be added in order that the resulting mixture contains 28% alcohol?

This would be challenging to solve without a diagram for even an experienced mathematics teacher. But Figure 5.7 shows an appropriate diagram that can certainly clarify the direction of the solution to this problem.

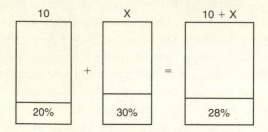

Figure 5.7

By assigning x to the number of quarts of the 30% mixture that will be added, the student can understand why the combined solution will contain $10 + x$ quarts. Once the student realizes that the amount of alcohol in the last container must be the sum of the amounts of alcohol in each of the first two containers, it is easier to understand that the appropriate equation becomes $(0.20)(10) + (0.30)(x) = (0.28)(10 + x)$. As always, the teacher should strongly encourage that the student check the answer of $x = 40$.

As with most examples for which a diagram is used, the diagram is an excellent visual tool for understanding the relationship among the pieces of information. This pictorial representation clarifies the problem so that students can better determine the required steps for arriving at a solution.

Chapter 5 Quiz

1. Consider the following three statements:

    (a) $1 + 3 = 2^2$, (b) $1 + 3 + 5 = 3^2$, and (c) $1 + 3 + 5 + 7 = 4^2$.

    Using inductive reasoning, which one of the following would apply?

    (A) The sum of the first n consecutive positive odd integers equals n^2.

    (B) The sum of any consecutive odd integers equals n^2.

    (C) The sum of the squares of the first n positive odd integers equals $(n - 1)^2$.

    (D) The sum of the squares of any consecutive odd integers equals $(n + 1)^2$.

2. Look at the following diagram

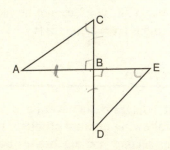

    If $\overline{DC}$ is perpendicular to $\overline{AE}$, $\overline{DB} \cong \overline{AB}$. and $\angle E \cong \angle C$, which of the following must be true?

    (A) $AB = (2)(BE)$ (C) $BC = (\frac{2}{3})(BD)$

    (B) $BC = AC$ (D) $BC = BE$

3. Given that $X = \{$all prime numbers between 10 and 20$\}$ and $X \cup Y = \{$all positive odd integers less than 20$\}$, what is the minimum number of elements in Y?

    (A) 5   (C) 7

    (B) 6   (D) 8

4. Look at the following geometric proof.

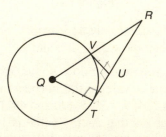

    Note: The figure is not drawn to scale.

Given: A circle with point Q as the center, $\overline{RT}$ is tangent to the circle at point T, and $\overline{UV}$ is perpendicular to $\overline{RT}$.

Prove: $m\angle RVU = m\overparen{VT}$

Statements	Reasons
1. A circle with point Q as the center, $\overline{RT}$ is tangent to the circle at point T, and $\overline{UV}$ is perpendicular to $\overline{RT}$	1. Given
2. $m\angle QTR = 90°$	2. A tangent to a circle is perpendicular to a radius at the point of contact.
3. $m\angle VUR = 90°$	3. Definition of perpendicular lines.
4. $\overline{QT}$ is parallel to $\overline{UV}$	4. Two lines that are perpendicular to the same line are parallel.
5.	5.
6.	6.
7. $m\angle RVU = m\overparen{VT}$	7. Substitution

Which of the following pairs of statements and reasons would be most appropriate in Steps 5 and 6?

(A)

Statement	Reason
5. $\angle R \cong \angle R$	5. Identity
6. $\triangle RVU \sim \triangle RQT$	6. AAA postulate

(B)

Statement	Reason
5. $m\angle Q = m\angle RVU$	5. When parallel lines are crossed by a transversal, the corresponding angles are equal.
6. $m\angle Q = m\overparen{VT}$	6. An interior angle of a circle has the same measure as its intercepted arc.

(C)

Statement	Reason
5. $\angle R \cong \angle R$	5. Identity
6. $m\angle Q = m\overparen{VT}$	6. An interior angle of a circle has the same measure as its intercepted arc.

(D)

Statement	Reason
5. $m\angle Q = m\angle T$	5. Base angles of an isosceles triangle are equal.
6. $m\angle Q = m\overparen{VT}$	6. AAA postulate

5. Look at the following figure.

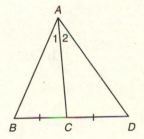

Note: The figure is not drawn to scale.
If $BC = BD$, which piece of additional information would <u>not</u> be sufficient to conclude that $\overline{AC}$ is perpendicular to $\overline{BD}$?

(A) $\angle B \cong \angle D$

(B) $\triangle ABC$ is equilateral

(C) $AB = AD$

(D) $\angle 1 \cong \angle 2$

6. Look at the following figure.

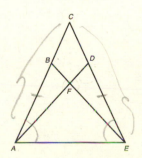

If $AC = CE$ and $AB = DE$, which of the following statements must be true?

I. $AB = FE$

II. $\angle ABE \cong \angle EDA$

III. $\triangle ABE \cong \triangle ACD$

(A) I, II, and III   (C) II only

(B) II and III only   (D) I only

7. Suppose set M is a proper subset of set N. Set M has 15 elements and set N has 25 elements. The Universal Set, of which M and N are proper subsets, has 45 elements. If set P is also a proper subset of the Universal Set, but contains no elements from set N, what is the maximum number of elements in P?

(A) 5   (C) 20

(B) 10   (D) 25

8. Look at the following figure.

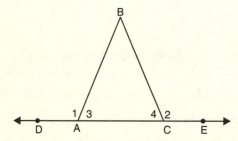

Given that the points D, A, C, and E are collinear, $\angle 1 \cong \angle 2$, and $\angle 1$ is obtuse, which of the following is <u>not</u> necessarily true?

(A) The measure of $\angle B$ is less than the measure of $\angle 3$

(B) $AB = BC$

(C) $\angle 4$ is acute

(D) $DE = DA + AC + CE$

9. Consider the following four statements to be true.

1. All people who exercise have blue eyes.

2. All people who have blue eyes enjoy movies.

3. People who have brown eyes enjoy baseball.

4. Sarah has blue eyes.

Based on these statements, which of the following <u>must</u> be true?

(A) Sarah has brown eyes.

(B) Sarah enjoys movies.

(C) Sarah exercises.

(D) Sarah enjoys baseball.

10. Look at the following figure, in which points F, G, and H are collinear.

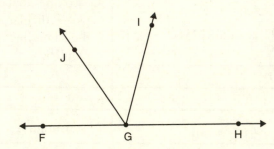

Which of the following statements <u>must</u> be true?

(A) $\angle FGJ$ and $\angle JGH$ are supplementary angles.

(B) $\angle FGJ$ and $\angle JGI$ are complementary angles.

(C) $\angle FGJ$ and $\angle IGH$ are vertical angles.

(D) $\angle FGJ \cong \angle JGI$

Chapter 5 Quiz Solutions

1. (A)

"The sum of the first n consecutive positive odd integers equals n^2" expresses the relationship that exists in each of the three examples.

2. (D)

If $\overline{DC}$ is perpendicular to $\overline{AE}$, then each of $\angle ABC$ and $\angle DBE$ must measure 90°. Then $\triangle ABC \cong \triangle DBE$ by the Side-Angle-Angle postulate. Therefore, $BC = BE$, since they are corresponding sides of congruent triangles.

3. (B)

X contains four elements, namely 11, 13, 17, and 19. $X \cup Y$ contains ten elements, namely 1, 3, 5, 7, 9, 11, 13, 15, 17, and 19. Then Y <u>must</u> contain at least the six elements 1, 3, 5, 7, 9, and 15.

4. (B)

After establishing that $\overline{QT}$ is parallel to $\overline{UV}$, the next step should be to state that the corresponding angles ($\angle Q$ and $\angle RVU$) are congruent. Then, to prove that $m\angle RVU = m\overarc{VT}$, it is necessary to establish that $m\angle Q = m\overarc{VT}$. This is accomplished by noting that the measure of a central angle is equal to the measure of its intercepted arc.

5. (D)

If $\angle 1 \cong \angle 2$, then triangles ABC and ACD would have two pairs of congruent sides and a pair of non-inclusive congruent angles. This would be insufficient to prove that the triangles are congruent. As a consequence, we could not conclude that $\angle ACB$ is congru-ent to $\angle ACD$. Thus, we could not conclude that $\overline{AC}$ is perpendicular to $\overline{BD}$.

Note that each of answer choices (A), (B), and (C) would be sufficient information to conclude that triangles ABC and ACD are congruent. So, $\angle ACB$ would be congruent to $\angle ACD$ by corresponding parts of congruent triangles, which would force each of these angles to measure 90°. As a consequence, $\overline{AC}$ would be perpendicular to $\overline{BD}$.

6. (C)

From the given information, $\angle CAE \cong \angle CEA$, because the sides opposite them are congruent. Since $AE = AE$, $\triangle ABE \cong \triangle EDA$ by the Side-Angle-Side postulate. Therefore, $\angle ABE \cong \angle EDA$ because they are corresponding angles of congruent triangles. None of the other statements are necessarily true.

7. (C)

Since no elements of P belong to N, this means that P and M also share no elements. There are $45 - 25 = 20$ elements in the Universal Set that belong to neither M nor N; this is the maximum number of elements in P.

8. (A)

From the given information, $\angle 3 \cong \angle 4$ because they are supplementary to congruent angles $\angle 1$ and $\angle 2$, respectively. This means that $\triangle ABC$ is isosceles, so $AB = BC$. By the Addition Postulate, $DE = DA + AC + CE$. Finally, since $\angle 1$ is obtuse, both $\angle 3$ and $\angle 4$ must be acute. However, we do not have sufficient information to determine the comparison of the measures of $\angle B$ and $\angle 3$.

9. (B)

Answer choice (A) is wrong because it contradicts Statement 4. Answer choice (B) is correct because it combines Statements 2 and 4. Answer choice (C) is wrong because the implication given is that if a person exercises, then that person has blue eyes. The converse is not necessarily true. Answer choice (D) is wrong because Statement 3 assures us that people with brown eyes enjoy baseball. We cannot draw any conclusion about whether people with blue eyes also enjoy baseball.

10. (A)

By definition, two adjacent angles whose exterior sides lie on the same line are supplementary. Answer choice (B) is wrong because we do not know whether $\angle FGI$ is a right angle. Answer choice (C) is wrong because vertical angles are opposite angles that are formed by two intersecting lines. Answer choice (D) is wrong because we cannot determine whether $\overrightarrow{GJ}$ bisects $\angle FGI$.

Practice Test 1

GACE 013 MIDDLE GRADES MATH

ANSWER SHEET FOR PRACTICE TEST 1

1 _____	16 _____	31 _____	46 _____
2 _____	17 _____	32 _____	47 _____
3 _____	18 _____	33 _____	48 _____
4 _____	19 _____	34 _____	49 _____
5 _____	20 _____	35 _____	50 _____
6 _____	21 _____	36 _____	51 _____
7 _____	22 _____	37 _____	52 _____
8 _____	23 _____	38 _____	53 _____
9 _____	24 _____	39 _____	54 _____
10 _____	25 _____	40 _____	55 _____
11 _____	26 _____	41 _____	56 _____
12 _____	27 _____	42 _____	57 _____
13 _____	28 _____	43 _____	58 _____
14 _____	29 _____	44 _____	59 _____
15 _____	30 _____	45 _____	60 _____

ANSWER SHEET FOR CONSTRUCTED-RESPONSE QUESTIONS

1. What part of $\frac{4}{5}$ is $\frac{1}{3}$?

   A. $\frac{4}{15}$ C. $\frac{17}{15}$

   B. $\frac{5}{12}$ D. $\frac{12}{5}$

2. If in ΔDEF, $DE = EF$ and angle D has measure 54°, then angle E has measure

   A. 50°   C. 72°

   B. 54°   D. 90°

3. What is the factorization of $12ab + 14a - 6b - 7$?

   A. $(-2a - b)(6b - 7)$ C. $(6b + 7)(2a + 1)$

   B. $(6b - 7)(2a + 1)$ D. $(6b + 7)(2a - 1)$

4. The graph below shows the frequency of test scores on a history exam.

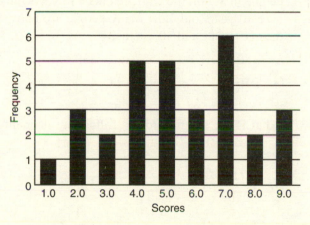

   What is the mode of the history scores?

   A. 4   C. 7

   B. 6   D. 9

5.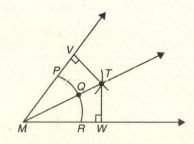

In the diagram above, $\angle PMR$ is acute. At point M, an arc PR is drawn so that $MR = MP$. Arc $\overset{\frown}{PR}$ is then bisected at point Q by the construction shown at point T. The ray joining M, Q, and T is drawn and a perpendicular segment is drawn from T so that $\overline{TV} \perp \overline{MV}$ and $\overline{TW} \perp \overline{MW}$. Which of the following may be **false**?

A. $TV = TW$

B. $m\angle VMW = m\angle VTM$

C. $m\angle VTM = m\angle WTM$

D. $MW > MP$

6. In the figure below, which transformation will map ΔABC onto ΔDEF?

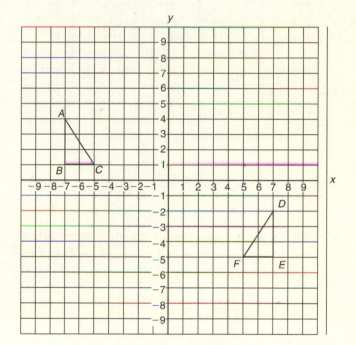

A. Reflect ΔABC over the y-axis and slide up 6 spaces.

B. Reflect ΔABC over the x-axis and slide up 6 spaces.

C. Reflect ΔABC over the y-axis and slide down 6 spaces.

D. Reflect ΔABC over the y-axis, reflect over the x-axis and slide down 2 spaces.

7. Which of the following numbers is <u>not</u> between 0.25 and 0.26?

A. $0.25\overline{1}$

C. 0.259

B. $0.\overline{259}$

D. 0.261

8.

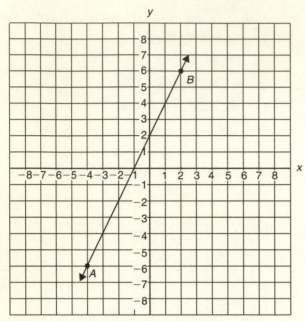

What is the slope of the line shown above?

A. -2

C. $\dfrac{1}{2}$

B. $-\dfrac{1}{2}$

D. 2

9. Which of the following decimals corresponds to the percentage of the cells that are shaded in the diagram below?

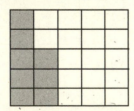

A. 0.40

C. 0.25

B. 0.32

D. 0.08

10. Assuming that $m, n \neq 0$, the quotient of $\dfrac{3n^2 + 14n - 24}{5mn + 30m}$ is equivalent to

A. $\dfrac{3n - 4}{5m}$

C. $\dfrac{3n + 8}{5m}$

B. $\dfrac{3n + 4}{5m}$

D. $\dfrac{3n - 8}{5m}$

11. What is the ratio of 6 feet to 30 inches?

A. $\dfrac{5}{1}$

C. $\dfrac{5}{12}$

B. $\dfrac{12}{5}$

D. $\dfrac{1}{5}$

12. Age Distribution of People Living in Smallville

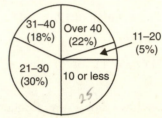

Using the above pie chart, if there is a total of 282 people in Smallville who are under 11 years old or over 40 years old, how many people are between the ages of 11 and 30, inclusive?

A. 180

C. 330

B. 210

D. 460

13. What is the solution to the following inequality?
$2 + 3(x - 2) > 7$

A. $\left(-\dfrac{11}{3}, \infty\right)$

C. $\left(\dfrac{3}{11}, \infty\right)$

B. $\left(-\dfrac{3}{11}, \infty\right)$

D. $\left(\dfrac{11}{3}, \infty\right)$

14. What is the domain of the function defined by $f(x) = \sqrt{-x + 1} + 5$?

A. $\{x \mid x \geq 0\}$

C. $\{x \mid 0 \leq x \leq 1\}$

B. $\{x \mid x \leq 1\}$

D. $\{x \mid x \geq -1\}$

15. The polygons shown in the figure below are similar. What is the length of m?

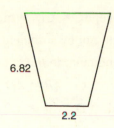

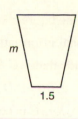

A. 2.80   C. 4.20

B. 3.15   D. 4.65

16. A survey asked a group of children to name their favorite flavor of ice cream. The results from this survey are shown in the following chart.

Favorite Ice Cream

Ice Cream	Number of Children
Chocolate	18
Mint Chocolate Chip	7
Rocky Road	12
Strawberry	20
Vanilla	23

If one child were randomly selected from this survey, what is the probability that the child's favorite flavor of ice cream is rocky road?

A. 5%   C. 15%

B. 10%   D. 25%

17. $(3)(9 + 4) = (3 \times 9) + (3 \times 4)$ is an example of which property of numbers?

A. Associative   C. Distributive

B. Commutative   D. Inverse

18.

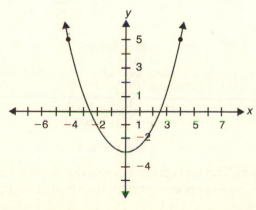

Which equation represents the above graph?

A. $y = \frac{1}{2}x^2 + 3$ C. $y = \frac{1}{2}x^2 - 3$

B. $y = -\frac{1}{2}x^2 - 3$ D. $y = -\frac{1}{2}x^2 + 3$

19. In the figure shown below, line l is parallel to line m.

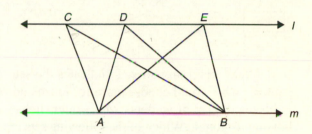

If the area of triangle ABC is 40 square centimeters, what is the area of triangle ABD?

A. Exactly 40 square centimeters

B. Less than 40 square centimeters

C. More than 40 square centimeters

D. Cannot be determined from the given information

20. Which of the following is an irrational number?

A. $\sqrt{7}$ C. $\frac{2}{15}$

B. $\sqrt{9}$ D. -2.57

21. Point C has coordinates $(2,3)$ and point D has coordinates $(0,6)$. To the nearest tenth, what is the distance between point C and point D?

A. 2.1   C. 3.6

B. 2.7   D. 4.5

22. The number missing in the series 14, 23, 29, 38, 44, x, 59 is:

A. 50   C. 54

B. 53   D. 58

23. Use the diagram below to answer the question that follows.

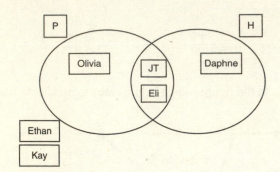

In the Venn diagram above, P indicates the set of students who would choose pizza for lunch and H indicates the set of students who would choose a hot dog for lunch. Which of the following sets represents the complement of (P ∪ H)?

A. JT, Eli

B. Olivia, JT, Eli, Daphne

C. Ethan, Kay

D. Olivia, Daphne

24.

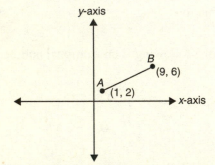

In the graph shown above, if $\overline{AB}$ is reflected about the x-axis, what will be the reflected coordinates of the midpoint of $\overline{AB}$?

A. (5, 4)   C. (5, −4)

B. (−5, −4)   D. (−5, 4)

25.

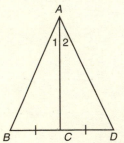

In the figure shown above, BC = CD. Which additional information would <u>not</u> be sufficient to conclude that $\overline{AC}$ is perpendicular to $\overline{BD}$?

A. $\angle B \cong \angle D$ C. $AB = AD$

B. $\triangle ABC$ is equilateral   D. $\angle 1 \cong \angle 2$

26. In a northern city, the winter temperature differed by 12 degrees from one day to the next. Which of the following could be the two temperature readings?

A. −10° and 2°   C. −4° and 7°

B. −5° and 4°   D. −1° and 9°

27. The figure shown below is a rectangular solid.

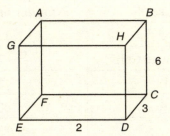

What is the length of the diagonal from point B to point E?

A. 11   C. $3\sqrt{5}$

B. 7   D. $2\sqrt{10}$

28. What is the value of x in the equation $\frac{2}{3}(x+5) = \frac{1}{4}(x+2)$?

A. $-\frac{34}{5}$ C. $-\frac{12}{5}$

B. $-\frac{34}{12}$ D. $-\frac{5}{12}$

29.   A-Plus Realty

Using the chart above, suppose that for this month, Kelly can improve her sales by 50% and André can improve his sales by 100%. Assume that Ted's and Maya's sales remain the same. For this month, what fraction of the total number of homes sold by A-Plus Realty will Kelly sell?

A. $\dfrac{1}{5}$

C. $\dfrac{3}{20}$

B. $\dfrac{3}{17}$

D. $\dfrac{1}{8}$

30. The input-output table below shows values for x and y.

Input (x)	Output(y)
−2	−6
0	2
2	10
3	14

Which equation could represent the relationship between x and y?

A. $y = 4x + 2$

C. $y = -x - 2$

B. $y = 2x + 1$

D. $y = x + 4$

31. If $f(x) = 3x - 5$ and $g(f(x)) = x$, then which of the following describes $g(x)$?

A. $\dfrac{x-5}{3}$

C. $\dfrac{2x+5}{3}$

B. $\dfrac{x+5}{3}$

D. $\dfrac{x+5}{4}$

32. Kathleen bought a gift for her best friend. The gift box she bought is pictured below. How much gift-wrap will she need to cover the box?

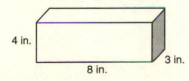

4 in.   3 in.
        8 in.

A. 96 square inches

B. 120 square inches

C. 136 square inches

D. 236 square inches

33. The figure below shows a number line, including point P.

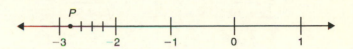

What is the value of P?

A. −2.9

C. −2.2

B. −2.8

D. −2.1

34. Allison wanted to find out what the students at her school believe about the new homework policy. Which of the following samples is most appropriate for surveying?

A. The first 46 students exiting the school

B. The girls in her math club

C. 25 students in Mrs. Jackson's English class

D. 6 students on her bus

35. What is the simplified expression for $\left(\dfrac{3}{a}\right)^2 \left(\dfrac{a^2}{3^2}\right)^2$?

A. $\dfrac{a^2}{9}$

C. $\dfrac{a}{3}$

B. $\dfrac{a^2}{2}$

D. $\dfrac{9}{a^2}$

36. Which of the following descriptions most accurately depicts the diagram?

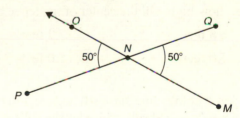

A. Line MO intersects with line PQ to create adjacent angles MNQ and PNO measuring 50°.

B. Line segment MO intersects with line segment PQ to create vertical angles MNA and PNO measuring 50°.

C. Line segment PQ intersects ray MO to create adjacent angles MNP and PNO measuring 50°.

D. Line segment PQ intersects ray MO to create vertical angles MNQ and PNO measuring 50°.

113

37. If $h(x) = 3x^2 - 2$, which of the following represents $h^{-1}(x)$?

    A. $\sqrt{\dfrac{x+3}{2}}$

    B. $\sqrt{\dfrac{x+2}{3}}$

    C. $\dfrac{\sqrt{x+3}}{2}$

    D. $\dfrac{\sqrt{x+2}}{3}$

38. The sum of the multiplicative inverses of 3 and 5 is equal to the multiplicative inverse of which number?

    A. $\dfrac{3}{5}$

    B. $\dfrac{5}{3}$

    C. $\dfrac{8}{15}$

    D. $\dfrac{15}{8}$

39. You roll a pair of dice. If the first die shows a 6, what is the probability that the sum of the dice is greater than 9?

    A. $\dfrac{1}{6}$

    B. $\dfrac{1}{3}$

    C. $\dfrac{1}{2}$

    D. $\dfrac{2}{3}$

40. Mrs. Landers wanted to make a life-size replica of a Comanche Indian tepee for her fourth grade class. The shape of the tepee is a cone. If the radius of the tepee is 5.1 feet and the slant height is 8.5 feet, how high will the center of the tepee be?

    A. 6.8 feet

    B. 7.0 feet

    C. 7.2 feet

    D. 8.0 feet

41. Given that (a) some shrubs flower, and that (b) an Alamanda is a shrub, which of the following can be logically deduced?

    A. An Alamanda flowers

    B. An Alamanda does not flower

    C. An Alamanda is not a shrub

    D. None of the above

42. A paramecium measures 0.000091 millimeters. How is this number written in scientific notation?

    A. -9.1×10^5

    B. 9.1×10^{-5}

    C. 91×10^{-5}

    D. -91×10^5

43. For their summer project, the student council officers at Cleveland High School volunteered to build a playground at the children's park. It would take 3 volunteers 96 hours of work time to build the playground. How many hours would it take to complete the playground if all 8 officers show up to work?

    A. 36

    B. 30

    C. 24

    D. 22

44. Which one of the following diagrams illustrates a reflection of $\triangle ABC$ to its image $\triangle A'B'C'$ over the line l_1?

    A.

    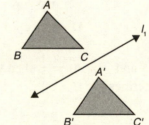

    B.

    C.

    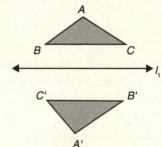

D.

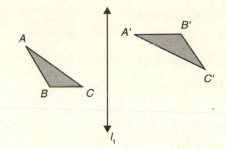

A. Cone   C. Cube

B. Cylinder   D. Pyramid

48. Exclusive of the numbers 1 and 984, how many factors are there for the number 984?

A. 8   C. 14

B. 10   D. 20

45. Ten people are to be seated in a row with 10 seats in a movie theater. Two of the people do not want to sit in either of the two end seats in this row. In how many accommodating ways can all ten people be seated?

A. 20,120   C. 2,257,920

B. 40,320   D. 3,628,800

46. Which polynomial represents the shaded area of the figure below?

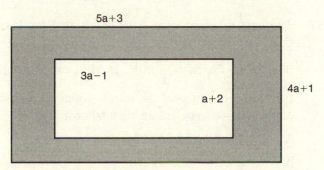

A. $17a^2 + 22a + 1$

B. $23a^2 + 22a + 1$

C. $9a^2 - 4a + 5$

D. $17a^2 + 12a + 5$

47. Look at the following diagram.

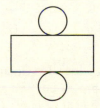

This represents the net of which geometric figure?

49. Using Algebra tiles, $(x + 2)(x + 1)$ can be represented as which of the following?

A.

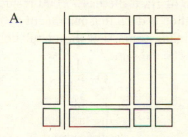

B.

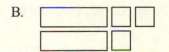

C.

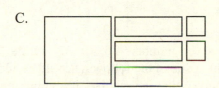

D.

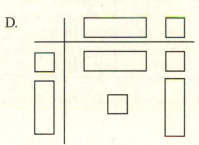

50. Southern Disposal picks up garbage in three areas of town on different days, with the following schedule:

South and East sides	Every 5 days
North and West sides	Every 9 days
Downtown	Every 6 days

How often will the garbage be picked up in all three areas of town on the same day?

A. Every 30 days

B. Every 90 days

C. Every 270 days

D. The garbage is never picked up in all three places on the same day.

51. The town of Cullman has a population of 50,000 residents, and is growing at a rate of 2,400 per year. The town of Hartselle has 77,000 residents, and the population is declining at a rate of 600 per year. In how many years will the population of these two cities be the same?

A. 7   C. 9

B. 8   D. 10

52. Point Q is located at $(2, -3)$. If Q is rotated 90° clockwise about the origin, what will be the new coordinates of Q?

A. $(3, 2)$ C. $(-2, -3)$

B. $(2, 3)$ D. $(-3, -2)$

53. Given the seven numbers 26, 30, 32, 32, 28, 21, and 21, which one of the following could be added to this group so that the median of all eight numbers is 27?

A. 23   C. 29

B. 27   D. 31

54. What is the fractional equivalent of the decimal $0.1\overline{24}$?

A. $\dfrac{6}{25}$ C. $\dfrac{124}{999}$

B. $\dfrac{41}{330}$ D. $\dfrac{31}{250}$

55. The owner of a theater wants to make a scale model of his small performance stage for a display. The stage in the theater measures 15 feet long by 12 feet wide. The model will be made by using a scale factor of $\dfrac{1}{10}$. Find the area of the model stage.

A. 3.6 square feet

B. 8 square feet

C. 1.8 square feet

D. 18 square feet

56. Which steps could be used to solve the equation $\dfrac{3}{8}x - 7 = 10$?

A. Multiply both sides by the reciprocal of $\dfrac{3}{8}$, and then add 7 to both sides.

B. Divide both sides by the reciprocal of $\dfrac{3}{8}$, and then add 7 to both sides.

C. Add 7 to both sides, and then divide both sides by the reciprocal of $\dfrac{3}{8}$.

D. Add 7 to both sides, and then multiply both sides by the reciprocal of $\dfrac{3}{8}$.

57. The cost of a cab ride with the Built-Rite Taxi Company is as follows: An initial cost of $2.50, plus $0.15 for each $\dfrac{1}{4}$ mile. If Mike takes a cab ride for a distance of 20 miles, which equation could be used to calculate his total cost (T)?

A. $T = (\$2.50 + \$0.15)(20)$

B. $T = (\$2.50 + \$0.60)(20)$

C. $T = \$2.50 + (\$0.15)(20)$

D. $T = \$2.50 + (\$0.60)(20)$

58. In calculating the value of $4 \div 2 + 3^2 - (8 + 2) \times 3$, which order of operations should be performed <u>last</u>?

A. Subtracting   C. Dividing

B. Multiplying   D. Squaring

59. The manager of Joe's Ice Cream Shop orders waffle cones that are 14 cm. tall and have a diameter of 6 cm. To the nearest cubic cm, what is the volume of these cones?

A. 305   C. 132

B. 150   D. 424

60. What is the range of the function $g(x) = \sqrt{16 - x^2}$?

   A. All numbers between 0 and 4, inclusive

   B. All numbers between −4 and 4, inclusive

   C. All numbers less than or equal to 4

   D. All numbers greater than or equal to 0

Constructed-Response Questions

61. A small housing community consists of three dwellings, as shown below.

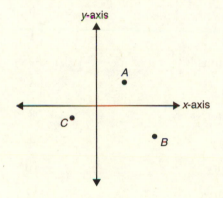

The town planner wants to construct a clubhouse that is equidistant from each dwelling.

- Using only a straightedge and a compass, how would you determine the exact location of the clubhouse?
- The distance between the clubhouse and each of points A, B, and C is 114 feet. A direct walkway will be built between the clubhouse and each dwelling. Each walkway is rectangular in shape and will be 4 feet wide. If the cost of the walkway is $15 per square foot, what is the total cost of all three walkways?

62. At the Sleep-Easy Motel, a senior citizen is given a $10 per night discount, calculated by taking the cost of each night's lodging, adding an 8% sales tax, then deducting $10 per night.

At the Rest-Well Motel, a senior citizen is also given a $10 per night discount. The discount is first applied to each night's lodging, then the 8% sales tax is added.

At either motel, one night's lodging (before discounts) costs $90.

- What is the cost for a senior citizen to stay at the Sleep-Easy Motel for four nights?
- What is the cost for a senior citizen to stay at the Rest-Well Motel for four nights?
- In order for the cost to be the same at each motel, how much of a discount, in dollars and cents, should be offered at the Rest-Well Motel?

ANSWER KEY – MATHEMATICS PRACTICE TEST 1

Question Number	Answer	Chapter	GACE Test Objective
1	B	Number and Operations	3
2	C	Measurement and Geometry	5
3	D	Patterns, Algebra, and Functions	8
4	C	Data Analysis and Probability	10
5	B	Math Processes and Procedures	5
6	C	Measurement and Geometry	6
7	A	Number and Operations	1
8	D	Patterns, Algebra, and Functions	9
9	B	Number and Operations	2
10	A	Patterns, Algebra, and Functions	8
11	B	Measurement and Geometry	4
12	B	Data Analysis and Probability	10
13	D	Math Processes and Procedures	12
14	B	Patterns, Algebra, and Functions	7
15	D	Measurement and Geometry	5
16	C	Data Analysis and Probability	11
17	C	Number and Operations	3
18	C	Patterns, Algebra, and Functions	9
19	A	Math Processes and Procedures	13
20	A	Number and Operations	2
21	C	Measurement and Geometry	6
22	B	Patterns, Algebra, and Functions	7
23	C	Data Analysis and Probability	11
24	C	Measurement and Geometry	6
25	D	Math Processes and Procedures	13
26	A	Number and Operations	1
27	B	Measurement and Geometry	5
28	A	Patterns, Algebra, and Functions	8

Question Number	Answer	Chapter	GACE Test Objective
29	C	Data Analysis and Probability	10
30	A	Math Processes and Procedures	12
31	B	Patterns, Algebra, and Functions	9
32	C	Measurement and Geometry	4
33	B	Number and Operations	2
34	A	Data Analysis and Probability	10
35	A	Number and Operations	3
36	D	Math Processes and Procedures	12
37	B	Patterns, Algebra, and Functions	9
38	D	Number and Operations	3
39	C	Data Analysis and Probability	11
40	A	Measurement and Geometry	4
41	D	Math Processes and Procedures	13
42	B	Number and Operations	2
43	A	Patterns, Algebra, and Functions	7
44	C	Measurement and Geometry	6
45	C	Data Analysis and Probability	11
46	D	Patterns, Algebra, and Functions	8
47	B	Measurement and Geometry	4
48	C	Number and Operations	1
49	A	Math Processes and Procedures	12
50	B	Number and Operations	1
51	C	Patterns, Algebra, and Functions	8
52	D	Measurement and Geometry	6
53	A	Data Analysis and Probability	10
54	B	Number and Operations	2
55	C	Measurement and Geometry	4
56	D	Math Processes and Procedures	13
57	D	Patterns, Algebra, and Functions	9
58	A	Number and Operations	3

Question Number	Answer	Chapter	GACE Test Objective
59	C	Measurement and Geometry	4
60	A	Patterns, Algebra, and Functions	7
61	–	Constructed Response: Measurement and Geometry	–
62	–	Constructed Response: Patterns, Algebra, and Functions	–

Practice Test 1 Progress Chart

Objective 0001   # + operations   2/4 50

7	26	48	50
✓	+	+	–

− + − +   50%

Objective 0002   4/5 = 80

9	20	33	42	54
+	+	+	+	–

3/3   + + + + ⊥   # + operations   100

Objective 0003   3/5 60%

1	17	35	38	58
+	–	+	–	+

+ + + +   # + operations   + 100

Objective 0004   4/6 = 67%

11	32	40	47	55	59
✓	+	+	+	–	+

+ + + + + +   meas. geom.   100%

Objective 0005   3/4 = 75%

2	5	15	27
+	+	+	–

+ + ⊤ −   meas + geom

Objective 0006   4/5 – 80%

6	21	24	44	52
–	+	+	+	+

− + + + −   meas. geom

Objective 0007   1/4 25%

14	22	43	60
–	+	✓	–

Ⓣ + + +   patterns, alg. , function

Objective   0008

patt, alg. function   3 /5 60%

3	10	28	46	51
+	+	+	—	—

+ + — + +

Objective   0009

patt./alg/ funct.   3 /5 60%

8	18	31	37	57
+	—	+	—	—

+ + — — +

Objective   0010

data analysis + prob.   4 /5 80%

data analysis + prob

④	12	29	34	53
+	—	+	+	+

+ + + + +

Objective   0011

1 /4 25%

16	23	39	45
+	—	—	—

+ — + —

Objective   0012

4 /4 100

Math Process + Procedure

13	30	36	49
+	+	+	+

+ + + +

Objective   0013

1 /4 25%

19	25	41	56
—	—	—	+

75%

+ — + +

Detailed Solutions

1. B.

To determine the part of $\frac{4}{5}$ that $\frac{1}{3}$ is, divide $\frac{1}{3}$ by $\frac{4}{5}$. Then $\frac{1}{3} \div \frac{4}{5} = (\frac{1}{3})(\frac{5}{4}) = \frac{5}{12}$.

2. C.

Because $DE = EF$, this figure is an isosceles triangle. Therefore, the measures of both $\angle D$ and $\angle F$ is 54°. Since the sum of all three angles of a triangle is 180°, the measure of $\angle E = 180° - 54° - 54° = 72°$.

3. D.

To factor $12ab + 14a - 6b - 7$, group terms that have common factors together. $(12ab - 6b) + (14a - 7)$. Then, factor out any common factors. $6b(2a - 1) + 7(2a - 1)$. Combine the "factored out" terms into one factor in parentheses $(6b + 7)$. The other factor is the common one of $(2a - 1)$. Therefore, the answer is $(6b + 7)(2a - 1)$.

4. C.

When analyzing data, the mode is the number that occurs most frequently. The value 7.0 occurs six times, which is more frequent than any of the other numbers.

5. B.

By the construction, $m\angle VMT = m\angle WMT$. There is already a right angle in each of triangles VMT and WMT. Since $\overline{MT}$ is an angle bisector, $TV = TW$. By the construction of the arc $\overset{\frown}{PR}$, we also know that $MP = MR$. Since $MW > MR$, it follows that $MW > MP$. Although it may appear that $m\angle VMW$ is greater than $m\angle VTM$, there are no numerical values to verify this statement. We would need to know the relationship between $m\angle VMT$ and $m\angle VTM$. Regarding these two angles, we can only state that $m\angle VMT + m\angle VTM = 90°$.

6. C.

Reflecting triangle ABC over the y-axis moves it to Quadrant 1. To move it to the position of triangle DEF, slide the triangle down six spaces.

7. A.

$0.\overline{25} = .252525\dots$, and $0.\overline{251} = .251251251$ $\dots$ Since $0.\overline{251}$ is actually less than $0.\overline{25}$, it cannot lie between 0.25 and 0.26.

8. D.

Choose any two points on the graph, for example (-1, 0) and (0, 2). The slope is equal to the change in y values divided by the change in x values, which is $\frac{2-0}{0-(-1)} = 2$.

9. B.

There are 25 squares in the grid, and 8 shaded squares represent $\frac{8}{25}$ of the total. $\frac{8}{25} = \frac{32}{100} = 0.32$.

10. A.

To determine the quotient, first factor the numerator and denominator to get $\frac{(3n-4)(n+6)}{(5m)(n+6)}$. Cancel the $(n + 6)$ from the numerator and denominator, which results in $\frac{3n-4}{5m}$.

11. B.

Convert 6 feet to inches (6 x 12 = 72 inches). Then, the ratio of $\frac{72}{30}$ can be reduced to $\frac{12}{5}$ by dividing the numerator and denominator by 6.

12. B.

The percent of people age 10 or less is $(100 - 5 - 22 - 18 - 30)\% = 25\%$. Thus, 25% + 22% = 47% of the people are either under 11 years old or over 40 years old. Let x represent the total population of Smallville. Then $0.47x = 282$, which means that $x = 600$. Since 5% + 30% = 35% of the population is between the ages of 11 and 30 inclusive, the number of people in this age bracket is $(0.35)(600) = 210$.

13. D.

First, distribute the 3 into the terms within the parentheses.

$2 + 3(x - 2) > 7$
$2 + 3x - 6 > 7$

Then, combine like terms and isolate the variable.

$3x - 4 > 7$
$3x > 11$

Divide both sides by 3 to get x $> \frac{11}{3}$. In set notation, this is equivalent to $(\frac{11}{3}, \infty)$.

14. B.

The restriction for the domain is that the quantity under the square root must be at least zero. This is equivalent to $-x + 1 \geq 0$, which can be simplified to $x \leq 1$.

15. D.

The lengths of corresponding sides of similar polygons are proportional. Therefore: $\frac{2.2}{1.5} = \frac{6.82}{m}$. Cross-multiply to get $2.2m = (1.5)(6.82) = 10.23$. Thus, $m = 4.65$.

16. C.

There are a total of 80 children who were surveyed. Since there were 12 children who chose rocky road as their favorite flavor, the required probability is $\frac{12}{80} = 15\%$.

17. C.

The distributive property of numbers states that for all real numbers a, b, and c, $a(b + c) = ab + ac$. In this example, $a = 3$, $b = 9$, and $c = 4$.

18. C.

This parabola faces upward, so the coefficient of the x^2 term must be positive. In addition, the graph passes through the point $(0, -3)$. Only answer choice (C) satisfies both of these conditions. As a check, note that the points $(2, -1)$ and $(-2, -1)$ lie on this graph. Both points satisfy the equation $y = \frac{1}{2}x^2 - 3$.

19. A.

Triangles ABC and ABD share a common base AB. Their heights are numerically equal, because they are represented by the perpendicular distance from line l to line m. Since the corresponding bases and heights are equal, the areas are the same.

20. A.

An irrational number is one that cannot be written as a quotient of two integers. Choice (B) is wrong because $\sqrt{9} = 3 = \frac{3}{1}$. Choice (C) is wrong because it is already written as a quotient of two integers. Choice (D) is wrong because $-2.57 = -\frac{257}{100}$. Choice (A) $\sqrt{7}$, cannot be written as the quotient of two integers.

21. C.

The distance (d) between any two points (x_1, y_1), (x_2, y_2) in the coordinate plane is: $d =$ square root of $(x_1 - x_2)^2 + (y_1 - y_2)^2$.

The problem can be calculated as: $d =$ square root of the quantity $(2 - 0)^2 + (3 - 6)^2 = \sqrt{4 + 9} = \sqrt{13}$.

The square root of 13 is approximately 3.6.

22. B.

In this pattern, the difference between the first two numbers is 9, the difference between the second and third number is 6, and the pattern continues. (A difference of 9, followed by a difference of 6.) After the number 44, the next number needs to be a difference of 9; thus, the answer is 53. Notice that the last number is 59, which is a difference of 6, and thus in agreement with this pattern.

23. C.

(P ∪ H) is the set that includes the children who would choose either pizza or a hot dog, or both. The complement of (P ∪ H) is the set containing the children who would choose neither pizza nor a hot dog. This set consists of Ethan and Kay.

24. C.

The midpoint of $\overline{AB}$ is located at $(\frac{1+9}{2}, \frac{2+6}{2}) = (5,4)$. When a point is reflected about the x-axis, its x value remains unchanged and its y value simply changes sign. Thus, the reflection of $(5, 4)$ is $(5, -4)$.

25. D.

If $\angle 1 \cong 2$, then triangles ABC and ACD would have two pairs of congruent sides and a pair of non-inclusive congruent angles. This would be insufficient to prove that the triangles are congruent. This means that we cannot conclude that $\angle ACB \cong \angle ACD$, which further implies that we cannot conclude that $\overline{AC}$ is perpendicular to $\overline{BD}$.

Answer choice (A) would imply that $\triangle ABC \cong \triangle ADC$ by side-angle-side, so $\angle ACB \cong \angle ACD$ by corresponding parts. This would imply that $\overline{AC}$ is perpendicular to $\overline{BD}$.

Answer choice (B) would already establish that since $\angle B \cong \angle D$, $\angle ACB \cong \angle ACD$. Thus, we would conclude that $\overline{AC}$ is perpendicular to $\overline{BD}$.

Answer choice (C) would imply that $\triangle ACB \cong \triangle ACD$ by side-side-side, so $\angle ACB \cong \angle ACD$ by corresponding parts. This would imply that $\overline{AC}$ is perpendicular to $\overline{BD}$.

26. A.

To solve this problem, find two numbers whose difference is 12. We note that $2 - (-10) = 12$. For each of the other answer choices, the difference between the two given numbers is less than 12.

27. B.

The value of EC, which is a diagonal of the base, is found by using the Pythagorean theorem. So, $EC = \sqrt{2^2 + 3^2} = \sqrt{13}$. Using the Pythagorean theorem for $\triangle BEC$, $BE = \sqrt{6^2 + (\sqrt{13})^2} = \sqrt{49} = 7$.

28. A.

To solve for x, first distribute the fractions to eliminate the parentheses to get $\frac{2}{3}x + \frac{10}{3} = \frac{1}{4}x + \frac{1}{2}$.

Multiply each term by 12, which is the least common multiple. This operation yields $8x + 40 = 3x + 6$. This equation simplifies to $5x = -34$, so $x = -\frac{34}{5}$.

29. C.

If Kelly improves her sales by 50%, she will sell $2 + (0.50)(2) = 3$ homes. If André improves his sales by 100%, he will sell $3 + (1.00)(3) = 6$ homes. Ted will still sell 5 homes and Maya will still sell 6 homes. This means that A-Plus will sell a total of $3 + 6 + 5 + 6 = 20$ homes, so that the fraction of homes that Kelly will have sold is $\frac{3}{20}$.

30. A.

Using the ordered pair $(0, 2)$, each of the answer choices (B), (C), and (D) can be shown to be wrong. However, each of the ordered pairs satisfies the equation in answer choice (A).

31. B.

Since $g(f(x)) = x$, $g(x)$ must represent the inverse function of $f(x)$. Let $y = 3x - 5$. In order to find the inverse function, switch the variables. Then $x = 3y - 5$. The next step is to solve for y. So, $3y = x + 5$, which means that $y = \frac{x+5}{3}$. This is the expression for $g(x)$.

32. C.

To find the amount of gift paper needed to cover the box, find the surface area. This prism has two rectangular faces that measure 8 inches by 4 inches, two rectangular bases that measure 8 inches by 3 inches, and two rectangular bases that measure 4 inches by 3 inches. Therefore, the surface area is $(2)(8)(4) + (2)(8)(3) + (2)(4)(3) = 64 + 48 + 24 = 136$ square inches.

33. B.

The interval between -2 and -3 is broken into 5 equal intervals. Therefore, each interval is equal to $\frac{1}{5}$ or 0.2. Therefore, point P is located at $-3 + 0.2 = -2.8$ on the number line.

34. A.

The first 46 students exiting the building would provide the most random representative sample, because there would most likely be a mix of genders and grade levels. In choice (B), Allison would only ask girls, which is not a representative sample of the population of the school (assuming it is not a girls-only school). In choice (C), the 25 students in Mrs. Jackson's English class are not a representative sample, because they all come from one class. In choice (D), the six students on the bus might be somewhat representative, but six students is not an adequate sample size.

35. A.

To simplify this expression, follow the order of operations, which means eliminate the parentheses first. This results in $\dfrac{3^2}{a^2} \times \dfrac{a^4}{3^4}$. Then, use the rules of division of exponents to reduce this product to $\dfrac{a^2}{3^2} = \dfrac{a^2}{9}$.

36. D.

A line segment has two endpoints, whereas a ray begins with an endpoint and extends indefinitely in one direction. Therefore, we can eliminate answer choice (A), which defines ray MO as a line. We can also eliminate answer choice (B), which defines ray MO as a line segment. We can eliminate answer choice (C) because the measure of $\angle MNP$ is $180° - 50° = 130°$, not $50°$. The marked angles are vertical angles because they are not adjacent, and they are formed by two intersecting lines. Choice (D) is the only remaining choice that identifies those angles as vertical.

37. B.

Rewrite the original function as $y = 3x^2 - 2$. In order to determine the inverse function $h^{-1}(x)$, switch the positions of x and y. Then $x = 3y^2 - 2$, which can be written as $3y^2 = x + 2$. Upon dividing both sides by 3, we get $y^2 = \dfrac{x+2}{3}$. Thus, $y = \sqrt{\dfrac{x+2}{3}}$.

38. D.

The multiplicative inverses of 3 and 5 are $\dfrac{1}{3}$ and $\dfrac{1}{5}$, respectively. Their sum is $\dfrac{5}{15} + \dfrac{3}{15} = \dfrac{8}{15}$. This is the multiplicative inverse of $\dfrac{15}{8}$.

39. C.

If the first die shows a 6, you need to determine how many possibilities on the second die would result in a sum greater than 9. In this case, you would need to roll a 4, 5, or 6. This represents three of the six possible numbers that you could roll. Therefore, the required probability is $\dfrac{3}{6} = \dfrac{1}{2}$.

40. A.

To determine the height of the center of the tepee, use the Pythagorean theorem. In this case, the base of the triangle is 5.1 feet and the hypotenuse is 8.5 feet. Set up an equation, with h being the height of the tepee. Then $(5.1)^2 + h^2 = (8.5)^2$, which becomes $26.01 + h^2 = 72.25$. So, $h^2 = 72.25 - 26.01 = 46.24$. Thus, $h = \sqrt{46.24} = 6.8$ feet.

41. D.

Neither of answer choices (A) and (B) can be deduced because only some shrubs flower. Answer choice (C) is a contradiction of statement B. Thus, answer choice (D) is correct.

42. B.

To write 0.000091 in scientific notation, move the decimal point to the right until there is only one nonzero digit to the left of the decimal point (in this case 9.1). Count the number of places you moved the decimal. The number of places you moved the decimal will be the exponent in the power of ten (in this case, five places). Since you moved the decimal point to the right, the exponent will be negative.

43. A.

The first step in the solution is to determine how many hours of work there are to complete. Since it would take 3 volunteers 96 hours, we know that $3 \times 96 = 288$ hours of work are needed. If 8 volunteers showed up to work, divide 288 by 8 to determine how many hours the job would take. Thus, the number of hours required is $288 \div 8 = 36$.

44. C.

In a reflection over l_1, it must be true that l_1 is the perpendicular bisector of any segment PP', where P' is the image of P.

45. C.

The number of ways to assign the left-most seat is 8, since two people cannot be seated there. The number of remaining ways to assign the right-most seat is 7, since one person has already been assigned to the left-most seat. Remember that there are an additional two people who cannot be assigned to either end seat. Since there are no restrictions on the assignment of the remaining 8 seats, they can be assigned in $8! = (8)(7)(6)(\dots)(1) = 40,320$ ways. Thus, the number of ways to seat all ten people is $(8)(8!)(7) = 2,257,920$.

46. D.

The area of the shaded region is equal to the area of the large rectangle minus the area of the small rectangle. That is represented by:

$(5a + 3)(4a + 1) - 3a - 1 (a+2)$

Using the FOIL method, eliminate the parentheses.

$20a^2 + 17a + 3 - 3a^2 - 5a + 2$

Combine like terms to get $17a^2 + 12a + 5$, which represents the part of the large rectangle that is shaded.

47. B.

The net of a cylinder consists of a rectangle and two circles.

48. C.

The number 984 can be written as $2^3 \times 3^1 \times 41^1$. The total number of factors is determined by increasing each exponent by 1, then multiplying those numbers together. In this case $(4)(2)(2) = 16$. However, this number includes the factors of 1 and 984. Remove these numbers to get the answer of 14 factors.

49. A.

$(x + 2)$ is represented on the top row and $(x + 1)$ is represented on the left-most column. The long side of each rectangle is x and the short side is 1. Each square also has a side of 1. The multiplication is shown by the combined areas of one large square (x^2), three rectangles ($3x$), and two small squares (2).

50. B.

We need to find the least common multiple of 5, 9, and 6. This can be accomplished by writing the prime factorization for each number. 5 is already factored into its prime form.

$9 = 3 \times 3$
$6 = 2 \times 3$

Now, identify the highest power of each prime factor, and multiply them together. Thus, the least common multiple is $2^1 \times 3^2 \times 5^1 = 90$.

51. C.

First, find expressions that represent the population for each city in future years.

Cullman: In y years, the population will be $50,000 + 2400y$ (the current population plus 2400 residents yearly).

Hartselle: In y years, the population will be $77,000 - 600y$ (the current population minus 600 residents yearly).

The population of these two cities will be the same when the two expressions are equal. Therefore, set the expressions equal to each other and solve for y.

$50,000 + 2400y = 77,000 - 600y$
$2400y + 600y = 77,000 - 50,000$
$3000y = 27,000$
$y = 9$

Thus, it will take 9 years for the populations to be the same.

52. D.

If a point located at (x, y) is rotated 90° clockwise about the origin, its new location is given by $(y, -x)$. Thus, the point $(2, -3)$ becomes $(-3, -2)$.

53. A.

When 23 is added, the numbers will appear in ascending order as follows: 21, 21, 23, 26, 28, 30, 32, 32. The median will equal the mean of the middle two numbers. Therefore, the median equals $\frac{26+28}{2} = 27$.

54. B.

Let $N = 0.1\overline{24}$. Then $100N = 12.4\overline{24}$. By subtraction, the repeated digits denoted as $\overline{24}$ will "subtract out." Thus, $12.4\overline{24} - 0.1\overline{24}$ becomes equivalent to $12.4 - 0.1 = 12.3$. Then $99N = 12.3$. Thus, $N = \frac{12.3}{99} = \frac{123}{990}$, which reduces to $\frac{41}{330}$.

55. C.

To find the area of the model, first find the length and width of the model, using the scale factor.

$$\text{length} = \frac{1}{10} \times 15 = 1.5$$

$$\text{width} = \frac{1}{10} \times 12 = 1.2$$

Then, multiply the length times the width to get the area.

$$1.5 \times 1.2 = 1.8 \text{ square feet}$$

56. D.

The first step in solving this equation is to put all x terms on one side of the equation. This can be accomplished by adding 7 to both sides. The equation is then simplified to $\frac{3}{8}x = 17$. The final step is to divide each side by $\frac{3}{8}$, which is equivalent to multiplying by the reciprocal of $\frac{3}{8}$. (Note that the reciprocal of $\frac{3}{8}$ is $\frac{8}{3}$.)

57. D.

$0.15 per one-fourth mile is equivalent to $0.60 per mile. Since Mike is traveling 20 miles, his total cost will be the sum of the initial cost and $0.60 per mile for each mile. This is equivalent to the expression $2.50 + ($0.60)(20)$.

58. A.

Remembering the mnemonic *Please Excuse My Dear Aunt Sally* for the order of operations will help you find the answer. The sequence of steps is: Parentheses, Exponents, Multiply, Divide, Add, Subtract. Therefore, in this expression, the subtraction is last. (The actual answer is -19.)

59. C.

To find the volume of the cone, first find the area of the circular base. $B = \pi r^2$. The diameter of the cone is given as 6 cm. Therefore, use half of that (3) as the radius. Thus, $B = \pi 3^2 = 9\pi$. Then, use B to find the volume.

$$V = \frac{1}{3}(B \times h)$$

$$V = \frac{1}{3}(9\pi \times 14)$$

$$V = \frac{1}{3}(126 \times 3.14)$$

$$V = \frac{1}{3}(395.64)$$

$V = 131.88$ cubic cm., which is rounded off to 132.

60. A.

The graph of $g(x)$ is a semicircle that passes through $(-4, 0)$, $(0, 4)$, and $(4, 0)$. The segment whose endpoints are $(-4, 0)$ and $(4, 0)$ is the diameter. The lowest y value is zero, and this value is found at each endpoint of the diameter. The highest y value is found at $(0, 4)$. Thus, the range is all numbers between 0 and 4, inclusive.

Constructed-Response Items

61.

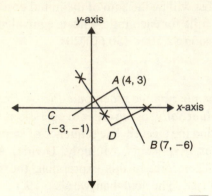

- Draw the line segments $\overline{AC}$ and $\overline{AB}$. Construct the perpendicular bisector of each of these segments, as shown above. The point of intersection D of these perpendicular bisectors is equidistant from A, B, and C. Point D is the center of the circle that contains points A, B, and C.

- The area of each walkway is $(114)(4) = 456$ square feet. The cost of each walkway is $(\$15)(456) = \$6840$. Thus, the cost of three walkways is $\$20,520$.

62.

- At the Sleep-Easy Motel, the cost for a single night, including the 8% tax followed by the $10 discount, is $(\$90)(1.08) - \$10 = \$87.20$. So, the cost for four nights is $\$348.80$.

- At the Rest-Well Motel, the cost of a single night, including the discount followed by the 8% sales tax, is $(\$90 - \$10)(1.08) = \$86.40$. So, the cost for four nights is $\$345.60$.

- Let x represent the discount at the Rest-Well Motel. In order for the cost to be the same at both motels for a single night, we need to solve the equation $(\$90 - x)(1.08) = \$87.20$. This equation can be written as $97.20 - 1.08x = 87.20$. Then $1.08x = 10$, so $x \approx \$9.26$.

Practice Test 2

GACE 013 MIDDLE GRADES MATH

ANSWER SHEET FOR PRACTICE TEST 2

1 _____	16 _____	31 _____	46 _____
2 _____	17 _____	32 _____	47 _____
3 _____	18 _____	33 _____	48 _____
4 _____	19 _____	34 _____	49 _____
5 _____	20 _____	35 _____	50 _____
6 _____	21 _____	36 _____	51 _____
7 _____	22 _____	37 _____	52 _____
8 _____	23 _____	38 _____	53 _____
9 _____	24 _____	39 _____	54 _____
10 _____	25 _____	40 _____	55 _____
11 _____	26 _____	41 _____	56 _____
12 _____	27 _____	42 _____	57 _____
13 _____	28 _____	43 _____	58 _____
14 _____	29 _____	44 _____	59 _____
15 _____	30 _____	45 _____	60 _____

ANSWER SHEET FOR CONSTRUCTED-RESPONSE QUESTIONS

1. Which of the following is equivalent to 50^{24}?

   A. $(50^6)^4$ C. $(5^6)^4$

   B. $50^6 \times 50^4$ D. $5^5 \times 50^4$

2. Triangle *DEF* has two congruent angles. What information must be true about these congruent angles?

   A. They are acute.

   B. They are right.

   C. They are obtuse.

   D. There is insufficient information to determine the answer.

3. What is the simplified form for $\dfrac{6b^3}{5c^5d^4} \div \dfrac{1}{15c^3d}$?

   A. $\dfrac{2b^3}{c^2d^3}$ C. $\dfrac{18b^3d^3}{c^2}$

   B. $\dfrac{12b^3c^2}{d^3}$ D. $\dfrac{18b^3}{c^2d^3}$

4. Which of the following groups of data has two modes?

   A. 2, 2, 3, 3, 4, 4, 5, 6, 7

   B. 2, 2, 2, 3, 3, 4, 4, 4, 5

   C. 2, 3, 3, 4, 4, 4, 5, 5, 6

   D. 2, 3, 3, 3, 3, 4, 5, 6, 6

5. Louis is a landscaper. Everyone who uses Louis's Landscaping Service has a beautiful yard. Betty has a beautiful yard. What can you deduce about Betty?

   A. Betty always uses Louis's Landscaping Service.

   B. This week, Betty used Louis's Landscaping Service.

   C. You cannot deduce anything for certain about whether Betty uses Louis's Landscaping Service.

   D. Betty does not use Louis's Landscaping Service.

6. What are the coordinates of the midpoint of a line segment with endpoints $(-8, 5)$ and $(16, -17)$?

   A. $(4, 6)$ C. $(4, -6)$

   B. $(-4, 0)$ D. $(-4, -6)$

7. Which of these numbers is the largest prime number less than 60?

   A. 47   C. 57

   B. 51   D. 59

8. What is the solution for x in the inequality $2x^2 - x - 3 < 0$?

   A. $-1 < x < \dfrac{3}{2}$ C. $-\dfrac{3}{2} < x < 1$

   B. $x > \dfrac{3}{2}$ or $x < -1$ D. $x > 1$ or $x < -\dfrac{3}{2}$

9. A bacterium is about 2.8×10^{-3} mm in length. What is this number in standard notation?

   A. 0.028 mm   C. 0.28 mm

   B. 0.0028 mm   D. 0.00028 mm

10. What is the range of values for which $|8x + 3| \leq 7$ is satisfied?

    A. $-\dfrac{1}{2} \leq x \leq \dfrac{5}{4}$ C. $-\dfrac{5}{4} \leq x \leq -\dfrac{1}{2}$

    B. $\dfrac{1}{2} \leq x \leq \dfrac{5}{4}$ D. $-\dfrac{5}{4} \leq x \leq \dfrac{1}{2}$

11. Jared ran the mile run in $6\dfrac{3}{10}$ minutes. The school record for that distance is $5\dfrac{4}{5}$ minutes. How far is Jared from matching the school record?

    A. 15 seconds   C. 30 seconds

    B. 20 seconds   D. 45 seconds

12. An AP statistics teacher wants to provide her students with a concrete example of a data set that illustrates the normal curve. Select her best choice from the examples below.

   A. The shoe sizes of the 15 students in her class

   B. The weight of all the 17 year olds in the country

   C. The number of times out of one hundred that a flipped penny will land on heads

   D. The height of the students in the high school

13. Which expression means "multiply the sum of six cubed and −9 by −3"?

   A. $(-3)(6+(-9))^3$

   B. $(-3)(6^3+(-9))$

   C. $(-3) \times 6^3 + 9$

   D. $(6^3)(-9 \times -3)$

14. Which number comes next in the following sequence: 3, 5, 9, 17, 33, ___?

   A. 60

   B. 65

   C. 66

   D. 63

15. If the hypotenuse of a right triangle is $x + 1$ and one of the legs is x, then the other leg is

   A. $\sqrt{2x+1}$

   B. $\sqrt{2x}+1$

   C. $\sqrt{x^2+(x+1)^2}$

   D. $\sqrt{2x}-1$

16. Eight red chips and 10 yellow chips are in a bag. If a girl pulls one chip from the bag at random, what are the odds in favor of her drawing a yellow chip?

   A. 8:20

   B. 10:20

   C. 10:8

   D. 18:8

17. In calculating the value of $3 + 6^2 \div (7 \cdot 2 - 2) \cdot 4$, which one of the following operations would not be used?

   A. Dividing 36 by 12

   B. Subtracting 2 from 14

   C. Multiplying 3 by 4

   D. Adding 3 to 36

18. Which shaded region represents the conditions $x \geq 0$ and $-3 < y < 3$?

A.

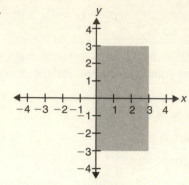

B.

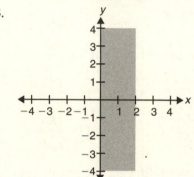

C.

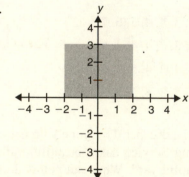

D.

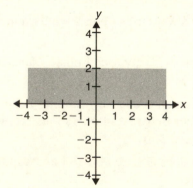

19. Consider the following statements:

    All people wearing hats have green eyes.

    Some of the people have brown eyes.

    All people who have green eyes like hamburgers.

    People who have brown eyes like pizza.

    Patrick has green eyes.

    Which of the following statements must be true?

    A. Patrick likes hamburgers.

    B. Patrick is wearing jeans.

    C. Patrick likes pizza.

    D. Patrick is wearing a hat.

20. The decimal $0.1\overline{5}$, expressed as a fraction in lowest terms is:

    A. $\dfrac{3}{20}$

    B. $\dfrac{15}{100}$

    C. $\dfrac{5}{33}$

    D. $\dfrac{1}{6}$

21. Consider the following figure.

    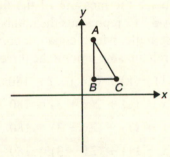

    Which of the following triangles $A' B' C'$ is the image of triangle ABC that results from reflecting triangle *ABC* across the *y*-axis?

    A.

    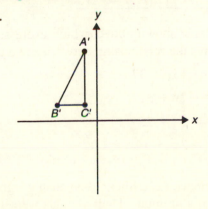

    B.

    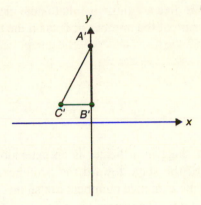

    C.

    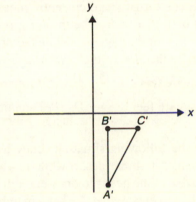

    D.

    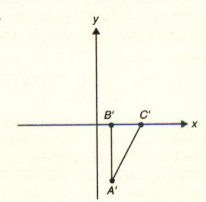

22. What is the range of the function $f(x) = -x^2 - 3x + 4$?

    A. All numbers less than or equal to -1.5

    B. All numbers between -1 and 4, inclusive

    C. All numbers less than or equal to 6.25

    D. All numbers between -4 and 1, inclusive

23. If two fair dice are thrown, what is the probability that the sum of the number of dots on the top faces will be 5?

A. $\dfrac{1}{12}$ C. $\dfrac{1}{4}$

B. $\dfrac{1}{9}$ D. $\dfrac{5}{12}$

24. A thrust stage in a theater is an extension of the middle of the stage toward the audience, so that some of the audience members can sit on each side to view the performance. The Cleveland Community Theater's thrust stage currently measures 12 feet long by 8 feet wide. The theater group wants to enlarge the thrust stage by a scale factor of 1.25. What will be the area of the new thrust stage?

A. 96 square feet   C. 150 square feet

B. 124 square feet   D. 192 square feet

25. Consider the following situation: Lucy has a bag that contains 5 red marbles, 5 white marbles, and 5 blue marbles. She needs to draw enough marbles from the bag to ensure that she has a matching pair (2 reds, 2 whites, or 2 blues). Which strategy would be most appropriate to use to solve this problem?

A. Construct a table   C. Work backwards

B. Guess and check   D. Draw a diagram

26. Antonio opened a checking account at his neighborhood bank. To use his ATM card, he needed to establish a 4-digit PIN. His birthday is June 24, 1986, and he decided to use the least common multiple of the numbers in his birthday, which are 6, 24, and 86. What is Antonio's PIN?

A. 1,024   C. 1,048

B. 1,032   D. 1,064

27. In the figure below, the two horizontal lines are parallel. What is the value of a?

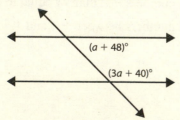

A. 20   C. 23

B. 22   D. 30

28. Two pounds of pears and one pound of peaches cost \$1.40. Three pounds of pears and two pounds of peaches cost \$2.40. How much is the combined cost of one pound of pears and one pound of peaches?

A. \$1.90   C. \$1.30

B. \$1.60   D. \$1.00

29. The mean of a group of 20 numbers is 9. If one number is removed, the mean of the remaining numbers is 7. What is the value of the removed number?

A. 16   C. 40

B. 25   D. 47

30. The sum of 3 angles of a triangle is 180°. The second angle is 11° less than the first angle. The third angle is twice the measure of the first angle increased by 3. If x represents the number of degrees in the first angle, which equation correctly represents the relationship among the three angles?

A. $x + (11 - x) + (2x + 3) = 180$

B. $x + (x - 11) + 2(x + 3) = 180$

C. $x + (x - 11) + (2x + 3) = 180$

D. $x + (x - 11) + (2x - 3) = 180$

31.

x	1	2	3	4
y	24	17	−2	−39

In the table shown above, which expression best represents the relationship between x and y?

A. $y = -13x + 37$

B. $y = -7x + 31$

C. $y = -x^3 + 25$

D. $y = -7x^2 + 14x + 17$

32. For a science experiment, Savannah weighed four pieces of aluminum. Their weights were 15.64 g,

15.69 g, 0.01566 kg, and 0.01565 kg. What is the average weight of these pieces of aluminum?

A.   15.70g

B.   15.66 g

C.   0.1569 kg

D.   0.1568 kg

33.

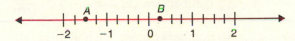

Using the number line shown above, which one of the following is the best approximation to the product of the numbers associated with points A and B.

A. $-\dfrac{5}{4}$

C. $-\dfrac{5}{8}$

B. $-\dfrac{3}{4}$

D. $-\dfrac{3}{8}$

34.   Read the graph below, then answer the question.

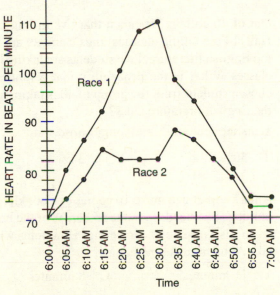

A runner has her heartbeat recorded for two 10.1-mile races run in the same park near her home, held on different days, and both starting at 6:00 a.m. Which of the following is true at 6:20 a.m. for the recorded heart rates for Race #1 and Race #2?

A.   Both recorded heart rates are increasing.

B.   Both recorded heart rates are decreasing.

C.   The recorded heart rate for Race #1 is increasing, and the recorded heart rate for Race #2 is stable.

D.   The recorded heart rate for Race #1 is stable, and the recorded heart rate for Race #2 is increasing.

35.   Kathleen wanted to make an international phone call. The cost of the call is $0.40 for the first three minutes and $0.13 for each additional minute. To the nearest minute, how long can Kathleen talk for $5.00?

A.   30 minutes

B.   35 minutes

C.   38 minutes

D.   42 minutes

36.   Consider the following graph.

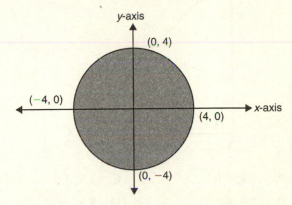

Which of the following inequalities describes the shaded region?

A. $x^2 + y^2 \leq 16$

B. $x^2 - y^2 \leq 16$

C. $x^2 + y^2 \geq 16$

D. $x^2 - y^2 \geq 16$

37.   What is the equation of the line that is parallel to $6x + 3y = 4$ and has a y-intercept of -6?

A. $y = 2x - 6$

C. $y = -2x - \dfrac{4}{3}$

B. $y = 2x + \dfrac{4}{3}$

D. $y = -2x - 6$

38.   Which of the following identities uses <u>both</u> the distributive and commutative properties of numbers?

A. $(8)(6 + 5) = (8)(5) + (8)(6)$

B. $(4)(3 + 2) = (4)(3) + (4)(2)$

C. $(5)(6 + 4) = (6 + 4)(5)$

D. $(7)(2 + 5) = (7)(2) + 5$

39.   How many games would it take a baseball coach to try every possible batting order with his nine players?

A. 9

B. 45

C. 81

D. 362,880

40. In triangle *ABC*, angle *A* is a right angle, and the length of *BC* is 7.0. What are the lengths of sides *AB* and *AC*?

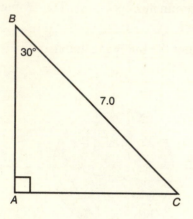

A. 4.9, 4.9

B. 2.0, 6.1

C. 3.5, 4.9

D. 3.5 , 6.1

41.

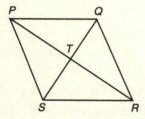

In the figure above, which of the following describes sufficient conditions in order for PQRS to be classified as a rhombus?

A. $\overline{PQ} = \overline{QR} = \overline{RS} = \overline{SP}$

B. $\overline{SP}$ is parallel to $\overline{QR}$ and $\overline{PQ}$ is parallel to $\overline{RS}$

C. $\overline{PR}$ and $\overline{QS}$ are perpendicular bisectors of each other

D. $\angle QPS \cong \angle QRS$ and $\angle PSR \cong \angle PQR$

42. In July 2004 there were approximately 293,000,000 people living in the United States. How is this number written in scientific notation?

A. 29.3×10^7

B. 293.0×10^6

C. 2.93×10^8

D. 29.3×10^9

43. What is the domain of the function $\dfrac{(2x^2 + 13x - 15)}{(2x^2 - x - 15)}$?

A. All numbers except $-\dfrac{13}{2}$ and 1

B. All numbers except $\dfrac{5}{2}$ and -3

C. All numbers except $-\dfrac{5}{2}$ and 3

D. All numbers except $\dfrac{15}{2}$ and -1

44. Rectangle *ABCD* is bisected by line *MN*, which contains the midpoints of two opposite sides. Suppose rectangle *ABCD* is rotated 360° around the axis of line *MN*. What shape does this generate?

A. Sphere

B. Cube

C. Rectangular prism

D. Cylinder

45. Out of 40 college freshmen that live in Lagrange Hall, 14 are taking classical music and 29 are taking English literature. Five students are taking both classes. What is the probability that a randomly chosen student from the group of 40 is taking only the English literature class?

A. 60%

B. 50%

C. 40%

D. 30%

46. Anna's copier can make 10 copies of a booklet in 2 minutes. She needs to make 55 copies of the booklet to disseminate at a meeting. How long will it take Anna to make the copies?

A. 11 minutes

B. 10 minutes

C. 8 minutes

D. 12 minutes

47. A rectangular piece of cloth has an area of 24 square inches and a perimeter of 22 inches. Which of the following are possible dimensions of the cloth?

A. 6 inches by 4 inches

B. 8 inches by 3 inches

C. 24 inches by 1 inch

D. 12 inches by 2 inches

48. What is the smallest positive even number that is the product of five different prime numbers?

    A. 15,015   C. 2310

    B. 10,395   D. 1890

49. Which one of the following represents an experiment for which the probability is equal to $\frac{1}{221}$?

    A. Drawing two aces, one at a time, with no replacement, from a deck of 52 cards

    B. Drawing two jacks, one at a time, with replacement, from a deck of 52 cards

    C. Drawing two slips of paper, numbered 13 and 17, one at a time, with no replacement, from a jar with 17 slips of paper numbered 1 through 17

    D. Drawing two slips of paper, numbered 13 and 17, one at a time, with replacement, from a jar with 30 slips of paper numbered 1 through 30

50. Larkwood Public Library identifies its books with a special number. They use a 6-digit code, where the number named by the first five digits is divisible by the sixth digit. Which of the following books does not belong to Larkwood Public Library?

    A. 12561-3   C. 38470-5

    B. 29648-4   D. 51352-6

51. Which one of the following has the same value as $-|-8-(-5)|$?

    A. $|-8-5|$

    B. $|-8-(-5)|$

    C. $-|5-(-8)|$

    D. $-|5-8|$

52. The vertices of triangle DEF are located at points D: (3, 1), E: (−2, 6) and F:(− 3,0). Which is the best description for this triangle?

    A. Right triangle

    B. Isosceles triangle

    C. Scalene triangle

    D. Equilateral triangle

53. The four exam scores for each of five students are given in the chart below. If student #3 takes a fifth exam, what score is needed so that this student achieves an average score of 90?

Student	Exam Scores				Total
#1	75	85	80	92	332
#2	67	80	75	82	304
#3	83	88	95	90	356
#4	94	82	87	77	340
#5	83	70	78	85	316

    A. 90   C. 94

    B. 92   D. 96

54. How many digits are in the number $2^{31} \times 5^{27}$?

    A. 31   C. 28

    B. 29   D. 26

55. Select the solid figure from the four choices which would result when the flat paper pattern below is folded up.

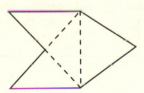

A.   C.

B. 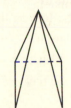   D.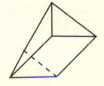

56.

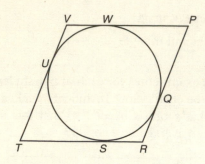

Note: Figure is not drawn to scale.

In the figure above, $\overline{PR}$, $\overline{RT}$, $\overline{TV}$, and $\overline{VP}$ are tangents to the circle at points Q, S, U, and W, respectively. The perimeter of $PRTV$ is 28 and $PW = 4$. Which of the following must be true?

A. $PR = RT$

B. $VW = 3$

C. $PR + TV = 14$

D. $m\angle P = m\angle T$

57. A function contains the points $(8, 3)$, $(-1, -3)$, $(-2, 6)$, and $(7, 6)$. Which one of the following must be a point belonging to the inverse of this function?

A. $(3, -8)$ C. $(-2, 7)$

B. $(1, 3)$ D. $(6, 7)$

58. In order to evaluate $4^2 - \dfrac{3}{4} \div \dfrac{2}{3} + \dfrac{1}{2} \times \dfrac{3}{5}$, for which number would the calculation of its reciprocal be required?

A. $\dfrac{3}{4}$ C. $\dfrac{3}{5}$

B. $\dfrac{2}{3}$ D. $\dfrac{1}{2}$

59. A cat is stuck on a limb of a tree. A firefighter places a 26-foot ladder against the tree, with the top of the ladder on the limb, and the bottom of the ladder placed 24 feet from the tree. What is the distance from the bottom of the tree to the limb where the cat is stuck?

A. 10 feet   C. 14 feet

B. 12 feet   D. 20 feet

60. At South College, the average male high jumper is 6'4" and averages 6'10" in his high jumps. At nearby East Central Junior High, the average height of the female high jumpers is 5'6". To the nearest inch, how high should the female athletes jump in order that the ratio of height to distance jumped is the same ratio as for the male athletes?

A. 5'8"   C. 5'11"

B. 5'10"   D. 6'2"

Constructed-Response Questions

61.

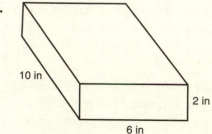

- Find the volume of this box. Show how you found your answer.
- Find the surface area of this box. show how you found your answer.
- Find the dimensions of a box that has the same volume but less surface area. Show how you found your answer.

62. Two trucks leave a warehouse at the same time. Truck A travels east at 50 mph and Truck B travels north at 60 mph.

- If Truck A reaches its destination in 2 hours and Truck B reaches its destination in 3 hours, how many miles apart will they be?
- Suppose Truck C travels from Truck A's destination to Truck B's destination. If Truck C travels at 40 mph for half the distance of this trip, how fast will it need to travel for the remaining distance in order to complete its entire trip in 4 hours? (Figure to the nearest $\dfrac{1}{10}$ mph.)
- Using the first quadrant of an xy-coordinate system, draw a representation of the trip of each truck. Use the y-axis to represent the path of truck B and the x-axis to represent the path of truck A. Each axis should be labeled: *Miles*.

ANSWER KEY – MATHEMATICS PRACTICE TEST 2

Question Number	Answer	Chapter	GACE Test Objective
1	A	Number and Operations	3
2	A	Measurement and Geometry	5
3	D	Patterns, Algebra, and Functions	8
4	B	Data Analysis and Probability	10
5	C	Math Processes and Procedures	13
6	C	Measurement and Geometry	6
7	D	Number and Operations	1
8	A	Patterns, Algebra, and Functions	9
9	B	Number and Operations	2
10	D	Patterns, Algebra, and Functions	8
11	C	Measurement and Geometry	4
12	D	Data Analysis and Probability	10
13	B	Math Processes and Procedures	12
14	B	Patterns, Algebra, and Functions	7
15	A	Measurement and Geometry	5
16	C	Data Analysis and Probability	11
17	D	Number and Operations	3
18	A	Patterns, Algebra, and Functions	9
19	A	Math Processes and Procedures	13
20	C	Number and Operations	2
21	A	Measurement and Geometry	6
22	C	Patterns, Algebra, and Functions	7
23	B	Data Analysis and Probability	11
24	C	Measurement and Geometry	6
25	D	Math Processes and Procedures	13
26	B	Number and Operations	1
27	C	Measurement and Geometry	5
28	D	Patterns, Algebra, and Functions	9

Question Number	Answer	Chapter	GACE Test Objective
29	D	Data Analysis and Probability	10
30	C	Math Processes and Procedures	12
31	C	Patterns, Algebra, and Functions	9
32	B	Data Analysis and Probability	10
33	D	Number and Operations	2
34	C	Data Analysis and Probability	10
35	C	Patterns, Algebra, and Functions	9
36	A	Measurement and Geometry	6
37	D	Patterns, Algebra, and Functions	9
38	A	Number and Operations	3
39	D	Data Analysis and Probability	11
40	D	Measurement and Geometry	5
41	C	Measurement and Geometry	5
42	C	Number and Operations	2
43	C	Patterns, Algebra, and Functions	7
44	D	Measurement and Geometry	6
45	A	Data Analysis and Probability	11
46	A	Patterns, Algebra, and Functions	8
47	B	Measurement and Geometry	4
48	C	Number and Operations	1
49	A	Data Analysis and Probability	11
50	D	Number and Operations	1
51	D	Number and Operations	3
52	B	Measurement and Geometry	6
53	C	Data Analysis and Probability	10
54	B	Number and Operations	2
55	A	Measurement and Geometry	4
56	C	Math Processes and Procedures	13
57	D	Patterns, Algebra, and Functions	9
58	B	Number and Operations	3

Question Number	Answer	Chapter	GACE Test Objective
59	A	Measurement and Geometry	5
60	C	Patterns, Algebra, and Functions	7
61	–	Constructed-Response: Measurement and Geometry	
62	–	Constructed-Response: Patterns, Algebra, and Functions	

Practice Test 2 Progress Chart

Objective 0001   _4_ /4 100%

7	26	48	50
+	+	+	+

Objective 0002   _5_ /5 100%

9	20	33	42	54
+	+	+	+	+

Objective 0003   _5_ /5 100%

1	17	38	51	58
+	+	+	+	+

Objective 0004   _3_ /3 100%

11	47	55
+	+	+

Objective 0005   _5_ /6 83%

2	15	27	40	41	59
+	+	+	+	–	+

Objective 0006   _4_ /6 67%

6	21	24	36	44	52
+	–	–	+	+	+

Objective 0007   _3_ /4 75%

14	22	43	60
+	–	+	+

Objective   0008

3/3 100%

3	10	46
+	+	+

Objective   0009

5/7 71%

8	18	28	31	35	37	57
+	+	+	+	−	+	−

Objective   0010

3/6 50%

4	12	29	32	34	53
+	−	−	+	+	−

Objective   0011

4/5 80%

16	23	39	45	49
+	−	+	+	+

Objective   0012

2/2 100%

13	30
+	+

Objective   0013

2/4 50%

5	19	25	56
+	+	−	−

Detailed Solutions

1. A.

When an expression involving a base and an exponent is raised to an exponent, the base remains unchanged and the exponents are multiplied. Thus, $(50^6)^4 = 50^{24}$.

2. A.

If triangle DEF had two right angles or two obtuse angles, then the sum of all three angles would be greater than 180°. This is impossible, since the sum of the angle measures of a triangle is exactly 180°.

3. D.

In a division problem, we multiply by the reciprocal of the second quantity. Also, the exponents of common bases are subtracted. Thus, the solution becomes $\dfrac{6b^3}{5c^5d^4} \times \dfrac{15c^3d}{1} = \dfrac{90b^3c^3d}{5c^5d^4} = \dfrac{18b^3}{c^2d^3}$.

4. B.

The two modes are 2 and 4. Answer choice (A) is wrong since it has three modes. Answer choice (C) is wrong since 4 is the only mode. Answer choice (D) is wrong since 3 is the only mode.

5. C.

It is impossible to deduce anything for certain about Betty's use of Louis's Landscape Service. Just because she has a beautiful yard, that does not mean that Louis created it. It is possible, but nothing can be deduced for certain from the given information.

6. C.

The coordinates of the midpoint are given by

$\left(\dfrac{x_1 + x_2}{2}, \dfrac{y_1 + y_2}{2} \right)$. By substitution, the coordinates

are $\left(\dfrac{-8 + 16}{2}, \dfrac{5 + (-17)}{2} \right) = \left(\dfrac{8}{2}, \dfrac{-12}{2} \right) = (4, -6)$.

7. D.

A prime number is a number that can only be divided by 1 and itself. The largest prime number less than 60 is 59, which is choice (D). In choice (A), 47 is prime, but it is not the largest prime number less than 60. In choice (B), 51 is not prime because it can be divided by 3. In choice (C), 57 is not prime because it can also be divided by 3.

8. A.

Factor the left side of the inequality to get $(2x - 3)(x + 1) < 0$. If $2x - 3 > 0$ and $x + 1 < 0$, we get $x > \dfrac{3}{2}$ and $x < -1$, which is impossible. If $2x - 3 < 0$ and $x + 1 > 0$, we have the actual solution of $-1 < x < \dfrac{3}{2}$.

9. B.

Because the exponent in this expression is negative, move the decimal point in 2.8 to the left. Because the exponent has the number 3, move the decimal point 3 places. Moving the decimal point in 2.8 to the left three places results in 0.0028.

10. D.

By the definition of absolute value, $|8x + 3| \le 7$ is equivalent to $-7 \le 8x + 3 \le 7$. Subtract 3 from each part of this double inequality to get $-10 \le 8x \le 4$. Then $\dfrac{-10}{8} \le x \le \dfrac{4}{8}$, which simplifies to $\dfrac{-5}{4} \le x \le \dfrac{1}{2}$.

11. C.

To find the difference between these two times, change each number to a decimal. So, $6\dfrac{3}{10}$ becomes 6.3 and $5\dfrac{4}{5}$ becomes 5.8. Then subtract to get $6.3 - 5.8 = 0.5$. Finally, 0.5 of a minute is 30 seconds.

12. D.

The students in the statistics class have a reasonable chance at being able to sample a large enough portion of the students at their high school to get a reasonable estimate of the population. Data collected would produce a normal curve under these circumstances. Therefore the choice is concrete and mathematically correct. Choice (A) is incorrect because there are not enough students and the data being collected is unlikely to yield a normal curve over such a small, homogeneous sample. Choice (B) does not work because there is no way to get the data. An internet source may provide a sample but the problem then becomes abstract — a mind exercise. Choice (C) is incorrect because the data collected would not produce a normal curve.

13. B.

Because the problem asks for the "sum of six cubed and −9," we know that this part of the expression goes in parentheses. Then, "multiply by −3", means to put the −3 outside the parentheses. Thus the answer becomes $(-3)(6^3 + (-9))$.

14. B.

In this sequence, the pattern is double the given number, then subtract 1.

3 doubled = 6; subtract 1 = 5
5 doubled = 10; subtract 1 = 9
9 doubled = 18; subtract 1 = 17
17 doubled = 34; subtract 1 = 33
33 doubled = 66; subtract 1 = 65

15. A.

If a, b, c are the sides of a right triangle, with c as the hypotenuse, the Pythagorean theorem states that $a^2 + b^2 = c^2$. Substitute x for a and substitute $x + 1$ for c. Then $x^2 + b^2 = (x + 1)^2$. This simplifies to $x^2 + b^2 = x^2 + 2x + 1$. So $b^2 = 2x + 1$. Finally, taking the square root of each side, $b = \sqrt{2x + 1}$.

16. C.

If an event can happen in p ways and fail to happen in q ways, then, if $p > q$, the odds are p to q in favor of the event happening. If $p < q$, then the odds are q to p against the event happening. In this problem, $p = 10$ and $q = 8$, thus $p > q$. Therefore, the odds in favor of the event of drawing a yellow chip are 10:8.

17. D.

First, calculate $7 \times 2 - 2 = 14 - 2 = 12$. Second, calculate $6^2 = 36$. Third, divide 36 by 12 to get 3. Fourth, multiply 3 by 4 to get 12. Finally, add 3 to 12 to get 15. In none of these steps is 3 added to 36.

18. A.

The inequality $x \geq 0$ identifies the region to the right of the y-axis, eliminating choices (C) and (D). The double inequality of $-3 < y < 3$ represents dotted horizontal lines passing through 3 and −3 on the y-axis with the area between the lines shaded. Of the two remaining choices, (A) is the only one which satisfies this constraint.

19. A.

The last statement in the list tells us that Patrick has green eyes. The third statement tells us that all people who have green eyes like hamburgers. Therefore, Patrick likes hamburgers.

20. C.

To change a repeating decimal to a fraction, first let $a = 0.\overline{15}$.

Then, $100a = 100 \times 0.\overline{15}$.

By subtraction: $100a - a = 15.\overline{15} - a$.

So: $99a = 15.\overline{15} - 0.\overline{15} = 15$.

Thus, $a = \dfrac{15}{99} = \dfrac{5}{33}$.

21. A.

Find the y-axis. Find the side of the figure closest to the y-axis and measure the distance that this side is from the y-axis. A reflection of the figure will put this side the same distance from the y-axis, but on the other side.

Also, notice the point labeled C. A reflection of this point across the y-axis will also be the same distance from the y-axis, but on the other side.

22. C.

The x-value of the vertex of this parabola is given by $-\dfrac{(-3)}{[(2)(-1)]} = -1.5$. The corresponding y-value $= -(-1.5)^2 - 3(-1.5) + 4 = 6.25$.

Since the coefficient of x^2 is negative, this parabola will have its highest point at the vertex, which is $(-1.5, 6.25)$. Thus, the range will be all numbers less than or equal to the y-value of the vertex, which is 6.25.

23. B.

When two dice are thrown, there are 36 possible outcomes. Four of these produce the sum of five: (4, 1) (3, 2) (2,3) and (1,4). Therefore, the probability is $\frac{4}{36}$, which reduces to $\frac{1}{9}$.

24. C.

To find the resulting area after dilation, first find the new length and width by multiplying each by the scale factor of 1.25.

Length = $(12)(1.25) = 15$ feet
Width = $(8)(1.25) = 10$ feet
Area = $(15)(10) = 150$ square feet

25. D.

Drawing a diagram would be most helpful when solving this problem. When drawing a diagram, you might show the first pull as a red marble, the second pull as a white marble, and the third pull as a blue marble. On the fourth pull, Lucy would have to pull a matching marble.

Constructing a table, guess and check, and working backwards would not be helpful strategies for solving this problem.

26. B.

First, find the prime factorization of the given numbers in Antonio's birthday.

$6 = 2 \times 3$, $24 = 2^3 \times 3$, and $86 = 2 \times 43$

Then, identify the highest power of each prime factor and multiply.

$2^3 \times 3 \times 43 = 1,032$

27. C.

If two parallel lines are intersected by a transversal, the same-side interior angles are supplementary. Therefore, add the measures of the two angles and set them equal to 180.

$a + 48 + 3a + 40 = 180$
$4a + 88 = 180$

$4a = 92$
$a = 23$

28. D.

Let x = the price per pound for pears and let y = the price per pound for peaches. Then, $2x + y = \$1.40$ and $3x + 2y = \$2.40$. Multiply the first equation by 2 to get $4x + 2y = \$2.80$. Now subtract the original second equation to get $x = \$0.40$. By substituating this value of x into the original first equation, we get $(2)(\$0.40) + y = \$1.40$. This results in $y = \$0.60$. Finally, $\$0.40 + \$0.60 = \$1.00$.

29. D.

The sum of the original group of 20 numbers was $(9)(20) = 180$. The sum of the new group of 19 numbers is $(7)(19) = 133$. Thus, the removed number is $180 - 133 = 47$.

30. C.

The second angle is 11° less than the first angle, so it can be represented by $x - 11$. The third angle is twice the measure of the first angle increased by 3, so it can be represented by $2x + 3$. Choice (C) shows that the sum of x, $x - 11$, and $2x + 3$ is 180.

31. C.

Each pair of values in the table will check the equation $y = -x^3 + 25$.

Answer choice (A) is wrong since (2, 17) and (4, −39) do not check the equation. Answer choice (B) is wrong since (3, −2) and (4, −39) do not check the equation. Answer choice (D) is wrong since (3, −2) does not check the equation.

32. B.

Before finding the average of these weights, they must all be converted into the same unit, namely grams. The numbers 15.64 and 15.69 are already in grams. Change 0.01566 kg to 15.66 g and change 0.01565 kg to 15.65 g. Then 15.64 + 15.69 + 15.66 + 15.65 = 62.64. Thus, 62.64 ÷ 4 = 15.66 grams.

33. D.

The number associated with point A is $-\frac{3}{2}$ and the number associated with point B is $\frac{1}{4}$. Then $\left(-\frac{3}{2}\right)\left(\frac{1}{4}\right) = -\frac{3}{8}$.

34. C.

In the interval of 6:20 A.M. to 6:30 A.M. one observes on the graph that for Race #1 the heart rate in beats per minute is increasing from 100 beats/minute to 110 beats/minute, as follows: (6:20, 100) (6:25, 108), (6:30, 110); while for Race #2 the heart rate in beats per minute is stable at 82 beats/minute, as follows: (6:20, 82), (6:25, 82), (6:30, 82).

Answere choice (A) is incorrect because the heart rate for Race #2 is steady. Answer choice (B) is incorrect because the heart rate for Race #1 is increasing, and the heart rate for Race #2 is steady. Answer choice (D) is incorrect because the answers are reversed: Race #2 is stable, and Race #1 is increasing.

35. C.

To solve this problem, set up an equation. In this equation, let x be the number of minutes Kathleen can talk. In the equation, 0.40 stands for the first 3 minutes of the phone call and $(x - 3)$ indicates the remaining number of minutes minus the first three minutes already accounted for in the $0.40.

$0.40 + 0.13(x - 3) = 5.00$
Eliminate the parentheses.
$0.40 + 0.13x - 0.39 = 5.00$
Combine like terms. $0.13x + .01 = 5.00$
Subtract .01 from both sides. $0.13x = 4.99$
Divide by .13 $x \approx 38.38$
To the nearest minute, Kathleen can talk for 38 minutes.

36. A.

The equation of the circle with center at $(0, 0)$ and a radius of 4 is $x^2 + y^2 = 16$. Since the shaded region lies inside this circle, the correct inequality is $x^2 + y^2 \le 16$.

37. D.

First, write $6x + 3y = 4$ in the slope-intercept form. By subtracting $6x$ from each side, we have $3y = -6x + 4$. Dividing by 3, the equation becomes $y = -2x + \frac{4}{3}$.

For this equation, the slope is -2 and the y-intercept is $\frac{4}{3}$. Since parallel lines have the same slope, the required equation will be in the form $y = -2x + b$. Finally, we know that the y-intercept of the new line is -6, so the required equation is $y = -2x - 6$.

38. A.

The distributive property states that $(a)(b + c) = ab + ac$. The commutative property states that $m + n = n + m$. By substituting the given numbers in answer choice (A), we can see that it satisfies both the distributive and commutative properties. Answer choice (B) only shows the distributive property and answer choice (C) only shows the commutative property. Answer choice (D) does not satisfy either property, and is actually an incorrect statement.

39. D.

The number of arrangements of nine players is defined as 9!, which is read as "9 factorial." The value of 9! is $(9)(8)(7)(6)(5)(4)(3)(2)(1) = 362,880$.

40. D.

This is a $30° - 60° - 90°$ right triangle. The hypotenuse ($\overline{BC}$) is twice the length of the shorter leg ($\overline{AC}$). So, $AC = \frac{BC}{2} = 3.5$. The length of the longer leg ($\overline{AB}$) is the product of the length of the shorter leg and $\sqrt{3}$. Thus, $AB = (3.5)(\sqrt{3}) \approx 6.1$.

41. C.

If $\overline{PR}$ and $\overline{QS}$ are perpendicular bisectors of each other, then all four angles at T are right angles. By using the side-angle-side (SAS) theorem, it can be shown that all four nonoverlapping triangles are congruent to each other. Since corresponding parts of congruent triangles are congruent, $\overline{PQ} = \overline{QR} = \overline{RS} = \overline{SP}$. Thus, $PQRS$ must be a rhombus.

42. **C.**

First move the decimal point so that the number is between 1 and 10. This means that the decimal point is placed between the 2 and 9. Since the decimal point in the original number is at the far right, it has been moved 8 places to the left. Therefore, the scientific notation is 2.93×10^8.

43. **C.**

The domain is determined solely by the denominator. If the denominator is not zero, then the function has a real value. Thus, $2x^2 - x - 15 = 0$ will yield the excluded values of x. $2x^2 - x - 15 = (2x + 5)(x - 3)$. Solving $2x + 5 = 0$ yields $x = -\frac{5}{2}$. Solving $x - 3 = 0$ yields $x = 3$. These two numbers represent the excluded values of the domain.

44. **D.**

A cylinder is formed when a rectangle is rotated 360° around an axis.

45. **A.**

To solve this problem, use a Venn diagram. We know that 5 students are taking both courses, so place 5 in the middle section. There are 29 students taking English literature, so there must be $29 - 5 = 24$ students who are taking only English literature. Thus, the required probability is $\frac{24}{40} = 60\%$. The complete Venn diagram appears as follows:

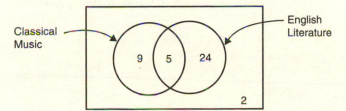

46. **A.**

To solve this problem, set up the proportion, with copies in the numerator and minutes in the denominator. Let x represent the unknown number of minutes.

Then $\frac{10}{2} = \frac{55}{x}$. Cross-multiply to get $10x = 110$. Thus, $x = 11$.

47. **B.**

The perimeter (P) = 2(length) + 2(width). For all of the answer choices, the area is equal to 24 square inches. However, only answer choice (B) has a perimeter of 22 inches, since $2(8) + 2(3) = 22$. Choice (A) has a perimeter of 20 inches, choice (C) has a perimeter of 50 inches, and choice (D) has a perimeter of 28 inches.

48. **C.**

The five lowest prime numbers are 2, 3, 5, 7, and 11. Thus, the required number is $(2)(3)(5)(7)(11) = 2310$.

49. **A.**

The probability for the experiment in choice (A) is $\left(\frac{4}{52}\right)\left(\frac{3}{51}\right)$, which reduces to $\frac{1}{221}$. For choice (B), the probability would be $\left(\frac{4}{52}\right)\left(\frac{4}{52}\right) = \frac{1}{169}$. For choice (C), the probability would be $\left(\frac{2}{17}\right)\left(\frac{1}{16}\right) = \frac{1}{136}$. For choice (D), the probability would be $\left(\frac{2}{30}\right)\left(\frac{2}{30}\right) = \frac{1}{225}$.

50. **D.**

Choice (A) is divisible by 3 because the sum of the first five digits is divisible by 3. Choice (B) is divisible by 4 because the final two digits of the 5-digit number are divisible by 4. Choice (C) is divisible by 5 because it ends in 0. Choice (D) is not divisible by 6, because it is not divisible by both 2 and 3. Although it is divisible by 2 because it is even, it is not divisible by 3. Therefore, the book represented by choice (D) is not owned by Larkwood Public Library.

51. D.

    The value of the item in the stem is $-|-8 + 5| = -|-3| = -3$. Answer choice (D) also has a value of -3. The values of answer choices (A), (B), and (C) are 13, 3, and -13, respectively.

52. B.

    To determine the type of triangle that is formed with the given vertices, use the distance formula to find the lengths of the sides.

$$DE = \sqrt{(3-(-2))^2 + (1-6)^2} = \sqrt{5^2 + 5^2} = \sqrt{50} = 5\sqrt{2}.$$

$$EF = \sqrt{(-2-(-3))^2 + (6-0)^2} = \sqrt{1^2 + 6^2} = \sqrt{37}.$$

$$DF = \sqrt{(3-(-3))^2 + (1-0)^2} = \sqrt{6^2 + 1^2} = \sqrt{37}.$$

    Since $\overline{EF}$ and $\overline{DF}$ are congruent line segments, triangle DEF is isosceles.

53. C.

    The total of the scores for student #3 is 356. Let x represent this student's fifth score. Then $\frac{356+x}{5} = 90$. Multiply both sides of the equation by 5, so that $356 + x = (90)(5) = 450$. Thus, $x = 450 - 356 = 94$.

54. B.

    The number $2^{31} \times 5^{27}$ can be written as $2^4 \times (2^{27} \times 5^{27}) = 2^4 \times 10^{27} = 16 \times 10^{27}$. In scientific notation, this number becomes 1.6×10^{28}, which represents a total of 29 digits.

55. A.

    By folding the given pattern along the dotted lines, we would get a three-dimensional figure that has triangles for all four of its faces.

56. C.

    Given an external point from a circle, two tangents drawn to the circle from that point must be equal. So $PQ = PW$, $QR = RS$. $ST = TU$, $UV = VW$. Then $PQ + QR + TU + UV$ must repre-sent one-half the perimeter of $PRTV$, or 14. By substitution, we get $PR + TV = 14$. Note that $PRTV$ is not any specific kind of quadrilateral.

57. D.

    The inverse of the graph of any function is found by reflecting the graph across the line $y = x$. This means that for any point (x, y) on the original graph, the point (y, x) must be on the inverse graph. The point $(6, 7)$ is a point on the graph of the inverse since $(7, 6)$ is on the graph of the original function.

58. B.

    The number $\frac{3}{4}$ is divided by $\frac{2}{3}$, which requires the use of the reciprocal of $\frac{2}{3}$.

59. A.

    The triangle formed by the tree and the ground is a right triangle. Therefore, the lengths of the sides satisfy the Pythagorean property $a^2 + b^2 = c^2$, where a and b are the lengths of the legs of the right triangle and c is the length of the hypotenuse. In this problem, $a^2 + b^2 = c^2$ translates to: (length of the base)^2 + (height of the trec)^2 = (length of the ladder)^2. Then $24^2 + b^2 = 26^2$, which becomes $576 + b^2 = 676$. So $b^2 = 100$, which means $b = 10$. Thus, the limb on which the cat is stuck is 10 feet above the ground.

60. C.

    First, convert all measurements to inches, and then set up a proportion.

    The average male height is 6' 4" = 76 inches.

    The average high jump for males is 6' 10" = 82 inches.

    The average female height is 5' 6" = 66 inches.

    Let x represent the average high jump for females.

    The proportion becomes $\frac{76}{82} = \frac{66}{x}$. Cross-multiply to get $76x = (82)(66) = 5412$.

    Thus, $x \approx 71.2$ inches. Finally, convert 71.2 to feet and inches. The answer is 5 feet 11 inches.

Constructed-Response Solutions

61.

- Volume = $10 \times 6 \times 2 = 120$ cubic inches
- Surface area = $2(10 \times 6 + 10 \times 2 + 6 \times 2) =$ 184 square inches.
- A new box can be 10 inches by 4 inches by 3 inches.
  Volume of new box: $10 \times 4 \times 3 = 120$ cubic inches.
  Surface area of new box: $2(10 \times 4 + 10 \times 3 + 4 \times 3) = 164$ square inches.
  Another solution is $6 \times 5 \times 4$.

62.

- Truck A travels $(50)(2) = 100$ miles east.
  Truck B travels $(60)(3) = 180$ miles north.
  Distance apart:
  $$\sqrt{100^2 + 180^2} = \sqrt{42,400} \approx 206 \text{ miles}$$

- Truck C travels at 40 mph for 103 miles, which requires 2.575 hours.
  Then
  $$4 - 2.575 = 1.425 \text{ hours to cover the remaining miles.}$$
  Finally, $\dfrac{103}{1.425} \approx 72.3$ miles/per hour.

-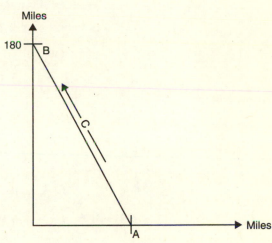

Index

Installing REA's TestWare®

SYSTEM REQUIREMENTS

Pentium 75 MHz (300 MHz recommended) or a higher or compatible processor; Microsoft Windows 98 or later; 64 MB available RAM; Internet Explorer 5.5 or higher.

INSTALLATION

1. Insert the GACE Middle Grades Mathematics (Test Code 013) CD-ROM into the CD-ROM drive.

2. If the installation doesn't begin automatically, from the Start Menu choose the RUN command. When the RUN dialog box appears, type d:\setup (where d is the letter of your CD-ROM drive) at the prompt and click OK.

3. The installation process will begin. A dialog box proposing the directory "C:\Program Files\REA\GACE_Math 013\" will appear. If the name and location are suitable, click OK. If you wish to specify a different name or location, type it in and click OK.

4. Start the GACE Middle Grades Math 013 TestWare® application by double-clicking on the icon.

REA's GACE Middle Grades Math 013 TestWare® is **EASY** to **LEARN AND USE**. To achieve maximum benefits, we recommend that you take a few minutes to go through the on-screen tutorial on your computer. The "screen buttons" are also explained here to familiarize you with the program.

TECHNICAL SUPPORT

REA's TestWare® is backed by customer and technical support. For questions about **installation or operation of your software**, contact us at:

Research & Education Association
Phone: (732) 819-8880 (9 a.m. to 5 p.m. ET, Monday–Friday)
Fax: (732) 819-8808
Website: www.rea.com
E-mail: info@rea.com

Note to Windows XP Users: In order for the TestWare® to function properly, please install and run the application under the same computer administrator-level user account. Installing the TestWare® as one user and running it as another could cause file-access path conflicts.